MOBILIZING SOCIAL MOVEMENT ORGANIZATIONS:
The Formation, Institutionalization, and Effectiveness of Ecumenical Urban Ministries

by

JAMES D. DAVIDSON

Department of Sociology and Anthropology
Purdue University

SOCIETY FOR THE SCIENTIFIC STUDY OF RELIGION
MONOGRAPH SERIES, NUMBER 6, STORRS, CONNECTICUT

Copyright © 1985 by The Society for the Scientific Study of Religion

All rights reserved. No part of this book may be reproduced or transmitted in any form or by any means, electronic or mechanical, including photocopying, recording, or by and information storage or retrieval system, without permission in writing from the compiler.

Library of Congress Number: 85-50402
International Standard Book Number: 0-932566-05-7

TO MY MOTHER AND FATHER

TO MY MOTHER AND FATHER

Series Editor's Introduction

The Society for the Scientific Study of Religion Monograph Series intends to make available significant work on religion from a variety of scientific disciplines and perspectives. *Mobilizing Social Movement Organizations: The Formation, Institutionalization, and Effectiveness of Ecumenical Urban Ministries*—the sixth monograph in the series—combines structural and resource mobilization approaches to the sociological understanding of social movements.

The heart of the monograph is an in-depth case study of an ecumenical urban ministry organization. James Davidson's penetrating analysis of the Lafayette Urban Ministry helps to explain the paradox that churches in the 1960s and 1970s often fostered social change despite the fact that the majority of their members opposed such change. The study has important implications for a variety of theoretical and practical problems faced by sociologists of religion, organizational sociologists, and leaders of religious and other voluntary organizations.

James R. Wood
Editor

TABLE OF CONTENTS

SERIES EDITOR'S INTRODUCTION..v
PREFACE..ix
CHAPTER 1   The Problem: The Formation, Institutionalization,
             and Effectiveness of Social Movement Organizations............1

        2   An Open System Approach: Structural Conduciveness
             and Resource Mobilization...............................15

        3   Method: A Case Study....................................29

        4   Description of LUM's Formation: From a Neighborhood
             Youth Group to an Ecumenical Urban Ministry.................35

        5   Analysis of LUM's Formation: Structures
             and Resources Converge..................................41

        6   Description of LUM's Institutionalization:
             A Volatile, Curvilinear Process..........................59

        7   Analysis of LUM's Institutionalization:
             Mobilizing the Resources.................................87

        8   Description of LUM's Effectiveness:
             Increasing Over Time....................................113

        9   Analysis of LUM's Effectiveness: Putting
             the Resources to Good Use...............................141

       10   Summary and Implications................................155

FOOTNOTES..171
APPENDIX A...181
APPENDIX B...185
REFERENCES 193
INDEX 200

PREFACE

Sociologists' interest in social movement organizations has grown in recent years (e.g., McCarthy and Zald, 1977; Jenkins, 1983). We have been intrigued by the special problems these organizations face as they are formed, struggle to survive, and try to achieve their goals. Research to date has provided some insights into these complicated issues, but we have a long way to go before we understand the formation, institutionalization, and effectiveness (in short, the mobilization) of social movement organizations.

The proliferation of ecumenical urban ministry organizations during the 1960s gave us a golden opportunity to explore these issues. Ecumenical urban ministries are social movement organizations which seek to increase local church involvement in social concerns, especially the causes and consequences of poverty. They do so by promoting social concerns programs within local congregations, and conducting social concerns programs on their behalf.

Several hundred urban ministry organizations were formed in cities throughout the country (Johnson, 1969). Some groups folded within a couple of years; others survived, but found it difficult to become permanent and effective forces within their communities; and some have become quite stable and influential organizations (VanderWerf, 1976; Takayama, 1977; Takayama and Darnell, 1979).

One of the more successful urban ministries is in Lafayette, Indiana. It evolved gradually between 1962 and 1971 and struggled to survive during the mid 1970s, but is now 14 years old and has made considerable progress in its efforts to increase Lafayette area churches' involvement in social concerns.

I had the good fortune of evaluating the Lafayette Urban Ministry (LUM) between 1975 and 1981. During that time, I formulated a theory to explain its formation, institutionalization, and effectiveness. The theory uses an open system approach, drawing heavily on traditional structural theories of social movement organizations and emerging theories stressing the process of resource mobilization. The structural emphasis calls attention to cultural patterns and institutional arrangements which can affect the development of social movement organizations. The resource mobilization perspective focuses attention on the availability of resources such as legitimacy, money, and leadership, and how they are mobilized. It took seven years to gather all the data I needed to test the theory.

This book summarizes what I learned. Chapter 1 describes the problems of formation, institutionalization, and effectiveness; Chapter 2 specifies my theoretical framework; and Chapter 3 summarizes the methods I used to gather data to test the theory. Chapter 4 describes and Chapter 5 analyzes LUM's formation. Chapter 6 describes and Chapter 7 analyzes its institutionalization. Chapter 8 describes and Chapter 9 analyzes its effectiveness. Chapter 10 summarizes the findings and explores their implications for future research on social movement organizations, and for religious leaders who wish to increase local church involvement in social concerns.

A great many people have contributed to this project. Rev. Ronald Elly (director of LUM from 1972 to 1977) and Rev. Judson Dolphin (director since 1978) deserve very special thanks for their support and cooperation throughout the project. I also want to thank all of LUM's other staff members, each of whom has helped me in specific ways, and well over 100 board members who have contributed to this project.

Rev. Elly, Rev. Donald Nead (a campus pastor), and Thomas Hull (a LUM board member) helped construct the model of urban ministry which was used in the 1975-76 phase of the evaluation and continues to shape LUM's experiences.

The project was funded mainly by Lilly Endowment, Inc. The first year of the project was part of a Lilly Faculty Open Fellowship. The last three years were made possible through a larger grant dealing with ecumenical groups throughout the state of Indiana. I am indebted to Laura Bornholdt (Vice President for Education) and Robert Lynn (Vice President for Religion) for their support. LUM and the Tippecanoe County Federation of Churches also made smaller financial contributions to the study.

An important part of this project was a survey of 30 local congregations. I want to thank the pastors and members who participated for their support and good will. Dennis Sorge and Marty Wortham also were very important parts of the survey, especially the sampling phase. Their interest and commitment are greatly appreciated.

Thanks also to the members of the Sorrento Seminar. Their spirit and support have been important factors in the completion of this project.

I am very grateful to James Wood and K. Peter Takayama for their guidance with the substantive and editorial aspects of preparing this volume.

Several people have helped with the typing of project reports, questionnaires, and this volume. These include Maria Broughton Wilcox, Bonnie Wilkerson, Carla Ade, Sue Nichols, and Holly Norman.

Finally, my folks have provided a great deal of motivation and a lot of their personal resources during the course of my education and career. They also have been important sources of my interest in religion and social concerns. My wife, Anna, has been a source of support and wisdom throughout this project. She and our children, Jay and Terry, have made sure that I devote as much time and attention to family as I do to work and the church.

CHAPTER 1

THE PROBLEM: THE FORMATION, INSTITUTIONALIZATION, AND EFFECTIVENESS OF SOCIAL MOVEMENT ORGANIZATIONS

Social movement organizations have two distinctive features: their emphasis on social change, and members whose participation is based on a strong belief in the changes the organizations are trying to make.[1] According to Zald and Ash (1966:37):

> A social movement is a purposive and collective attempt of a number of people to change individuals or societal institutions and structures. Although the organizations through which social movements can manifest themselves may have bureaucratic features, analytically they differ from 'full-blown' bureaucratic organizations in two ways. First they have goals aimed at changing the society and its members; they wish to restructure society or individuals, not to provide it or them with a regular service (as is typical of bureaucracies) . . .
>
> Second (and related to the goals of change), MO's are characterized by an incentive structure in which purposive incentives predominate . . . the values represented by MO's goals must be deeply held in order for the organization to command time and loyalty in the face of competition of work and the demands of family and friends.

There are at least two types of social movement organizations.[2] One type consists of *radical*, or utopian, groups which view themselves as alternatives to the prevailing social order, and feel they should not depend on "the enemy" for support (and probably quite rightly feel they could not obtain such support even if they were willing to receive it). This type of social movement organization prefers to be autonomous, depending as much as possible on its own resources and limiting its dependence on the organizations it seeks to change. The "challenge groups" in Gamson's (1975) study of social protest tended to be of this type. Their members tended to come from—and wanted to remain—outside the groups they were trying to influence (Gamson, 1975:17). I am *not* concerned with this type of group.

I *am* concerned with social movement organizations which view themselves as part of the social order and want to maintain close relationships with larger "parent" organizations, yet want to *reform* social policies and practices (including those of their parent organizations). They want to be a leavening influence, stimulating reform from within.

I am interested in these groups for several reasons. First, the sociological literature contains surprisingly little theory and research on the process of organizational formation (Ross, 1980; Myers, 1984). Several of the major texts on organizations hardly even mention the process (e.g., Champion, 1975; Hall, 1982). Thus, we know very little about the circumstances under which any kind of organization is *formed*, including social movement organizations. What societal conditions are likely to give rise to such groups? Where are they most likely to be formed? What kinds of people are most likely to

1

participate in their formation? What kinds of resources do these people need to get such groups started? Answers to these questions would advance our understanding of organizations in general and social movement organizations in particular.

Second, new organizations struggle to survive, and many do not make it (Stinchcombe, 1965; Hall, 1982). The problem of surviving is especially difficult for social movement organizations. They are "aggressive organizations in reluctant environments" (Maniha and Perrow, 1965; Takayama and Darnell, 1979). Their interest in reform is likely to provoke some defense of the status quo and actions intended to curtail their activities (e.g., attempts to discredit their leadership or reduce their funding). Siffin (1972:117) described the problem this way:

> There is an important difference between institutionalizing organizations for social change purposes, and establishing viable organizations within congenial settings. The essence of the difference is the hostility of the environment in the former case . . . In friendlier circumstances, it will be relatively easy to obtain suitable personnel, relatively well socialized, prepared and predisposed to behave in conformity with organizational needs and expectations.
>
> Likewise, in a friendly setting, the legitimacy of the organization and the possible utility of its output will be more or less self-evident. . . . But in hostile (or uncongenial environments) . . . [it] may be difficult and expensive to create the core of the organization: people will have to be socialized, as well as made skillful and knowledgeable. It is equally hard—perhaps harder—to maintain the organization. And it will be hardest of all to cause the organization's product to be accepted and used in the intended way.

The possibility of survival-threatening actions seems especially likely when social movement organizations are dependent on parent organizations which do not necessarily share their goals (Wood, 1972 and 1981; Jenkins, 1977). What parent organizations are willing to support groups wanting changes that are not important to the members of the parent organizations? What if some of the changes the reform groups want are incompatible with the social, economic, and political interests of people in the parent organizations? Can the reform groups survive and become enduring parts of the social fabric? Under what conditions can they become institutionalized? How much do they control their own fate? How much is their fate a function of conditions beyond their control? Evidence concerning these questions would add to our understanding of how organizations generally, and social movement organizations in particular, struggle to become viable entities.

Finally, there is the problem of *effectiveness*. As Siffin (1972) suggests, it is easier for service-oriented organizations to achieve their goals than it is for reform-oriented organizations. It may be especially difficult for social movement organizations at certain times or in certain places. However, success is possible, even likely, at other times and in other places. But, we do not know much about the conditions which affect effectiveness. How much impact do societal factors such as changing cultural values have? Or, what about the economy? Do local circumstances have much effect? To what extent can reform-oriented organizations beat the odds and be successful in hostile environments? What organizational factors have the most bearing on a group's effectiveness? These are questions sociologists need to pursue before we can fully understand the effectiveness of social movement organizations.

My goal in this volume is to report what I learned about these issues during a seven-year evaluation of a social movement organization seeking to increase church involvement in social concerns, especially the causes and consequences of poverty.

Ecumenical Urban Ministries

Several hundred new social movement organizations were formed in the 1960s to increase local churches' involvement in issues related to poverty (Johnson, 1969). Most of the groups were led by young, recently-ordained clergy; small staffs, often consisting of just a secretary; and volunteers who served as an advisory council or board of directors. They received most—if not all—of their support from churches; relatively little money came from other (e.g., federal) sources. As a rule, the groups were oriented toward (a) helping the poor *on behalf of* local congregations, and (b) fostering more social involvement *within* local congregations.

Most of these groups were called "urban ministries," signifying their nature as religious groups interested in the causes and consequences of urban poverty. When they were supported by several denominations or local congregations—as most were—they were "ecumenical urban ministries."

The proliferation of ecumenical urban ministries caused a number of social researchers (Johnson, 1969; Davidson, 1976; Takayama, 1977, Takayama and Darnell, 1979; Davidson, Elly, Hull, and Nead, 1979) to ask questions about their formation, institutionalization, and effectiveness.

Formation

Researchers were intrigued by the formation of ecumenical urban ministries for several reasons. First, research indicates that most local congregations do not sponsor many programs related to the social, economic and political problems in their communities. There is little evidence of social concerns programs in the annual reports of most local churches. Local churches often lack social concerns committees and seldom provide these committees with budgets to encourage and support meaningful action (Graham, 1970:153-175). The worship services, Sunday sermons, Sunday bulletins, and the activities calendars of most local churches emphasize the cultivation of personal faith and pay much less attention to the social concerns of the immediate community or the society as a whole. Thus, Glock and Stark (1965:183) concluded that "the church's emphasis is overwhelmingly on man's relationship to God. The implications of the faith for man's relation to man are left largely to the individual to work out for himself, with God's help but without much help of the churches." I reached essentially the same conclusion (Davidson, 1972:74), noting that "while churches provide a variety of means by which church members can relate their vertical beliefs [about the supernatural] to their personal lives (e.g., private prayer, devotional services, reading the Bible), they provide relatively few ways by which church members can translate their horizontal beliefs [about loving one's neighbor] into social action (Davidson, 1970)." Berger (1961:38) concluded that "organized religion is irrelevant to the major social forces which are operative in American society; it does not affect them, and it relates to them in an overwhelmingly passive way." Graham (1970:151) expressed it this way: "Societal practices that in their conception and execution are degrading to the Judeo-Christian view of man flourish in almost all of the states with no cry of protest from the leaders of organized religion."

Given the lack of local church involvement in social concerns, how can social researchers explain the formation of ecumenical urban ministries in local communities? What conditions give rise to organizations which seek to increase local congregations' involvement in issues they have not pursued in the past?

Second, studies of parishioners' priorities indicate that most lay people want their churches to focus on personal faith and enrichment more than on social concerns. For example, in a national study of Presbyterians, Hoge and Faue (1973:181-182) found that:

> Among the laymen, it is proclamation of the faith, religious education for children, and personal support which are most desired from the church. For them the main function of church membership seems to be individual and family support. Mission and outreach have lower priority. Among the ministers, congregational life and nurture are ahead of mission and outreach, but not so clearly as among the laymen. Individual social action and charity rank 6th and 8th respectively, ahead of maintaining moral standards and teaching theology within the congregation. The main conflict between laymen and ministers is over the *type* of church mission and outreach, and the secondary conflict is over the *place* of the mission and outreach in the total program of the church. The laymen want charity and evangelical missions clearly ahead of social action, and they place *all* mission items . . . below congregational life and nurture. The ministers give charity and social action equal priority, with both ahead of evangelical missions: they make mission slightly subordinate to congregational life and nurture. The priority of congregational life and nurture over mission found here is consistent with other research on Protestants (Brewer, *et al.*, 1967; Campbell and Fukuyama, 1970; Campolo, 1971; Johnson and Cornell, 1972).

Three years later, Hoge (1976:104) summarized the results from additional research on Presbyterian church members' priorities:

> (1) Personal and family support is the highest priority, and all programs serving these goals are ranked highest. (2) Evangelical missions, charity, and social service are given a moderate priority. (3) Prophetic ministry or social action implying a questioning of existing local economic structures is given a lowest priority or is met with hostility.

Dixon and Hoge (1979) found essentially the same pattern among members of three Catholic congregations: "the results were so similar to the results in surveys of Presbyterian laity that we interpret them in terms of basic needs which laity see the church as serving for them—mostly individual and family support."

Clearly, ecumenical urban ministries focus on activities that are low priority for most church members. How could social researchers explain the formation of organizations which strive to increase local churches' involvement in issues that are of little or no interest to their members?

Third, Judeo-Christian theology assumes that vertical beliefs about the supernatural are related to horizontal beliefs about human relationships. Beliefs about the existence of God, Christ, and a life after death are supposed to be related to beliefs about loving one's neighbor and doing good for others (Luke 10:27; Deuteronomy 24:17-22; Proverbs 21:13; Psalm 82:3-4; Matthew 25:31-45; Luke 4:16-21; Amos 5:21-24; and 1 John 3:14-18).

But studies done in such diverse places as the Bay Area of California, Oklahoma, and Indiana reveal that there is little or no connection between vertical and horizontal beliefs. In the Bay Area, Stark and Glock (1968) found a correlation of only .11 between vertical beliefs and horizontal beliefs among Catholics. The correlation among Protestants was -.02. Thus, the two types of belief did not overlap; they represented distinctly different dimensions of faith for both groups. My research (with D'Antonio and Schlangen, 1966) in two Oklahoma communities revealed a similar pattern. The groups which scored highest on measures of vertical belief did not necessarily score high on measures of horizontal belief. For example, 90 percent of the Baptists had a firm belief in God and 94 percent believed in the divinity of Christ, but only 31 percent said that "love of neighbor" was necessary for salvation. My (1975) research among Baptists and United Methodists in two Indiana communities revealed a negative correlation (-.45) between vertical and horizontal belief: those who believed in God, Christ, and a life after death were *less* likely to report that "loving thy neighbor" and "doing good for others" are important parts of their faith. Finally, in my study of Purdue students (with Knudsen, 1977:62) "there was virtually no relationship between the respondents' vertical beliefs and their horizontal beliefs: people who believed in God and the divinity of Christ were no more likely to believe in loving one's neighbor and doing good for others than were people who did not believe in God or Christ ($r = .09$)."

Given the fact that churchgoers' vertical and horizontal beliefs tend to be separate dimensions of faith, how can social researchers explain the formation of ecumenical urban ministries which want to bring these two worlds of belief together? What forces foster organizations which strive to integrate the vertical and horizontal dimensions of faith?

Finally, as a rule, religious involvement does not foster more compassionate social attitudes and activities among church members. In his study of Protestants and Catholics in Detroit, Lenski (1961) found that doctrinal orthodoxy seems "to foster the view that one's religious commitments are irrelevant to one's political and economic actions and other aspects of life." My analysis (with Knudsen, 1977) revealed that people who were most involved in religion were no more likely to believe in the need to love one's neighbor or do good for others than were people who were least involved. My (1975) study of Baptists and United Methodists in Indiana revealed no relationship ($r = .01$) between religion's "personal consequences" and its "social consequences": people who derived the most personally from their faith were no more likely to be involved for religious reasons in the social concerns of their community than those who benefited least from their religion. Wuthnow's (1973) review of the literature on religion and social attitudes revealed that, more often than not, church attendance, vertical belief, and involvement in church activities were unrelated to people's liberal and conservative beliefs in the social, economic, and political arenas.

Some other evidence indicates that, if religion is related to parishioners' social attitudes and activities, it tends to be in directions which seem inconsistent with Judeo-Christian concerns for love of neighbor and the willingness to seek remedies for social conditions fostering human misery (Quinn and Davidson, 1976). Several studies have found that churchgoers are more prejudiced than non-churchgoers (Keedy, 1958; Salisbury, 1962; Photiadis and Biggar, 1962; Photiadis and Johnson, 1963; Feagin, 1965; Glock and Stark, 1966; Gorsuch and Aleshire, 1974). Other studies have found that churchgoers are less willing to sympathize with persons involved in efforts to reform society and bring about social justice and equality (Marx, 1967; Bahr, et al., 1971; Gibbs et al., 1973; Rokeach, 1969). My study of Baptists and United Methodists revealed a *negative* correlation ($r = -.30$) between vertical belief and social consequences: persons who were *most* inclined to believe in God, Christ, and a life after death were *least* likely to report that their faith had inspired them to become more involved in community activities which would improve the lot of the poor. Thus, with Quinn, I (1976:347) concluded: "The evidence quite consistently indicates that religious orthodoxy [i.e., vertical belief] is either irrelevant to people's secular orientations, or it is associated with such orientations as ethnocentrism, prejudice, economic and political conservatism, authoritarianism, localism, and an unwillingness to support social change."

If involvement in most local churches does not bring about increased social compassion (indeed, may be associated with a lack of compassion), how can social researchers account for the formation of urban ministries which want the local churches and church-goers to be *more* involved in issues related to the causes and consequences of poverty? What conditions in society, local communities, and local congregations foster organizations which ask church members to engage in outreach activities which many church members are unprepared to do?

Answers to the questions of how and why social movement organizations such as these are formed will increase social researchers' knowledge of group and organizational behavior. They also will be instructive to religious leaders considering the formation of ecumenical urban ministries in their communities.

Institutionalization

Institutionalization is a never-ending process whereby a group seeks a configuration of organizational characteristics which will allow it to be a viable organization. It is a volatile process involving a constant search for some combination of characteristics that works.

Institutionalization also is a multi-dimensional process (Thomas, Potter, Miller, and Aveni, 1972). It occurs at two levels (structure and process), each of which encompasses several dimensions (see Table 1). The structural level concerns the development of relatively enduring policies and practices which constitute the more permanent and stable components of the organization. The process level pertains to the more dynamic and volatile aspects of organizational life: the relationships among people within the group and the group's relationships with other groups.

Eight *structural* dimensions of institutionalization need to be considered: purpose, membership, size, economic resources, formalization, complexity, bureaucratization and distribution of authority.

Purpose. Organizational theory and research stress the intrinsic importance of a clear sense of purpose and the impact it can have on many other dimensions of group life (Champion, 1975; Aldrich, 1979; Hall, 1982). A group's sense of purpose is indicated by its goals. Research on group goals emphasizes the need to examine a groups' "official" goals and its "operative" goals.

Official goals are "the general purposes of the organization as put forth in the charter, annual reports, public statements by key executives and other authoritative pronouncements" (Perrow, 1961:855; Hall, 1972:83). Operative goals have to do with groups' day-by-day operations. They "designate the ends sought through the actual operating policies and practices of the organizations; they tell us what the organization actually is trying to do, regardless of what the official goals say are the aims" (Perrow, 1961:855; Hall, 1972:83).

For a group to be highly institutionalized in terms of its purpose, two conditions should be met. First, the group's official goals should be clear. The group should have a clear definition of the problem(s) it wishes to address and the functions it wants to perform in

Table 1
MODEL OF INSTITUTIONALIZATION
FOR SOCIAL MOVEMENT ORGANIZATIONS

Dimensions	Institutionalization	
	Low	High
Structure		
Purpose	Unclear	Clear
Membership	Unclear	Clear
Size[a]	Small	Moderate/Large
Economic Resources[b]	Inadequate	Adequate
Formalization	Little	Some
Complexity[c]	Little	Some
Bureaucratization	None/Much	Some
Distribution of Authority	Highly (de)centralized	Somewhat centralized
Process		
Administrative Succession	Unsuccessful	Successful
Leadership	Weak	Strong
Stability	Little	Some
Flexibility	None	Some
Productivity	Low	High
Intra-Organizational Relations	Negative	Positive
Inter-Organizational Relations	Negative	Positive

[a] Assumes correlation between size of membership and size of staff
[b] From constituent or member groups and individuals
[c] Assumes programs related to group's purpose

relation to the problem(s). If it does not, the group will be confused from the start and will have great difficulty making decisions relating to other dimensions of institutionalization. Second, there should be a close connection between the group's official goals and its operative goals. The closer the connection between the group's vision or mission and the goals it pursues on a daily basis, the more highly institutionalized the group is.

Membership. Any organization needs to determine who its members will be and why they should belong. A group's purpose should determine its membership. The problem the group wishes to address and the functions it wants to perform in relation to these problems should indicate which groups and/or individuals are to be included. If these groups and individuals are included, the organization has taken an important step toward institutionalization. If they are *not* included (or if other groups and/or individuals who have little or nothing to do with the organization's purpose *are* included), the institutionalization of the group will suffer in this respect.

Size. Organizational size refers to the number of members and the number of staff a group has (Champion, 1975; Aldrich, 1979; Hall, 1982). Though the two aspects of group size are analytically separate (small groups can have large staffs, and large groups can have small staffs), the two tend to be related (Hall, 1982). Groups with few members tend to have small staffs, and groups with many members tend to have large staffs. Thus, the more consistent the two aspects are, the more highly institutionalized a group is on this dimension.

Social movement organizations start out with small memberships and small staffs. And because they are interested in social reform, they may remain relatively small for long periods of time. However, most observers (e.g., Thomas, Potter, Miller, and Aveni, 1972) also agree that to become institutionalized, such groups also should experience some increase in size. Thus, growth in membership and staff is one indication of institutionalization.

Economic Resources. An organization also must have enough resources to survive and pursue its goals. The question of economic resources actually involves three issues. First, where does the group's income come from? If funds come from groups which have an interest in the problems the group wants to address and the functions it wants to perform, the group is rather highly institutionalized in this respect. If its funds come from sources which have little or no interest in its goals and objectives, the organization is not highly institutionalized in this respect.

Second, has the group been able to obtain enough funds to meet its expenses? If the group's annual income is equal to or exceeds its annual expenses, the group has enough resources to function. If its annual expenses exceed its income, the group has not been institutionalized in this respect.

Finally, does the organization have a cash reserve or balance which it can use to absorb any short-run situations where expenses exceed income? If a group has reserves to draw on, it can get through emergency situations resulting from sudden shortfalls in income and/or sudden increases in expenses. If the group has no reserves, it is very vulnerable to sudden shifts in income and/or expenses.

Formalization. The process of institutionalization implies increased formalization over time. Formalization refers to the extent to which an organization's "rules, procedures, instructions, and communications are written" (Litterer, 1973:331; Champion, 1975:88; Pugh *et al.*, 1968). Informal groups seldom, if ever, codify or write down their policies and practices. Highly formalized groups, on the other hand, do codify their policies and practices. They conduct business according to rules and regulations which they specify in a variety of documents which they have on file. These documents include: a constitution and/or bylaws; papers indicating the group has been incorporated and the nature of its status with the Internal Revenue Service (e.g., that it is tax-exempt); job descriptions for staff members; personnel policies; minutes minutes of meetings; and records of income and expenses.

Complexity. Complexity refers to the extent to which a group is structurally differentiated into various departments, committees, and programs (Champion, 1975; Aldrich, 1979; Hall, 1982).

Differentiation of departments and programs occurs along two axes: vertical and horizontal. Vertical differentiation involves a proliferation of departments at the international, national, regional, state and local levels. Horizontal differentiation involves the development of departments and programs at any one of these levels.

One needs to consider both the extent and nature of differentiation at the various levels. The creation of new departments and programs is a sign of institutionalization; the lack of differentiation is a sign of organizational stagnation. But, new departments and programs also ought to be consistent with the group's goals. If they are not, they will inhibit the process of institutionalization.

Bureaucratization. Bureaucratization refers to the relationship between the personal qualities of group members and the tasks the organization wants to perform. It can be described as a continuum. At one end is a non-bureaucratic group which assigns high priority to its individual members and low priority to programmatic goals. At the other extreme is a very bureaucratic group which assigns high priority to group tasks and low priority to the needs of its individual members. Of course, between these poles are semi-bureaucratic groups which establish some balance between their attention to the needs of the organization and the needs of individual members.

Social movement organizations tend to be non-bureaucratic at the beginning. However, this state is problematic because it equates the group with individuals who may or may not be capable of the tasks that need to be accomplished and who may come and go.

To become institutionalized, social movement organizations must create positions with clear expectations related to organizational goals, and expect people in the positions to fulfill these expectations. At the same time, social movement organizations must be flexible enough to redefine the positions when circumstances call for it. They also must take their members' talents and needs into account when appraising their performance.

Distribution of Authority. Distribution of authority refers to the (de)centralization of responsibility among various positions within an organization. In a highly centralized organization, top management retains control over decisions affecting many aspects of organizational life. In a highly decentralized organization, top management delegates the responsibility for many decisions to lower levels of authority.

Both extremes would be problematic in most social movement organizations. Centralization of authority would tend to foster alienation among group members, while decentralization might lead to chaos. Thus, we assume that a social movement organization becomes more highly institutionalized to the extent that group members participate directly in the formulation of policies and program *and* group leaders (e.g., board and staff) have the right to make decisions for the group.

The *process* dimensions of institutionalization have more to do with the actions or behaviors of the group and/or its members at any given time. These dimensions include: administrative succession, leadership, stability, flexibility, productivity, intra-organizational relations, and inter-organizational relations.

Administrative Succession. Administrative succession refers to the replacement of people in key positions of administrative responsibility (Champion, 1975; Hall, 1972:253-260). In social movement organizations, administrative responsibility resides mainly in the hands of the group's director, who is head of the staff.

Organizations which fail to replace directors or have difficulty replacing them are not highly institutionalized. On the other hand, groups which can and do find people to fill key administrative posts are highly institutionalized. Not only do they have positions; they also can recruit people to succeed others who leave without disrupting the normal flow of organizational life.

Leadership. Leadership involves "the ability, based on personal qualities of the leader, to elicit the followers' voluntary compliance on a broad range of matters" (Etzioni, 1965:690-691). But, leadership is not simply a personality trait (Hall, 1972:246). It also involves the utilization of talents which are appropriate to prevailing organizational circumstances (Hall, 1972:247). Thus, the question is whether an organization has been able to recruit people who have the talents that are needed to lead at various stages in the organization's life. This is an important matter, because "in organizations [like social movement organizations] that are relatively loosely structured and where it is expected that the leadership will have a great deal to do with what goes on in the organization, leadership behavior will have a large impact" (Hall, 1972:259).

In social movement (ecumenical urban ministry) organizations, two types of leadership are especially important: the leadership of the director and the leadership of the board.

Previous research suggests that four dimensions are useful in examining the leadership of the director. Each dimension represents a different emphasis, not mutually exclusive alternatives. Thus, two leaders are likely to have a lot in common, but they also are likely to differ in some observable ways which can affect organizational behavior.

First, the director might assume that he/she is personally responsible for most aspects of organizational life. Such a person will try to do almost everything for the group. This has been called "focused leadership." Or the director might assume that many people in the organization have responsibility for various aspects of the group. Such a person will engage a larger number of people in the planning and execution of group activities and decisions. This type of leadership is called "distributed leadership."

Second, a leader can become involved in many diverse activities which relate in one way or another to the group. For example, he/she may take on responsibilities in other organizations because their programs and activities have consequences for one's own group. This style of leadership is called "fragmented" because the leader's attention becomes divided among many different groups and sometimes unpredictable events. Another style of leadership involves greater concentration on matters within one's own group. In this case, the leader limits his/her involvement in other groups so he/she will not be "spread too thin."

Third, one style of leadership stresses the importance of developing new programs to accomplish group goals. This style places high priority on the "initiation of structures." Another leadership style places more emphasis on the well-being of individuals and/or their relationships with others. This style stresses "consideration" and "deeper concern for group members' needs."

Finally, leaders can use different incentives or rewards to foster compliance. Normative incentives stress the importance of work as a "calling" or "ministry." Thus, one is motivated by "higher values" and a view that one's work has a larger purpose. Remunerative incentives stress the importance of work as a source of income. Work is not a "calling," it is a "job." The importance of the job and one's attitude toward one's responsibilities vary with the financial benefits one derives from the job.

Board leadership involves two issues. Board members exhibit leadership by attending meetings. Thus, one needs to examine the annual attendance rates of board members to see how this aspect of leadership varies over time. But there also is a qualitative component to board leadership. How wise are the board's decisions? Does the board do its "homework?" To what extent does it explore and understand the causes and consequences of its actions? How decisive is the board? Does it facilitate or obstruct the organization's business? In short, how "strong" or "weak" is the board?

Stability. All groups seek stability (i.e., continuity among members and staff over time). Stability among members increases the predictability of support. And stability among staff permits the formulation and proper execution of programs. Thus, stability among members and staff is an indication of institutionalization.

Any organization experiences at least some turnover among members and staff. Such turnover is not necessarily problematic. However, rapid turnover can be. Rapid turnover among members fosters unpredictable support. Rapid turnover among staff disrupts continuity and the execution of programs and activities.

Flexibility. Flexibility concerns the extent to which an organization is able to adapt to changing conditions inside and/or outside the group (Champion, 1975:100). Ordinarily some degree of flexibility contributes to institutionalization. It allows a group to respond to emerging issues and to reduce its investments in areas that no longer require as much attention as they might have at some earlier time.

With their interest in social issues and social change, it is especially important that social movement organizations be flexible enough to increase their involvement in some areas and/or curtail their involvement in others. Organizationally, they cannot afford to be so committed to particular programs that they are unable to respond to emerging issues or changes in their environments. To be highly institutionalized, they must be able to phase out their investments in some areas (perhaps turning them over to other groups which could sponsor them on a longer term) and phase in others (which they could experiment with before turning them over to other groups).

Productivity. According to Champion (1975:118), productivity usually means:

> the extent to which an organizational member satisfactorily performs his role or fulfills the expectations of higher-ups. Individuals who accomplish much in relation to their role expectations are said to be "high producers." Those who fail to achieve the minimal standards of their role set by administrative definition are viewed as "low producers."

I prefer to deal with the issue at an organizational level. How productive is the group? How much work is the staff as a whole putting out? These questions are important within an organization, but they also are likely to be important to other groups which support the organization financially. They often want to know whether they are "getting their money's worth."

As a rule, groups which are not highly productive do not fulfill the expectations of their boards or "higher-ups"; their lack of productivity jeopardizes their survival. Groups which produce are more likely to fulfill the expectations of their boards and support groups. Their productivity is an indication—and source—of their institutionalization.

Intra-Organizational Relations. "Intra-organizational relations" is a behavioral concept referring to the relationships among the members and staff of an organization (Champion, 1975; Davidson, Brown, Hofmann, 1978). If these relationships involve mutual respect, a willingness to interact in a free and open manner, and friendliness, the organizational climate is "positive." If people in the group do not respect one another, harbor suspicions of one another, avoid one another and/or are in frequent conflict, the climate is "negative."

Any organization hopes to minimize negative relationships among its members because they can threaten the group's survival and the achievement of its goals. This is especially true in social movement organizations which tend to be relatively small and where people tend to work rather closely together in relation to group goals. Thus, to be highly institutionalized, such a group must do all it can to promote positive relations among group members.

Inter-Organizational Relations. Inter-organizational relations pertain to the quality of relationships with *other* groups and *their* members (Hall, 1982). If the relationships between a social movement organization and some other group involve respect, a willingness to interact in a free and open manner, and friendliness, the inter-organizational relationships can be characterized as "positive." If the relationships between the groups involve suspicion, distrust, avoidance, and conflict, the inter-organizational relationships are "negative."

It is very difficult, if not impossible, for an organization to maintain positive relations with all other groups, and in the case of social movement organizations, negative relationships with some groups might even be expected. Because of their interest in social change, social movement organizations might need to challenge the prevailing policies and practices within some other social groups. Such challenges are likely to be based on some suspicions about their motives, or at least the consequences of their behavior. They also are likely to produce avoidance and/or conflict.

If such negative relationships are with groups which belong to the organization or are related to the organization's goals and objectives, these relationships are problematic. However, if the negative relations are with other groups which are not members or constituent groups, the negative relations might be far less damaging; in some cases, they might even be signs that the organization is performing the functions its members expect it to perform. Under these circumstances, the organization's survival might not be threatened; it might even be enhanced.

Thus, recognizing that some negative relations are likely to occur and may even be beneficial, I assume that positive inter-organizational relations—especially with members and constituent groups—contribute to the institutionalization of ecumenical urban ministries.

In summary, to become more highly institutionalized, an urban ministry should struggle to develop a clear sense of purpose and a clear definition of who its members will be; grow in size; secure enough resources to support its programs and provide some security for dealing with periods of uncertainty and change; develop some formality with regard to record keeping; develop a variety of committees and programs related to its purpose; become somewhat bureaucratic in style of operation, while retaining a concern for individual needs; and develop a somewhat decentralized style of decision making. It also: must succeed in replacing its original leader; seek strong leadership; create a stable membership and staff; have some flexibility in its programs; strive for high productivity; cultivate positive relationships within the group; and develop positive relationships with other groups in its inter-organizational environment, especially the groups most closely related to the group's purpose.

But, how can an ecumenical urban ministry wanting to reform local churches and society ever develop such characteristics? Won't community forces with vested interests in prevailing social arrangements want to defend the status quo? Won't they do all they can to challenge the urban ministry's legitimacy, limit its resources, and disrupt its functioning? If local churches are as uninvolved in social concerns as the literature suggests, won't many of them refuse to support urban ministries? Won't others limit their support to some token amount? If more important needs arise, won't they cut their support altogether?

Knowledge of the conditions affecting the institutionalization of ecumenical urban ministries will add to sociologists' knowledge of social movement organizations generally; it also will offer some guidance to religious leaders who are responsible for policies relating to such groups.

Effectiveness

Effectiveness is the "degree to which [an organization] realizes its goals" (Etzioni,

1964:8). The effectiveness of ecumenical urban ministries is problematic for several reasons. Because local congregations have not been actively involved in social concerns, they are not used to it, and may not know how. They may be timid, even fearful, of "getting their feet wet." Some may feel it is not in their best interest to be involved. Others may even oppose it, feeling such activity either is not an integral part of faith or, at least, not congregational life. Thus, ecumenical urban ministries might experience great difficulty trying to foster social concern programs within local congregations.

Also, churches sometimes have acted in ways which are contrary to the social, economic, and religious interests of low-income people (Graham, 1970). As a result, some low-income people have very negative images of churches; many simply choose not to belong. Thus, ecumenical urban ministries may have difficulty convincing low-income people of their sincerity and identifying low-income people who would be willing to participate in their activities. As a result, ecumenical urban ministries may have difficulty conceptualizing programs that accurately reflect the needs and interests of low-income people; they also may have difficulty carrying out the programs they *are* able to devise.

Yet, some ecumenical urban ministries have been relatively successful in achieving their goals (Takayama and Darnell, 1979; Davidson, Elly, Hull, and Nead, 1979). Thus, researchers must determine under what conditions these groups can cultivate more social concerns programs within local congregations, increase the priority parishioners attach to social concerns, integrate the vertical and horizontal dimensions of faith, and bring about a situation wherein religious involvement does foster social compassion. Under what conditions can they reform social policies that foster poverty, cultivate bonds with the poor, extend services to low-income people, and respond to the emergency needs of the poor?

Answers to these questions can tell us something about the impact of social movement organizations in general; they also can have programmatic implications for religious leaders who want to know what goals ecumenical urban ministries can achieve most readily and what types of strategies and programs might be most effective.

Conclusion

Sociologists are seeking answers to questions about the formation, institutionalization, and effectiveness of social movement organizations. I was able to explore these issues while evaluating a social movement organization in Lafayette, Indiana. The organization was one of several hundred ecumenical urban ministries which evolved in cities throughout the country during the 1960s and early 1970s. As a social movement organization, it faced special problems getting started, surviving, and achieving its goal of increasing local churches' involvement in social concerns. Chapter 2 describes the theoretical framework I used to explore these issues.

CHAPTER 2
AN OPEN SYSTEM APPROACH:
STRUCTURAL CONDUCIVENESS AND RESOURCE MOBILIZATION

The theoretical approach I used to explain the formation, institutionalization, and effectiveness of ecumenical urban ministries stresses an open system approach, drawing heavily from structural and resource mobilization approaches to social movement organizations. I will briefly summarize the assumptions on which the theory is based, then specify the research hypotheses derived from these assumptions.

Open System Approach

The literature on social movement organizations suggests the value of using an open system approach (c.f., McCarthy and Zald, 1977; Zald and McCarthy, 1979; Takayama and Darnell, 1979; Aldrich, 1979; Takayama, 1980; Scherer, 1980; Hall, 1982; Jenkins, 1983). In contrast to a closed system approach, which assumes organizations are self-sufficient units containing all the resources they need to operate, the open system approach assumes factors outside of organizations have important effects on what transpires within them. Also, whereas a closed system approach stresses the permanence of internal organizational structures, the open system approach assumes that organizational goals and procedures tend to change in relation to environmental influences. Finally, a closed system approach assumes that, if an organization's members do what they are expected to do, the group will achieve its goals in an orderly and efficient manner. An open system approach, on the other hand, assumes organizational effectiveness depends on how other groups respond to the group's activities. In short, the open system approach calls attention to "what comes into [an organization] in the form of input, . . . what transpires inside the organization and . . . the nature of the environmental acceptance of the organization and its output" (Hall, 1972:25).

Structural Conduciveness

A traditional line of inquiry has suggested that structural conditions in society and/or local settings can affect the formation, institutionalization, and effectiveness of social movement organizations (e.g., Smelser, 1963; Champion, 1975; Aldrich, 1979; Hall, 1982; Wood and Jackson, 1982). These conditions include the prevailing policies and practices within institutions and the relationships between spheres. They also encompass the relationships between groups in a given social setting. Finally, they include the outcomes of these structures and processes (e.g., the distribution of wealth, income, power, and prestige).

Structural conditions may be conducive to the growth of social movement organizations at some *times* ("periods") more than others. Period factors include *societal* conditions such as rates of social change (e.g., slow vs. rapid). They also include conditions within particular institutional spheres (e.g., the extent to which traditional religious beliefs and practices are widely accepted or are being challenged).

Structural conditions in some *localities* ("places") also may be more conducive to social movements than others. For example, social movements are more likely to develop in urban areas than rural areas (Wood and Jackson, 1982; Tilly, 1974). But, social conditions within some urban areas may be more conducive than others. For example, in one city Roman Catholic and Protestant churches may get along very well, while in another there might be a history of interfaith conflict.

Structural conditions in society and in local communities are important because they can influence the likelihood of *any* social movement organizations occurring, the localities where they are most likely to evolve, and the nature of those which are formed. They also can influence the viability of groups which are formed and their ability to achieve their goals.

However, there has been growing awareness that understanding the structural context is not enough. Social movement organizations do not always evolve in contexts which seem most conducive to their growth. And, sometimes, they are formed in contexts which are not conducive to their growth. Thus, there has been increased interest in other perspectives which might supplement our understanding of social movement organizations.

Resource Mobilization

The approach which has attracted the most attention stresses the importance of resources and the extent to which they are mobilized (McCarthy and Zald, 1973, 1977; Zald and McCarthy, 1979; Knoke and Wood, 1981; Jenkins, 1983).

Resources are units which can be called upon to pursue some end. These units can include tangible entities such as money, facilities, and people. They also can include intangibles such as ideas, legitimacy, and leadership.

These resources are more available at some periods and in some places than others. However, their availability does not necessarily correspond with the structural conditions discussed above. Resources *might* be most plentiful in a period and place where structural conditions are most conducive to the growth of social movement organizations, but they might not be. Conversely, they might be most available when and where structural conditions are least conducive to social movement organizations.

Analysts who stress the importance of resources assume the greater the availability of resources, the greater the chance that social movement organizations will be formed, institutionalized, and effective (even in contexts which otherwise are not conducive to such outcomes).

But, the availability of resources is no guarantee that social movement organizations will evolve. Emergent organizations must mobilize the resources they need. They need to secure the resources, incorporate them into the organization's structures and processes, and put them to good use. If they fail to do so, their chances of being formed, institutionalized, and effective are minimal.

Combining the structural conduciveness and resource mobilization perspectives, I identified a list of factors to help explain the formation, institutionalization, and effectiveness of ecumenical urban ministries (see Table 1). These factors pertain to three levels of analysis: societal, local, and organizational.

Societal ("Period") Factors

I divided period factors into four categories: structural conditions in the secular realm and in the religious sphere, and resources in the secular realm and religious sphere.

Structural Conditions: Secular Realm

Social Conditions. If the society's values, political arrangements, and economic institutions are being taken for granted and, thus, are the basis on which all other behaviors "naturally" occur, society is not likely to spawn or tolerate groups which want to challenge the legitimacy of that order. Such conditions also are likely to limit the effectiveness of such groups by stifling new programatic ideas and the willingness of people in various constituencies to become involved.

On the other hand, if the society's values, political arrangements, and economic institutions are being questioned, it is more likely that religious organizations expressing dissident views also will arise. A liberal, change-oriented social climate in the society as a whole would liberate people within the religious sphere to consider forming such groups (Takayama, 1977). Zald (1970) argued that urbanization and the sense of uprootedness which accompany it, contributed to the growth of the YMCA movement in England and the United States in the 1800s. And Gamson's (1975) data on challenge groups reveals that "[al]most three quarters of the groups [N = 39] began during relatively turbulent periods, periods characterized by major social movements and many new and diversified challenges." Wilson (1978:112) says: "New religious movements do not arise out of stable contexts, rather they rise out of a changing social order."

Social change also should contribute to the effectiveness of reform groups like LUM. The dissident ideas which tend to increase in time of social change could suggest new goals and/or new programatic ideas; they also should increase the likelihood that people in various constituencies would be willing to experiment with new programs.

Structural Conditions: Religious Sphere

Policies and Practices. The policies and practices of secular institutions are often reflected in the values and interests of religious groups. As long as secular policies and practices are accepted, the corresponding policies and practices in the religious sphere also will tend to be accepted. Under these conditions, there is little or no reason to expect the religious sphere to form or support reform organizations to challenge prevailing norms. If there is consensus that churches "ought to stay out of politics," there is little basis for institutionalizing groups to increase church involvement in social concerns. And if such groups already exist, prevailing policies and practices supporting the status quo would limit their effectiveness.

However, if secular policies and practices are being challenged, these challenges almost necessarily will have some influence on church people in positions which interface most directly with the broader challenges to societal policies and practices (Wilson, 1978:371). These people, in turn, will begin to question the prevailing policies and practices within the religious sphere. Their challenges to the legitimacy of prevailing norms are likely to stimulate an interest in forming and supporting groups which might experiment with alternative policies and practices. The persistence of such questioning also should contribute to the effectiveness of such groups, increasing the likelihood that others in the church would consider the alternative ideas (Stinchcombe, 1965).

Table 1
FACTORS EXPECTED TO AFFECT THE FORMATION, INSTITUTIONALIZATION, AND EFFECTIVENESS OF ECUMENICAL URBAN MINISTRIES

	Formation	Institution-alization	Effect-iveness
Period Factors			
A. Structural Conditions: Secular Realm			
Social Conditions (change)	+	+	+
B. Structural Conditions: Religious Sphere			
Policies and Practices (changing)	+	+	+
Cooperation (possible)	+	+	+
C. Resources: Secular Realm			
Economic Conditions (prosperity)	+	+	+
D. Resources: Religious Sphere			
Economic Resources (abundant)	+	+	+
Ideological Justification (possible)	+	+	+
Personnel (available)	+	+	+
Place Factors			
A. Structural Conditions: Secular Realm			
Political Climate (liberal)	+	+	+
B. Structural Conditions: Religious Sphere			
Problem (exists/persists)	+	+	+
Cooperation (possible)	+	+	+
Competition (little)	+	+	+
C. Resources: Secular Realm			
Community Size (large)	+	+	+
D. Resources: Religious Sphere			
Support Groups (exist)	+	+	+
Resources in Support Groups (abundant)	+	+	+
Organizational Factors			
A. Fostering Formation			
Leadership (secured)	+	NA	NA
Lay Support (secured)	+	NA	NA
Clergy Support (secured)	+	NA	NA
Economic Resources (secured)	+	NA	NA
B. Fostering Institutionalization and Effectiveness			
Institutionalization	NA	+	+
Effectiveness	NA	+	0

\+ : Positive relationship expected
0 : No relationship expected
NA : Not applicable, or is subsumed under another variable

Cooperation. If the experimental group is to have its own administrative structure but be supported (financially and in other ways) by other member organizations which have representatives on a council governing the group's activities (Warren, 1967), these other organizations must be willing to cooperate with one another (e.g., talk about issues of common concern, share financial resources in joint ventures over which each would have only partial control, and conduct programs together). If that willingness does not exist, a new "federated" group is not likely to emerge, grow, or be effective over time. However, if groups *are* willing to cooperate, a federated group can develop, has a better chance of surviving, and might be effective.

In the sphere of religion, cooperation among groups means ecumenism (i.e., interaction between two or more religious groups for sake of either learning more about one another's traditions or working together to accomplish some goal the groups have in common). Ecumenism can involve groups from different traditions (e.g., Protestants, Catholics, and Jews). Or, the groups can be different subunits within a single religious tradition (e.g., Orthodox, Conservative, and Reform Judaism; the many denominations within Protestantism).

Zald (1970:26) noted the important role that interfaith cooperation played in the formation and development of groups such as the YMCA and other American Protestant benevolent associations.

Resources: Secular Realm

Economic Conditions. When a nation's economy is weak (i.e., the Gross National Product is down, the stock market is down, unemployment is high, and personal disposable income and personal savings are down), established institutions suffer a decline in their resources. They struggle to maintain existing programs and often have to cut back. Under these conditions of scarcity, established groups are not likely to plow their limited resources into new, possibly risky, organizations (Zald, 1970:192). Many individuals also are out of work, unable to provide their families with what they consider "the basics," and do not feel they have the extra resources to "squander" on "frills" and "luxuries" such as "entertainment, voluntary associations, and organized religion and politics" (McCarthy and Zald, 1977:1224). People grow uncertain about the future, their donations for institutional development become problematic, and their participation in "non-essential" or "non-productive" organizations declines (McCarthy and Zald, 1977). Under these conditions, it is unlikely that new organizations requiring support from other organizations and individuals will be formed, grow, or be effective in achieving their goals.

On the other hand, when the economy is strong (i.e., the GNP is up, the stock market is up, unemployment is low, and personal disposable income and personal savings are up), new organizations can flourish. As Hall (1972:302) has observed, "In periods of economic growth, organizations, in general, also grow . . ." Established institutions have excess resources, some of which they can afford to plow into new ventures. And individuals feel they have enough resources to fulfill their basic needs. They feel they can afford to share some of their extra resources with other persons and groups, including fringe or dissident groups which may be exploring alternatives to the prevailing social order. Under these conditions of abundance, movement organizations can be nourished (Zald, 1970; McCarthy and Zald, 1977; Takayama, 1977).

Economic prosperity not only affects the formation and institutionalization of such groups; it also affects their effectiveness. In Hall's (1982:301-302) words: "At some points in time [e.g., economic hardship], organizations appear to do little else than attempt to cope with [environmental] constraints. At other times [e.g., economic prosperity] the environment is more benign. In the latter situation, more attention can be given to matters such as goals and goal attainment." Thus, economic prosperity in the society as a whole should contribute to the formation, institutionalization, and effectiveness of social movement organizations like LUM.[1]

Resources: Religious Sphere

Economic Resources. If an institutional sphere is experiencing a scarcity of resources, it is not likely to spin off or support new organizations (Stinchcombe, 1965:167-168; Hall, 1972:311). If there is not enough money to cover current expenses, and little or no savings, institutional energies will be spent protecting existing groups and programs. Thoughts of building and institutionalizing new organizations and programs will be remote. Even if such thoughts occur, they are not likely to get very far because, as Zald (1970:192) has noted: "in a 'politics of scarcity,' in which new directions must be financed from a stagnant or declining resources base, any change in allocation must imply a loss to some older interest, at least for the short run." And most organizations are not likely to sacrifice established programs to pursue new and perhaps risky directions, especially in periods of economic hardship. Garrett (1980:355) notes that "during periods of economic stringency when denominational budgets tighten up, ecumenical contributions are generally one of the first items reduced or eliminated from denominational disbursements." Such cutbacks clearly limit ecumenical groups' potential for effectiveness (Takayama, 1977; Johnson, 1980).

However, as Zald (1970:192) tells us: "When a resource base is expanding and fund sources are changing slowly, it is possible that new directions and allocations can be grafted onto an organization's old economy without major shifts in allocation criteria (that is, an organization operating under 'politics of abundance' conditions may add new program interests with little harm to older ones)." Abundant resources imply a sense of future security and a willingness to expend excess resources on innovative projects. And as Johnson (1980:334) said, "financial support will be a key indicator of effectiveness." Some evidence for this thesis comes from the origins of the YMCA during a period in which there was a "sense of growing return to religion" (Zald, 1970:27).

Ideological Justification. A stable or growing institutional sphere might be able to expend its excess resources on many experimental groups. Assuming it cannot afford to support all these groups at once, it must find a way to differentiate between groups it will support and those it will not. The criterion most likely to be employed is the ability to justify the group in the context of the sphere's overall goals and interests (Stinchcombe, 1965:167-168; Hall, 1972:311; Bendix, 1956; Winter, 1977; Wood, 1981). To the extent there is ideological justification for reform groups, resistance to their ideas and programs will be less defensible and acceptance should be somewhat greater. Thus, urban ministries must be able to demonstrate that their goals are consistent with traditional religious concerns.

Personnel. Clergy are most likely to play key leadership roles in ecumenical urban ministries. If there were a shortage of clergy, most would be assigned positions where the need is felt to be greatest (e.g., parishes); few, if any, would be left over for experimental positions where the need is not as well established (e.g., urban ministries). On the other hand, if there were an adequate supply of clergy, the chances of starting and institutionalizing ecumenical urban ministries would be increased. There would be a supply of people within the sphere who are willing and able to assume the task of creating and leading them.

Such people might be located in positions of authority which liberate them from dependence on groups which might oppose their interests (e.g., bishops or denomination officials in national and regional offices [Harrison, 1959; Demerath and Hammond, 1969; Wood, 1970]).

Another possible source of leaders might be clergy who do not necessarily have much authority or control over many resources, but who are in positions where they either are expected to cultivate new ideas, or are likely to develop such ideas as a function of their associations with others. People in institutional think tanks, national study or planning committees, and campus ministries would be examples (Hadden, 1969; Quinley, 1974; Winter, 1977).

A third pool of personnel would be young people who are involved in, or recently have completed, training for careers in the institutional sphere. "Young turks" are encouraged to explore alternatives to existing organizational patterns. Some have opportunities to participate in pilot or experimental projects. While these younger personnel (e.g., seminarians) might lack the authority high-ranking church officials have, they might have ideas and motivations that, with some support, could be quite appropriate for leading new social movement organizations.

Local ("Place") Factors

Local factors fall into the same four categories discussed above.

Structural Conduciveness: Secular Realm

Political Climate. Local communities can have different political orientations or "climates" (Hall, 1982:229 and 232). Community organizations can have policies and practices stressing social order (conservative) or social change (liberal). If groups such as the major political parties, the business community, and the media are oriented toward maintaining the status quo, the political climate is not conducive to the formation, institutionalization, or effectiveness of social or religious groups wanting to foster change. Such groups will tend to be viewed as "deviant" and their goals will tend to be discredited.

On the other hand, if the political parties, business leaders, and media are inclined to be critical of local policies and practices—if they urge others in the community to understand the need for change—then the political climate is more conducive to the survival of reform groups. It will contribute to their legitimacy and the support they need to pursue their goals.

Structural Conduciveness: Religious Sphere

Existence of the Problem. The existence of a problem does not guarantee that efforts will be made to resolve it, but it increases the chances. Its existence is likely to stir the consciences of potential leaders and provide them with the evidence (however systematic or impressionistic) needed to persuade others that the problem is real and needs to be addressed. If the problem is sufficiently large in scope, its persistence would provide a rationale for efforts to institutionalize the new group and would cause people to respond more favorably to its programs (Hall, 1982:231; Ross, 1980).[2]

Studies of other communities provide some support for this hypothesis. Hadden and Longino (1975:37) have shown how racial inequality and turmoil in Dayton, Ohio, during the late 1960s, along with a pattern of churches not being involved in such issues, fostered the development of an experimental religious group called the Congregation of Reconciliation. Takayama and Darnell (1979) have argued that the strike of sanitation workers and the eventual assassination of Dr. Martin Luther King in 1968—which they describe as "a time of anxiety, despair and discouragement for many" in Memphis—were crucial factors in the formation of an ecumenical urban ministry in that city in 1968-69.

Cooperation. While a national spirit of ecumenism seems important, it might not penetrate all localities and, therefore, might not be a force in some communities (Johnson, 1980:331). If it does not exist at the local level, its absence represents a serious stumbling block to the formation, institutionalization, and effectiveness of groups which need interfaith support and hope to work with many local churches.

However, a national spirit of ecumenism tends to filter into many communities, especially those with substantial numbers of Roman Catholic and liberal Protestant churches. National and regional church offices tend to legitimize ecumenism and often stimulate and support ecumenical programs at the local level. If local churches have worked together on other programs, there is an increased chance that they would be willing to work together on an ecumenical urban ministry. Takayama and Darnell (1979) have demonstrated the important role that ecumenism played in the formation of the Metropolitan Interfaith Association in Memphis.

Competition. Emery and Trist (1967) have called attention to the effects which the "texture" of an organization's environment can have on its development (also see Aldrich, 1979; Pennings, 1980; Marrett, 1980; Hall, 1982). By texture, they mean the number of similar organizations in an area and what their presence does to a group's behavior.

Emery and Trist suggest there are four levels of competition. The first level involves no organized competition. A new group would be the only one of its kind in the area. The second level involves no organized competition, but more recognizable clusters of support and opposition. Under these conditions, a group tends to develop some strategy for dealing with its environment. "In the clustered environment," say Emery and Trist (1976:440), "the relevant objective is that of 'optimal location,' some positions being discernible as potentially richer than others . . ." Organizations under these conditions . . . tend to grow in size and also to become hierarchical, with a tendency toward centralized control and coordination."

Competition intensifies at level three. In Emery and Trist's words, "It is a type of environment in which there is more than one organization of the same kind; indeed, the existence of a number of similar organizations now becomes the dominant characteristic of the environmental field." The environment is "disturbed" as groups vie with one another for control over "turf." Under these conditions, organizations tend to develop tactics to maximize their own survival. "The flexibility required encourages a certain decentralization and also puts a premium on quality and speed of decision at various peripheral points" (Emery and Trist, 1967:440).

Finally, competition is most intense at level four. There "is a great deal of causal interconnection among elements in the environment" (Hall, 1982:234). But, according to Emery and Trist (1967:441), "the dynamics [of this level] arise not simply from the interaction of the component organizations, but also from the field itself. The 'ground' is in motion." Thus, they describe this stage of competition as "turbulent" and "increasingly unpredictable."

Following this approach, I expected that the limited competition in levels one and two is most conducive to the mobilization of ecumenical urban ministries. Under these conditions, new groups will be seen as unique organizations attempting to fulfill a need no other groups are fulfilling. They also should be able to obtain the resources they need to pursue their goals with relatively little worry about organized opposition from similar groups. For example, they could apply to their parent organizations for funds knowing there are few, if any, other groups in the area with similar goals also applying for support.[3]

Resources: Secular Realm

Community Size. Stinchcombe (1965), Tilly (1974), Aldrich (1979), Pennings (1980), and Hall (1982) have argued that urban areas are more fertile grounds than rural areas are for spawning new organizations. One reason has to do with the heterogeneity of urban populations. According to Aldrich (1979:173-174):

> Urbanization removes some constraints on the likelihood of ideas attracting enough interest to be turned into new organizational forms: also it increases the diversity of the organizational population by generating environmental heterogeneity and new niches (Fischer, 1975). Stinchcombe (1965, p. 151) stressed the consequences or urban social heterogeneity for the acceptance of new ideas: "Socially differentiated urban populations present alternatives to each other, and most innovations can find a home in some social segment." The secular city, with its universalistic standards and high rates of social mobility, is a favorable atmosphere for nurturing and sheltering new ideas until they can become forms. In this respect urbanization has the same effect as an increase in societal information-processing capacity (see Tilly, 1973).

Another reason urban areas are more fertile grounds for new groups concerns the "central place" function they perform: they become magnets for business offices, hospitals, political offices, legal services, shopping centers, leisure and recreation activities. These services attract people and new resources which foster the development of even more voluntary associations (Ullman, 1941; Aldrich, 1971). And because people in all areas are likely to turn to urban groups for information and assistance, this predisposition might contribute to the groups' effectiveness.

Resources: Religious Sphere

Support Groups. A community also must include a number of organizations which can justify a new group in terms of their traditional ideological commitments. In the religious sphere, this means there must be a pool of local churches which view social concern as a meaningful dimension of religious commitment.

Conservative and fundamentalist theologies (in addition to being suspicious of ecumenism generally—believing it requires groups to compromise on truths they believe should not be compromised)—stress individual salvation and personal reform to the virtual exclusion of social change. They assume personal commitment to Christ will foster social concern, an assumption which the data in Chapter 1 tend not to support. Thus, they foster a view that social problems are mainly spiritual, not economic and political, issues.

Roman Catholics and liberal Protestants have theologies which are more conducive to involvement in social concerns. They have religious teachings and programatic commitments in the area of social concerns. Both groups have issued more authoritative documents and sponsored more programs on social concerns than sectarian Protestant groups have. Catholic Charities, the National Campaign for Human Development, the National Council of Churches, and One Great Hour of Sharing are examples of Catholic and mainline Protestant efforts in the area of social concerns (Evans, 1979; Parella, 1975; Wilson, 1978:378-379; Jenkins, 1977; Hessel, 1979; Feagin, 1975; Amerson and Carroll, 1979). Clergy from these denominations were most active in social concerns activities during the 1960s (Hadden, 1969:124 and 170; Quinley, 1974; Stuhr, 1972:54; Blume, 1970). Takayama and Darnell (1979) indicate that liberal groups—Episcopal, Presbyterian, and United Methodist judicatories, along with eight congregations (three Catholic, one Episcopal, two United Methodist, one AME, and one Baptist)—were instrumental in forming the Memphis urban ministry.

Thus, a core of Roman Catholic and liberal Protestant churches in the area would seem necessary for an ecumenical urban ministry to be mobilized (Takayama, 1977).

Resources in Support Groups. If the potential support groups in the area are small and lack the finances the new group needs to function, the group will have a difficult time getting started, surviving over time, and achieving its goals. However, if the potential support groups have large memberships and are well off financially, the chances are much better that the group will be mobilized (Stinchcombe, 1965; McCarthy and Zald, 1977; Pennings, 1980; Hall, 1982). Larger and more affluent churches can provide more volunteers and generate more financial support through regular collections and special appeals. They also tend to have more physical facilities, which increase their chances of participating in the new group's programs, either because they volunteer use of their facilities or because the group asks to use them.

Organizational Factors

But, organizations need to mobilize these resources if they are to be formed. To remain viable over time, they also need to incorporate them into the structural and process dimensions of organizational life. Finally, they need to put the resources to good use if they are to be effective.

Factors Affecting Formation

Four factors seem most useful in explaining the formation of ecumenical urban ministries: leadership, support among lay members of potential support groups, support among clergy members of potential support groups, and economic resources.

Leadership. Analyses of leadership in the formation of religious groups often stress the crucial role of one person whose qualities transcend those of other people, whose personality is a force in the lives of others. Such analyses easily lend themselves to theories emphasizing the importance of charisma.[4]

While charisma may be helpful in explaining the formation of *some* religious groups, it probably has been over-emphasized. Ordinary people, in the right place at the right time, can play crucial roles in the formation of groups. According to Esman (1972), they need two resources: personal dedication ("commitment") to the goals of the group they want to form, and knowledge of problems involved and some possible ways in solving them ("competence").

A leader in the formation of a social movement organization needs to have a conviction that his/her "calling" is to solve a particular problem by creating a new group. This sense of over-riding urgency produces a willingness to persist in the difficult and time-consuming tasks required to form a group.

But, personal dedication is not enough. A dedicated, but misguided, person will have great difficulty persuading others that one's message is valid and/or that he/she knows how to solve the problem. Knowledge about the problem and some reasonable courses of action also is necessary (Hall, 1972:307).

Support Within Potential Support Groups. If potential support groups lack people with values, beliefs, and interests which are consistent with those of the new group, the new group will have a difficult time taking root. There will be few people to volunteer time and energy to the new group.

On the other hand, if the potential support groups contain people with values, beliefs, and interests which are consistent with those of the new group, the new group stands a better chance of taking root. A pool of supportive people can provide the resources needed to get the new group off the ground. They also can organize to put support of the new group on their churches' agenda. Finally, they can provide volunteers the new group needs even if their churches balk at providing formal support.

The group leader will seek the support of people who belong to his/her own congregation and denomination (Snow, Zurcher, and Ekland-Olson, 1980). He/she will have the most frequent interaction with members of these groups; will know their interests better than others; and will know the social, economic, and political resources they can contribute to the group.

Within congregations, support is most likely to come from lay people in professional occupations. Flacks (1971), Zald and Ash (1966), Hamilton (1972), Rothschild-Whitt (1976), and Vanfossen (1979) have stressed the important role professional workers can play in the formation of social movement organizations. For example, Vanfossen (1979:155) says:

> . . . while the upper-middle class generally is one of the most conservative classes politically, within it there is a substratum of radical and liberal intellectuals from educational, social service, and artistic circles, which commonly provides the leadership for radical social and political movements (Hamilton, 1972).

Rothschild-Whitt's (1976:79) data indicate that the growth of "participatory-democratic organizations" (which tend to be social movement organizations) is "facilitated by having a supportive and liberal professional base in the community." In her words,

> . . . the existence of a large pool of professionals, though usually taken for granted, appears to be a significant contributing factor in the growth of alternative service organizations in the area. Such professionals contribute to the maintenance of alternatives in a variety of ways.

In short, "an alternative organization located in a town without a base of relevant professional support . . . may expect to encounter many difficulties" trying to establish itself (Rothschild-Whitt, 1976:80).[5]

Another group which may include a disproportionate share of supportive people would be the spouses of professional people. Professional people tend to marry people with college educations and, quite frequently, advanced degrees. Some of these spouses tend to adopt a traditional role of homemaker, either on a short-term basis while the children are young, or on a permanent basis. In either case, they tend to be highly educated, creative people who often have an interest in contributing to the community in some way. They tend to seek out opportunities to make use of their education and skills. They can be a force either for creating reform groups which are in areas of interest to them or mobilizing support for such groups.

Support of Professional Staffs in Potential Support Groups. An ecumenical urban ministry also can benefit from the support of people who hold leadership positions in potential support groups. In church circles, that means obtaining the support of pastors and other clergy.

Studies indicate that several factors may predispose local clergy to support the formation of ecumenical urban ministries. These include: having professional positions which insulate them from negative ramifications of their words and actions (Wilson, 1978:378-379; Jenkins, 1977; Evans, 1979; Hammond and Mitchell, 1966; Hadden and Rymph, 1966; Earle, *et al.*, 1975:253; Hadden, 1969:185; Quinley, 1974); association with the leader of the incipient group, mainly along denominational lines, though not exclusively (Snow, Zurcher, and Ekland-Olson, 1980); being relatively young (Hadden, 1969; Nelsen, *et al.*, 1973; Quinley, 1974); theological beliefs stressing the intrinsic importance of "loving one's neighbor" and "doing good for others" (Stark and Foster, 1970; Hadden, 1969; Nelsen, *et al.*, 1973); belief that involvement in community and social issues is an integral part of one's ministerial role (Blizzard, 1956a and b; 1958a and b; 1959; Campbell and Pettigrew, 1959; Cox, 1968; Nelsen, *et al.*, 1973; Winter, 1977); liberal political beliefs (Johnson, 1967; Hadden, 1969; Nelson, *et al.*, 1973; Quinley, 1974); a tendency "to take as [their] primary reference group not the congregation they serve, but their ministerial colleagues" (Wilson, 1978:386; Martin, 1972:30; Quinley, 1974:142; Hadden and Rymph, 1966); and the perception that such involvement is in their own best interest (Pope, 1942:195; Earle, *et al.*, 1976:286; Hadden and Longino, 1974:47).

Economic Resources. Finally, an ecumenical urban ministry must secure the economic resources it needs to support its staff and programs. It must obtain enough money to cover start-up costs, such as salaries and program expenses. If it cannot obtain these resources, the organization is not likely to be formed.

An ecumenical urban ministry is most likely to seek economic support from its parent organizations. Thus, it is most likely to approach denominations, congregations, and people who have been involved in its formation in other ways (e.g., drawing up its constitution and bylaws). However, in its eagerness to get started, it also is likely to accept support from a wide variety of other groups which want to support one or more of its proposed activities.

Factors Affecting Institutionalization

I assume six structural and process dimensions (especially those pertaining to resources) play key roles in the institutionalization of social movement organizations. These dimensions include: purpose, economic resources, administrative succession, leadership, intra-organizational relations, and inter-organizational relations.

Sense of purpose can affect nearly all other aspects of group life, but its most obvious effects are to clarify a group's definition of who should belong and who should not (membership); indicate from where the group should get its resources and the amount of resources it will be able to obtain from those sources; influence the number and nature of the group's programs (complexity); increase its chances of finding replacements for its key leaders; stabilize its membership and staff; maintain flexibility in its programs; increase leadership and productivity; and foster positive relations among group members and between the group and other organizations related to its goals and objectives.

The more economic resources the group has, the more staff it can afford; the more programs it can sponsor; the more stable its membership and staff are likely to be; and the more positive relationships are likely to be among group members and with other organizations (especially those which can affect its resources).

Administrative succession is crucial because the replacement of key leaders can stabilize group membership and economic resources; increase or maintain the leadership of board and staff members; increase productivity; and foster more positive intra- and inter-organizational relations.

Most research points to the importance of leadership in voluntary and social movement organizations (e.g., Esman, 1972; Hall, 1982; Wood, 1981). This research suggests that leadership tends to improve the group's economic resources, the number and nature of its programs, bureaucratization, the distribution of authority, productivity, intra-organizational relations, and inter-organizational relations.

Positive intra-organizational relations also are important because they can improve productivity; foster stability among group members and staff; promote leadership; and improve relations with other groups.

Finally, positive inter-organizational relations tend to improve economic resources, the stability of membership, the ability to replace key administrative leaders, leadership of the board and staff, productivity, and relations among group members.[6]

I also assumed that the more effective an organization is in achieving its goals, the more highly institutionalized the group would become; the less effective it is, the less institutionalized it would be. In Johnson's (1980:334) words:

> . . . people who are paying for a program are not going to remain silent when that program is non-productive. For example, it is unlikely that contributions can be expected for funds to support 'economic justice' when there are no evident results from such a program.

Within this context, I assumed that some dimensions of an urban ministry's effectiveness would influence its institutionalization more than other dimensions would. Effectiveness increasing local churches' *own* involvement in social concerns should contribute the most to institutionalization. The more effective an urban ministry is in increasing churches' own involvement in social concerns, the clearer its sense of purpose would be, the clearer its commitment to churches as members would be, the more churches would join, the greater its economic resources would be, the more successful it would be replacing its key administrative leaders, the more stable its church memberships would be, the more positive relations would be among its members, and the more positive its relationships would be with local churches.

Effectiveness working with low-income people *on behalf of* local churches is likely to have a mixture of positive and negative effects on institutionalization. Effectiveness in this area might foster a clear sense of purpose, a greater commitment to low-income people, more positive relations within the group, and more positive relations with the poor. However, success in advocating social changes that would benefit the poor also might cause local churches to reduce their support, thus contributing to "deinstitutionalization" (Wood, 1972; Jenkins, 1977).

Factors Affecting Effectiveness

Highly institutionalized social movement organizations should have a greater chance of achieving their goals than less institutionalized groups. Among other things, more highly institutionalized groups would have a clarity of purpose, economic resources, a variety of programs, leadership, and productivity—all of which should enable them to sponsor activities that would contribute to the fulfillment of their goals. Less highly institutionalized groups would lack the clarity of purpose, economic resources, programs, leadership, and productivity to do a good job.

Ecumenical urban ministry organizations have tended to pursue two goals: working with low-income people on behalf of local churches and/or trying to increase local congregations' own involvement in issues related to poverty (Johnson, 1969). Following Hall (1982), I assumed these goals tend to be independent of one another. Success in one area is not likely to have much impact on an organization's success in another. Thus, rather than assuming accomplishments in one area will spill over into another, effective organizations develop programs specifically designed to accomplish each of its goals.

Conclusion

My theoretical framework for explaining the formation, institutionalization, and effectiveness of ecumenical urban ministry organizations was based on an open system approach, drawing heavily from literature stressing the importance of structural determinants and resource mobilization. I specified seven structural and seven resource factors I thought might have some effect.

Structural factors at the societal level which I thought would be conducive to the growth of ecumenical urban ministries included: changing societal norms and values; changing policies and practices within the religious sphere; and a spirit of ecumenism. Structural factors at the local level included a liberal political climate; the existence/persistence of a problem (in this case, churches not being involved in issues related to the causes and consequences of poverty); cooperation among local churches; and the absence of other organizations with similar goals.

Resource factors at the societal level included a healthy economy; an abundance of economic resources within the religious sphere; religious justification for social reform; and a supply of religious personnel who might want to be leaders in urban ministry organizations. Local resources included a large, urban population; the existence of Roman Catholic and mainline Protestant churches which might support an urban ministry; and an abundance of resources within these support groups.

Finally, I argued that social movement organizations have some control over their own fate. To the extent they mobilize the leadership, support, and economic resources they need, they can be formed. Once formed, several structural and process dimensions (especially those having to do with resources) should promote institutionalization, which should promote effectiveness. Effectiveness, in turn, should promote institutionalization, but a group's success in pursuing any one of its goals is not likely to have much impact on its success achieving others.

CHAPTER 3
METHOD: A CASE STUDY

This chapter discusses my reasons for using a case study approach (including why I studied the Lafayette Urban Ministry), the specific methods I used, and my plan for presenting and analyzing the data in Chapters 4 through 9.

The Case Study Approach

There are two main ways to examine social movement (urban ministry) organizations: conducting a survey of many different groups, and doing an in-depth analysis of one which has survived and been relatively successful. Johnson (1969) used the survey approach in his study of experimental ministries. Takayama (1977) has proposed a longitudinal survey which could provide many important insights into the various conditions under which urban ministries are formed, develop different patterns of operating, and experience different amounts of success. Takayama and Darnell (1979) used the case study method in their analysis of an urban ministry organization in Memphis, Tennessee.

The case study approach was most consistent with my interest in obtaining first-hand experience with a religious group struggling with the issue of social inequality.[1] The experience demonstrated that the problems of formation, institutionalization, and effectiveness are real-life challenges to organizational leaders (and not just theoretical-academic issues). The experience also sensitized me to factors that needed to be considered if I was to describe and analyze an urban ministry's experiences. The longitudinal nature of the case study also allowed me the time needed to gather historical and qualitative, as well as quantitative, data related to my theoretical framework.

A convergence of opportunity and need led to the selection of the Lafayette Urban Ministry (LUM) as the group I would study.[2]

The case study approach also was compatible with LUM's needs. As evaluator, I was able to observe the problems LUM faced and the ways in which it tried to resolve these problems. Over time, group members came to trust my assessments and allowed me to make recommendations. A number of these changes proved beneficial.[3]

Specific Methods

Data-gathering methods included: participant observation, records and documents, interviews, a survey of local churches, an evaluation of the Tippecanoe County Federation of Churches, the local newspaper, and other literature and research. Table 1 summarizes how these methods were related to the issues I needed to examine.

Participant Observation[4]

Between 1975 and 1981, I attended almost all of LUM's monthly board meetings. From 1975 to 1976, I was strictly an observer. From 1977 to 1979, I attended as a participant-observer, serving as chairman of the Program and Planning Committee.

Table 1
SPECIFIC METHODS AND HOW THEY RELATE TO THEORETICAL ISSUES

	Independent Variables			Dependent Variables		
	Societal Conditions	Local Conditions	LUM Factors	Formation	Institutionalization	Effectiveness
Participant observation	–	✓	✓	–	✓	✓
Records and documents	–	–	✓	✓	✓	✓
Interviews	–	✓	✓	✓	✓	–
Church survey	–	✓	–	–	–	✓
Evaluation of Federation	–	✓	–	✓	–	–
Local Newspaper	✓	✓	–	–	–	✓
Other literature and research	✓	✓	–	–	–	–

✓ = Method used to gather data on this issue
– = Method not used on this issue

During that time, I was not formally considered a member of the board (I was not an elected representative), and I did not vote. Between 1980 and 1981, I did not chair any committees and, thus, was less active at board meetings (serving only as an at-large board member).

I also attended most monthly meetings of the Program and Planning Committee. From 1977 to 1979, I chaired the committee. Between 1979 and 1981, I was a regular member.

From 1975 to 1979, I attended most all monthly meetings of LUM's Executive Committee (i.e., its officers, committee chairpersons, and the director). Beginning in 1980, schedule conflicts prevented me from attending Executive Committee meetings on a regular basis, though I attended on occasion. The Executive Committee also reports to the full board every month, so I was aware of actions it took on behalf of the board.

Also, during 1975 and 1976, I attended all weekly staff meetings. After 1977, I did not attend staff meetings, though I maintained regular contact with individual staff members.

Finally, I became involved in many of LUM's activities. I participated in a special meeting LUM had with the Mission Committee of the presbytery of Wabash Valley in 1977 and a special presentation LUM made to the presbytery in 1979. I sat in on numerous meetings with the Personnel Policies and Salary Review Committee when its first director (Rev. Ronald Elly) resigned and the committee was trying to find a new one. I attended a special meeting involving LUM's Executive Committee and the Executive Committee of the Southside Community Center, when the two groups were quarreling over a summer camp program. I also attended most all the events and programs LUM sponsored between 1975 and 1981. Finally, I attended other meetings in the community which I thought might produce information pertaining to LUM, local churches, and/or low-income people.

I collected all the handouts and made detailed notes on actions which pertained to the variables in my theoretical framework.

Records and Documents

Records and documents used in the study included: minutes to all monthly board meetings; monthly staff and committee reports; brochures listing and explaining LUM's goals and activities; LUM's monthly newsletter *The Seed*; quarterly and annual financial budgets; LUM's applications to denominational funding agencies; and applications from people wanting to be considered for the job of director in 1977.

Interviews

I conducted a great many personal and telephone interviews. I tape recorded several in-depth interviews with LUM's two directors: Rev. Ronald Elly and Rev. Judson Dolphin.

Based on names obtained from LUM's records and interviews with Rev. Elly, I compiled a list of all the people who participated in LUM's formation. I then conducted telephone interviews with each of the poeple Rev. Elly thought most helpful in starting LUM.

As part of the evaluation of the Tippecanoe County Federation of Churches, several volunteers and I interviewed over 20 local religious and civic leaders. Portions of these interviews touched on the history of ecumenism in the Lafayette area, high and low points in interfaith cooperation during the 1960s and 1970s, and the relationship between the Federation and LUM.

Finally, I interviewed several pastors and other staff persons in churches to learn more about their churches' involvement in social concerns (e.g., programs they conduct, the costs and benefits of such programs for their congregations). I also had numerous opportunities to talk more informally with other pastors and staff members about similar issues.

Church Survey

I also conducted a survey of all the congregations which belonged to either LUM or the Federation of Churches and a sample of six churches which belonged to neither group. Altogether, 30 local congregations participated.

LUM and the Federation wanted information about a wide variety of subjects, and I needed data about a number of issues related to the theory in Chapter 2. I knew the questionnaire's length would reduce the overall response rate, but was willing to sacrifice some of the response rate (especially among less active members) for data on a wider variety of subjects (especially from more active members).[5]

In churches with fewer than 200 adult members, I sent questionnaires to all adults on the membership roll. In larger churches, I drew random samples of 200 adult members. Questionnaires were sent to a total of 4,855 church members in October 1979. Follow-up postcards were sent out in November. By the end of December, there were a total of 1,557 returns (32 percent).

Evaluation of the Federation

My evaluation of the Federation of Churches also included a thorough review of documents pertaining to its history, interviews with religious and civic leaders about directions the Federation might pursue in the future, discussions among Federation leaders about its present and future organizational characteristics, survey results on parishioners' involvement in the Federation, and survey results on church members' attitudes about interfaith activities. The evaluation contributed important information on the history of ecumenism in the Lafayette area and other conditions relating to the formation of LUM. The evaluation of the Federation also gave me some relative basis for assessing the strengths and weaknesses of LUM as an ecumenical organization.

Local Newspaper

The Lafayette area has one daily newspaper, the Lafayette *Journal-Courier*. With a circulation of about 45,000, it is a primary source of national and local news in the Greater Lafayette area. I clipped articles, editorials, and letters-to-the-editor related to LUM and/or conditions bearing on LUM. Excerpts from several articles, editorials, and letters will be presented as evidence in later chapters.

Other Literature and Research

I also used popular, governmental, and academic literature for evidence, especially in relation to societal and local conditions that might affect LUM. Included in this literature were: articles from news magazines such as *Time* and *Newsweek*; articles from the *New York Times, Washington Post* and *Indianapolis Star*; sociological studies in the areas of social stratification, complex organizations, and the sociology of religion; census data; and data pertaining to poverty in Indiana generally and Lafayette in particular. Takayama's (1977, 1979) work on urban ministries was especially helpful.

Plan of Analysis

Chapter 4 describes the 10-year process leading up to LUM's formation in 1971. Chapter 5 uses my theoretical framework to analyze the conditions that had the most to do with LUM's formation.

Chapter 6 describes the institutionalization process, presenting data on all 15 dimensions for the 10-year period 1972 to 1981. By the end of that chapter, I hope readers will have a good sense of LUM's struggle to survive and become a viable organization. Then, in Chapter 7, I use my theoretical framework to show which structural and resource factors had the most impact on the institutionalization process.

Chapter 8 presents evidence concerning the extent to which LUM succeeded in achieving its goals between 1972 and 1981. Once I have described LUM's success, I return (in Chapter 9) to my theoretical framework to help me explain LUM's effectiveness.

When the data in Chapters 5, 7, and 9 are consistent with my expectations, I will have demonstrated that there is some association between the independent and dependent variables. When I can present concrete evidence of causation, I will conclude that my theoretical framework is valid and that these variables deserve to be considered in future analyses of social movement (urban ministry) organizations. I also will use these relationships as bases for policy implications. When variables do not have the effects I expected, I cannot be sure these variables would not help explain the formation, institutionalization, or effectiveness of other urban ministries. However, unexpected findings will call attention to aspects of my theoretical framework which will require special scrutiny, perhaps revision, if used in future analyses. I also will not risk policy implications in these areas.

Conclusion

Chapter 1 raised three questions about ecumenical urban ministries: What conditions contribute to their formation? What factors affect their institutionalization over time? And, under what conditions can they achieve their goals of increasing local congregations' involvement in social concerns? Chapter 2 identified the conditions I felt were most important and explained how I thought they would affect these processes. The present chapter has described the methods used to gather data related to my hypotheses, and indicated how I will analyze these data. The next six chapters will describe and analyze LUM's formation, institutionalization, and effectiveness.

CHAPTER 4

DESCRIPTION OF LUM'S FORMATION: FROM A NEIGHBORHOOD YOUTH GROUP TO AN ECUMENICAL URBAN MINISTRY

This chapter describes LUM's formation during the late 1960s and early 1970s. The account starts with the formation of the Neighborhood Development Project at Hope Chapel Church in 1962 and concludes with the formation of LUM in December 1971.

Hope Chapel and the Neighborhood Development Project

Hope Chapel was founded in 1844 as a Presbyterian mission to the relatively low-income people living on the Southside of Lafayette. It operated under the supervision of larger nearby Presbyterian churches until 1924, when it became a separate church. In 1957, Rev. Peter Hanstra became pastor. He conducted a rather traditional, pastoral ministry—stressing the recruitment of new members and caring for members' personal-spiritual needs.

Hope Chapel's 1967 annual report indicates that there were 316 "active communicants" and 163 people enrolled in the Sunday School program. Rev. James Sala, regional presbyter, estimated that half of Hope Chapel's members came from the lower-working class in areas between downtown and the affluent suburbs, but "many of them," he said, "retain their loyalty to the church and exhibit it by their attendance and support." About 80 percent of the church's 316 members were 55 years of age or older.

The Neighborhood Development Project (NDP) was started at Hope Chapel in 1962 by Rev. Hanstra's wife and a Purdue University student. NDP consisted of crafts and camp programs for Southside youngsters, many of whom were in families which did not belong to Hope Chapel. There was an afternoon crafts program for youngsters from kindergarten to third grade; an evening crafts program for children in fourth to sixth grades; and a summer camp program.

During fall 1966, an advisory board was created to watch over NDP and its use of Hope Chapel's facilities. The functions which the church session (i.e., the decision-making body within the congregation) assigned to the advisory board reflected the church's ambivalence toward NDP:

1. Appoint the director or co-directors of the project from the workers in the project.
2. Participate in the basic planning and submit the program for approval by the Session.
3. Disseminate information to keep the congregation (and other supporters of the project) fully informed about the work being done and the needs of the project.
4. Receive periodic reports concerning all finances of the project and keep the congregation informed about these finances. (Project budget is separate from the church budget.)

5. Receive complaints concerning the project and see that they are adjusted satisfactorily. Consult with those who have questions concerning the project.
6. Seek to involve more people from Hope Chapel in the work of the project.

Thus, the session wanted some input into NDP programming; and it wanted NDP to be accountable to Hope Chapel, especially insofar as use of church property was concerned; but it did not want to be responsible for NDP's budget.

Rev. Hanstra retired from Hope Chapel in 1966, creating a vacancy which Hope Chapel and the presbytery of Crawfordsville had to fill. His retirement also left NDP without Mrs. Hanstra, its most effective leader. In its search for a new pastor, the Pulpit Nominating Committee learned that Ronald Elly, a student at Louisville Presbyterian Theological Seminary, was available and might be interested in the position.

Rev. Ronald Elly

Rev. Elly went to Maryville College, a Presbyterian school in Tennessee, where he majored in history and minored in English. After college, he went directly into Louisville Presbyterian Theological Seminary, where he stressed biblical studies and "church and society." During seminary, Rev. Elly worked with an interdenominational Downtown Neighborhood Council in New Albany, Indiana, which is just across the Ohio River from Louisville.

Rev. Elly's experience with the Downtown Neighborhood Council was so positive that he wanted "to do something like that somewhere else." So he began his search for an inner-city church in a medium-sized city where there was no history of "community ministry" but a possibility of developing one.

Rev. Elly and Hope Chapel: 1967-1971

Rev. Elly became the pastor at Hope Chapel in June, 1967. He soon found that he and the people of Hope Chapel had very different concepts of religion and the role of the church in society. In his words, he had a "servant" model of the church; they saw the church "as theirs for themselves." He viewed Sunday worship as "an inspiration to do something in the world; they viewed it as an inspiration to endure the world." He offered a rational-intellectual approach to biblical teachings; they wanted a religion that offered an emotional uplift.[1]

These differences affected, and were symbolized in, the different views Rev. Elly and the people of Hope Chapel had of NDP. On two occasions, he tried to incorporate NDP and the community service dimension of ministry into Sunday morning worship services. Both times, the congregation responded negatively. Reflecting on the second occasion—when he devoted a sermon to the past, present, and future of NDP as part of Hope Chapel's program—Rev. Elly said, "I thought it was a decent sermon, but the feedback was: 'Don't do that again!' "

A 1968-1969 report shows that, including Rev. Elly, nine people from Hope Chapel were involved in NDP programs. However, five of the nine were on the advisory board; only four were involved as counselors or helpers in the crafts or camping programs. Moreover, the nine Hope Chapel volunteers represented less than 3 percent of Hope Chapel's members and less than a third of all the volunteers working with NPD. Thus, as Rev. Elly observed, the people of Hope Chapel did not perceive NDP as an integral part of the congregation's life.

At the November 1968 meeting of NDP's advisory board, Rev. Elly moved "that the NDP under jurisdiction of our Session be submitted to the development and guidance of the Presbytery of Crawfordsville's National Missions Committee and through them to the Synod (as a Synod cause) and wider church; that we seek designation as a Presbytery Cause."

The session voted 5 to 0 with two abstentions to support an application for $1,000 in National Missions Funds. But in an 8 to 1 vote, session stipulated that NDP be considered a "non-parish" project. Rev. Elly could continue to work in community ministry, but that activity would be separate from his ministry to Hope Chapel's members. Rev. Elly later observed: "At that point in time, one of my own dreams about that ministry began to go down the tubes, because I conceived of a worshiping-service institution and not a worshiping institution doing Christian education and everything over here and a serving institution separate over there. There was no integration of those and that has been one of my concerns all the way along."[2]

Nineteen sixty-nine was a year of continued frustration for Rev. Elly and Hope Chapel. One long-standing member of NDP's advisory board felt that Hope Chapel could only support NDP if the children were being urged to participate in the church's Sunday School program. She felt NDP was not performing this function to the extent it should. Rev. Elly replied that "NDP has never been a recruitment program to get the children to come to Sunday School. The program tries to show Christian love and concern for the children in working with them." Her letter of resignation was read to the board at its March 1969 meeting.

Financial difficulties also arose in 1969. Hope Chapel's receipts had remained about the same (about $15,500) since 1965, but expenses were growing. The church's trustees responded by instituting measures designed to cut back on expenses. These measures included reducing the size of the bulletin, prohibiting long distance telephone calls, and using old envelopes for church offerings. The measures succeeded in bringing about some economic stability; in 1969 receipts exceeded disbursements for the first time since 1966. But, the measures did not increase Hope Chapel's revenues and produced a great deal of additional frustration for Rev. Elly.

With his commitment to a dual ministry, a growing awareness that the members of Hope Chapel were more interested in a traditional ministry, and realizing that the congregation's financial situation would not permit an expanding ministry to the community, Rev. Elly urged NDP to develop ties with other groups in the community.[3]

By September 1969, NDP's arts and crafts program was taking place in the nearby Southside Community Center rather than at Hope Chapel. People from Covenant, Bethany, and Faith Presbyterian churches joined NDP, making it "a multi-church ministry." By the end of 1969, NDP had its own constitution, bylaws, and incorporation papers. Except for Rev. Elly and a couple of board members, Hope Chapel and NDP were separate entities.

In 1970, the financial problems at Hope Chapel grew to the point where Rev. Elly, the session, trustees, and the congregation were openly specifying their frustrations and considering their "options for [Hope Chapel's] future." At a meeting in June 1970, the members agreed that "the congregation of Hope Chapel Presbyterian Church continue with a full-time pastor, seeking greater working together and greater resources within a time-limit to be determined by the session." The session voted for a one-year time limit.

At the same time, NDP's programs and its support from other groups in the Lafayette area continued to grow. At its February 1970 meeting, the advisory board unanimously adopted a resolution that "the NDP establish its area of concern to any person of low income throughout Lafayette" (not just in the Southside area). NDP voted to support the creation of a neighborhood newspaper in the Southside and one in another low-income area just north of downtown. By November 1970, NDP was involved in a Senior Citizens Visitation program. And, activities relating to "adult basic education" (tutoring), medical services, consumer credit counseling, and better housing were occupying increasingly prominent places on NDP meeting agendas.

NDP's financial support from the Committee on National Missions (of the presbytery of Crawfordsville) increased from the $1,000 in 1968 to $4,500 in 1970. Local contributions to NDP were almost $4,000. Presbyterian congregations gave about $1,500; United Methodist churches gave about $100; and a few other churches gave from $10 to $40 each. In addition, a local Hunger Hike contributed over $1,200; civic groups of various types offered about $700; individual contributions amounted to $200.

By the end of 1970, Rev. Elly considered leaving Hope Chapel. He was hoping to find a way of continuing his community ministry through NDP, but he also was looking seriously at other communities with a potential for continuing this style of ministry. The December 1970 NDP board minutes include the following entry:

> Rev. Elly, having decided that this should be the last year that he serves as both pastor of Hope Chapel and coordinator of NDP, considers the important objectives of 1971 should be: (1) to get Lafayette churches to contribute funds of approximately $10,000 for the salary and housing of a full-time director of NDP; (2) to receive approval from the Presbytery of the terms of a call to that position; and (3) to seek the co-operation of the United Methodist church and the Roman Catholic church in obtaining a second man for the urban ministry. The Presbyterian churches will need to approach other churches with a fairly definite plan and the question of whether they want to be included.

The effort to bring about a full-time urban ministry proceeded swiftly in 1971. At the February board meeting, Rev. Elly recommended "that a letter be sent early in March to the Presbyterian and Methodist churches in the area and to the Bishop of the Roman Catholic diocese here about an expanded urban ministry in downtown Lafayette." The NDP planning council volunteered to present a slide program and outlined the urban ministry to local churches. The NDP planning council also completed its proposal for a new organization called the Lafayette Urban Ministry (LUM). It also was reported that NDP would be housed at Central Presbyterian Church (in the downtown area) rather than at Hope Chapel, at least for the remainder of 1971.

At the April board meeting, Rev. Elly and Richard Schurr reported that the Board of National Missions Committee "voiced approval of NDP plans and indicated they would be ready to support these plans in the fall providing our preparations had been completed."

In September and October 1971, a job description was written for the first full-time urban minister. The job description was approved at the board's October 1971 meeting. Six board members were chosen to comprise "a committee to meet with Rev. Elly for the purpose of interviewing him as an applicant for the position of Director." Rev. Elly resigned from Hope Chapel on November 2, 1971, and at the NDP board meeting two weeks later, it was announced that the "Rev. Elly would be assuming [the] position [of urban minister] in January [1972]." The December 1971 board minutes include the final action in the formation of LUM.

> Mrs. Dee Tritschler moved and Les Gaylor seconded to change the name of the

Neighborhood Development Project to Lafayette Urban Ministry passing all the assets and liabilities of the one to the other. This was passed unanimously by all present. Rev. Beswick moved and Les Gaylor seconded to ask Central Presbyterian Church for office space in 1972. This passed unanimously.

Conclusion

I have described the circumstances within which a neighborhood youth group (NDP) lodged in—but not sponsored by—a Presbyterian mission church became an interfaith program for low-income people in the Greater Lafayette area (LUM). Chapter 5 examines the factors which contributed to LUM's formation.

CHAPTER 5
ANALYSIS OF LUM'S FORMATION:
STRUCTURES AND RESOURCES CONVERGE

My theoretical framework (Chapter 2) helps to explain LUM's formation. I will restate each hypothesis and present evidence relating to each one.

Societal ("Period") Factors

My theory included three structural conditions at the societal level: social change in the secular realm, change in religious policies and practices, and a spirit of cooperation among religious groups. It also included four resource factors: economic prosperity, abundant resources in the religious sphere, religious justification for social reform, and the availability of religious personnel.

Structural Conditions: Secular Realm

Social Conditions. This period factor concerns the legitimacy of existing social, economic, and political arrangements. If the nation's mood is to affirm traditional ways of life, it is not likely to encourage the formation of groups such as LUM which want to challenge prevailing social practices. However, *when the legitimacy of societal policies and practices is being challenged, these challenges can foster an interest in groups like LUM.*

The 1962-71 period was full of challenges to the status quo. The civil rights movement had national political consequences by the early 1960s (e.g., President Kennedy's famous television address to the nation, the 1964 Civil Rights Act, and the 1965 Voting Rights Act). President Kennedy's assassination in 1963 led to the inauguration of President Lyndon Johnson and, among other things, the War on Poverty. By 1964, the free speech and counter culture movements were underway in California and soon spread throughout the nation. By 1965, the anti-war movement had begun to grow. In 1966, Stokley Carmichael uttered the words "black power" and began a movement that was an even more volatile period in blacks' struggle for racial equality. By 1967-68-69, all of these movements rocked the nation, especially college campuses, and had enormous political consequences. In 1967, President Johnson chose not to run for a second term in 1968. In 1968, Robert Kennedy was assassinated during his run for the presidency, and Martin Luther King was killed in his support of the garbage workers in Memphis, Tennessee. Thus, the 1962-71 period was marked by a concentration of movements and events which—separately and together—provided a national context which was conducive to the formation of social movement organizations.

Structural Conditions: Religious Sphere

Religious Policies and Practices. If society is inclined to reaffirm its traditional policies and practices, this search for stability also will be reflected within social institutions. And

41

when not pressured by groups to change the system, leaders of the various institutions (including religion) will tend toward the reaffirmation of traditional ways. However, *if the society is experiencing significant challenges to the legitimacy of its traditional policies and practices, these challenges will tend to foster ferment within the religious sphere—which, in turn, will foster interest in religious groups oriented toward change.*

When the social upheavals of the 1960s challenged many traditional policies and practices in the nation's economic and political spheres, they also precipitated turmoil in religion. Many religious leaders questioned the silence of the churches on social issues, urging them to be more prophetic. Many of these so-called "new breed" clergy and lay people became actively involved in the civil rights movement of the late 1950s and early 1960s (Cox, 1968; Hadden, 1969; Winter, 1977). Many formed "underground churches" (Boyd, 1969). Some eagerly sought federal money to subsidize religious efforts to attack poverty (Greenwood, 1967). Some began to question traditional beliefs about the existence of God (Altizer and Hamilton, 1966).

Churches also were rocked by the demands of activists such as Angela Davis and James Foreman. Thus, "liberal" churches (e.g., Episcopal and Presbyterian) which espoused the value of brotherhood found themselves engaged in racial conflict over "reparations." Churches which stressed the value of equality frequently found themselves protecting interests they had accumulated in the context of racial and economic inequality (Bissaillion, 1972). Churches which espoused a value of peace often found themselves defending war in Vietnam and differing among themselves over issues of conscientious objection and amnesty. And evangelical churches, which had not been actively involved in social issues, found themselves exploring issues such as racism, poverty, and social inequality through new publications such as *Sojourners* and *The Other Side* (Hunter, 1980).

In short, social upheaval in society became a source of theological and social ferment within the sphere of religion. This ferment was conducive to experimentation with new forms of ecumenical ministry intended to express the churches' concern for the poor.

Cooperation. A spirit of cooperation must exist among relevant organizations if they are to share their resources and support the formation of a "federated" (in this case, ecumenical) organization. If they have not related to one another in the past, or if their past relations have been hostile, the situation is not conducive to interfaith cooperation.

There was a rapid increase in ecumenical activity during the 1950s and 1960s (e.g., Berger, 1963; Brown, 1969; Modras, 1968; Knapp, 1966; Lee, 1960; Cavert, 1968). The most significant expressions of this ecumenical thrust were the lessening of tensions between Christians and Jews (especially Vatican II documents absolving Jews of any responsibility for the crucifixion of Christ); increased dialogue between Protestants and Catholics; more programs of various kinds co-sponsored by several Protestant denominations (e.g., the National Council of Churches); efforts such as the Consultation on Church Union to unite some of Protestantism's largest denominations; and numerous mergers (e.g., the Evangelical United Brethren and the Methodists to form the United Methodist Church).

Johnson's (1969) data indicate that this ecumenical attitude contributed to the formation of specialized, experimental ministries; most were co-sponsored by member churches from several religious traditions. Takayama and Darnell (1979) also described the important role ecumenism played in the formation of the Memphis Interfaith Association (an ecumenical urban ministry similar to LUM). Thus, ecumenism alone does not foster groups like LUM, but under the right conditions, it can permit the development of urban ministries which are broadly based in several local churches.

Resources: Secular Realm

Economic Conditions. I argued (Chapter 2) that *a healthy economy is conducive to organizational formation* and that an unhealthy economy stifles it. And the nation's economy was soaring in the 1962-71 period when LUM was emerging out of NDP. The Gross National Product was rising at the fastest pace since the 1938-44 period (from 565.0 billion dollars in 1962 to 1,077.6 billion dollars in 1971). The stock market (Dow Jones Industrial Average) rose from 639.76 in 1962 to 884.76 in 1971. Personal income, personal disposal income, and personal savings were increasing (e.g., personal disposable income [using 1967 dollars] rose from 386.8 billion in 1962 to 751.8 billion in 1971). The nation's unemployment rate declined from 5.6 percent in 1962 to 3.5 percent in 1969, its sharpest drop since the World War II period of 1940-44 (though it rose to 5.9 percent again between 1969 and 1971). Thus, the nation was experiencing prosperity which permitted the channeling of some financial resources into the support of new social organizations.

Resources: Religious Sphere

Economic Resources. When resources are abundant in a sphere of life, existing organizations are likely to expand the number and types of projects they are willing to support. If the economic resources are small, the institutional sphere will place more emphasis on balancing its budgets and maintaining existing programs than on developing new ones.

There was an abundance of resources in the religious sphere during the 1950s and 1960s (Jacquet, annually; Gaustad, 1968; Demerath, 1968; Swanson, 1968; Johnstone, 1975; Wuthnow, 1976; Wilson, 1978). Church membership increased from 86.8 million in 1950 to 131.4 million in 1971. The percentage of the total population which belonged to a church also rose from 57 in 1950 to 62 in 1971. These increases fostered additional increases in church building, baptisms, and Sunday school enrollment (Demerath, 1968).

Per capita contributions to religion also rose sharply during the 1950s and 1960s (Jacquet, 1980:248). In 1961, per capita contributions to religion were $77.01 (using 1967 constant dollars to control for increases in the cost of living). They rose steadily to $82.38 in 1965 and $91.47 in 1968, before dipping somewhat between 1969 and 1971 (when they were $85.69)—11.3 percent higher than they had been in 1961.

Two other factors also need to be considered: churches' substantial corporate investments and the healthy stock market during this period. These factors yielded significant increases in church revenues. Demerath (1968:365) noted "a level of religious business assets in the U.S. that is almost double the combined assets of the nation's five largest corporations."

Thus, there was a marked increase in churches' human and economic resources during the 1950s and 1960s. This abundance helped form a context in which urban ministries could be formed.[1]

Justification. But, ferment and resources with a sphere are not enough. *For a group like LUM to be formed, the institutional sphere also must contain an ideological heritage which legitimates change.* If group leaders can claim that the changes they favor are legitimate within the institution's tradition, their ideas and programs cannot be totally dismissed.

The religious sphere contains such a prophetic heritage. Though it tends to be subordinate to other themes in the Judeo-Christian tradition, this prophetic heritage is rooted in the Bible and found in nearly two centuries of church teachings. Wilson (1978:369) says:

> Actually, there are several revolutionary themes within the Judeo-Christian tradition. They include (1) the death and resurrection of Christ and the early realization of a heavenly Kingdom by him; (2) apocalyptic thinking fostered by the persecution of the early Christians, with its images of closeness, release, and overturning; (3) the promise of eventual triumph over earthly suffering; (4) the vision of a future Golden Age, which is to be based on the principle of God's dominion and not on that of demonic powers; (5) the egalitarian message of grace and salvation for all, regardless of social condition; (6) the post-Aquinas teaching that tyrants can be rightfully usurped; (7) the exodus theme, with its message of liberation and deliverance; (8) the pilgrim people idea, with its message of temporary suffering and necessary sojourn in a world of troubles; (9) the idea of divine judgment, with its implication that all human institutions are corrupt and frail; and (10) the idea of God as Lord, whose domain is entirely separate from that of Ceasar's.

Biblical passages expressing this prophetic heritage (themes of love, justice, equality, freedom and escape from bondage) are numerous (Sider, 1977 and 1980; Santa Ana, 1979). According to Clark (1965:14): "the main thrust of the gospel as found in both the Old and the New Testaments is in the direction of deeply felt compassion and generous sharing of the blessings bestowed by God."

Personnel. If a sphere has an adequate supply of personnel who might lead in the formation of experimental, reform groups, such groups can be started. If the sphere lacks a supply of such personnel, it is unlikely that new, reform groups will be started (even if all the other conditions discussed so far are in place).

Seminaries were booming in the 1960s and there were more clergy of all kinds than ever before. For example, among Presbyterians and United Methodists (the two groups which contributed the most in starting LUM), there were sizable increases in the number of seminary graduates, clergy in parish positions, clergy in non-parish positions (such as church hierarchies or groups like LUM), and clergy in secular positions (Carroll and Wilson, 1980; Harrison 1959; Jenkins, 1977).

Moreover, seminarians and clergy in non-parish positions were playing a disproportionate role in efforts to increase churches' involvement in social concerns. Demerath and Hammond (1969:223-230) noted that people located in high-ranking positions of church authority are able to engage in prophecy more readily than local church functionaries. Stark and Glock (1969) indicated that church officials in virtually all major denominations had issued statements stressing the sinfulness of racial bigotry and the Christian obligation to love one's neighbor. Evans (1979) showed how Roman Catholic bishops led in the formation of the Campaign for Human Development. Wood (1972) and Jenkins (1977) documented the National Council of Churches' work on behalf of mainline Protestant churches in areas such as civil rights. Hammond and Mitchell (1965) demonstrated the tendency for campus ministers to have relatively liberal ideas compared with other members of the clergy (especially pastors of local congregations). Hadden and Rymph (1966) also showed that campus ministers were among the clergy who were most likely to participate in "radical" activities during the 1960s. Fichter (1968) showed how young seminary graduates in low-ranking parish roles often had ideas that were more liberal than those of the pastors they worked with. Johnson (1969) showed how leaders in the new social action ministries he studied tended to be recent graduates of places such as Yale Divinity School and Union Theological Seminary.

Thus, organized religion had large numbers of people in positions which were conducive to support of increased church involvement in social concerns, and these people were taking leadership roles in social action groups such as LUM.

Local ("Place") Factors

Chapter 2 specified four structural conditions at the local level: a liberal political climate, the existence of the problem, a spirit of cooperation among potential support groups, and a lack of competition with other groups with similar goals. There were three resource factors at the local level: an urban population, the presence of potential support groups, and an abundance of resources within these support groups.

Structural Conditions: Secular Realm

Political Climate. I expected that *communities with liberal political climates would be more conducive to reform groups like LUM than communities with conservative political climates would be.*

However, the political climate in the Lafayette area was *not* conducive to the formation of a group like LUM. The state of Indiana was quite conservative politically. In the 1968 presidential election, the state preferred Republican Richard Nixon to Democrat Eugene McCarthy. The state's two governors during the late 1960s and early 1970s (Roger Branigin and Edgar Whitcomb) were Republicans. The state General Assembly was heavily Democrat during the mid 1960s (following President Johnson's landslide victory over Barry Goldwater in 1964), but returned to its more usual Republican majority in the House by 1967 and in the Senate by 1969. State income taxes in 1970 were among the lowest in the United States (*Money*, February 1982:61), and Indiana ranked last among all states in the amount of money received from the federal government (*Statistical Abstracts*, 1972:44).

The Lafayette area also was quite conservative. The mayor of Lafayette was a Republican and all members of the city council, except one, were Republican. The mayor of West Lafayette was a conservative Democrat; the entire city council was Republican. And virtually all the township trustees (who are responsible for poor relief) were Republican.

The area's conservatism was apparent in the city elections of November 1971—one month before the NDP officially became LUM. The *Journal-Courier* endorsed six Republican candidates but only two Democrats in Lafayette. It endorsed six Republicans but only one Democrat in West Lafayette. In Lafayette, the Democratic candidate was elected mayor, partly because he objected to the tax rate which he said "seems to go up every year." In West Lafayette, the Republican candidate was elected. A Democrat "cracked the Republican City Council line up for the first time in [West Lafayette's] history" (*Journal-Courier*, November 3, 1971:A-1).[2]

This pattern was not consistent with my expectation that liberal political climates would be most conducive to the formation of groups like LUM. Though the expected pattern might have prevailed in other places where urban ministries were formed, LUM was formed *in spite of* a conservative political climate.

Structural Conditions: Religious Sphere

Existence of the Problem. According to my theory, *reform groups such as LUM must be able to demonstrate the existence of a problem if they are to gain the support they need to get started.* If there is no problem, they will have great difficulty establishing themselves. In LUM's case, as in the case of most urban ministries, the problem was the lack of church involvement in programs dealing with the causes and consequences of poverty.

The evidence concerning poverty in the Lafayette area reveals a paradox. On the one hand, the economy in the area was relatively healthy compared to the state as a whole and to nearby cities such as Kokomo and Anderson. Using the government's "official" definition of poverty ($3,743 for a non-farm family of four in 1959), 9.6 percent of all persons in Tippecanoe County were poor (the state average was 9.5; see Table 1). And the county unemployment rate was only 3.4 percent in 1970 (see Table 2), while the state average was 4.1 percent. The local newspaper and citizens frequently used these statistics as evidence that poverty was not a serious problem in the Lafayette area.

However, other evidence indicates there was considerable poverty in the Lafayette area. A number of writers have argued that half of the median family income is a fairer and more meaningful measure of poverty than the government's "official" measure (Fuchs, 1967; Hougham and Davidson, 1979; Davidson, 1985b). The median family income for Tippecanoe County as a whole in 1970 was $10,120. Half of that was $5,060. Using $5,000 as a cutting point, 4,064 families were poor (see Table 3). Since the average size of a county family was 3.38 persons, nearly 14,000 people were in families with incomes less than or equal to half of the median family income for the county. Poor "unrelated individuals" brought the total number of poor to almost 19,000.

Government figures in Table 1 indicate there were 9,389 poor people in Tippecanoe County. The largest number of these people (over 5,000) were part of 1,575 poor families (6.1 percent of all families), but 4,184 were "unrelated individuals" (40.3 percent of all unrelated individuals). The average income of all poor families was only $1,737; the average for unrelated individuals was $972. Only about 8 percent of poor families, and only 2 percent of unrelated individuals, received public assistance. Most poor people were white (approximately 9,000). But, poverty was most common (percentage-wise) among blacks (19.7 percent). The percentage of Spanish-speaking people who were poor was about the same as for the population as a whole (9.1 vs. 9.6 percent).

Government documents also estimate how many people are living in abject poverty by calculating the number of people with incomes "less than 75 percent of poverty." The data in Table 4 indicate that 68 percent of all poor people (N = 6,399) in Tippecanoe County were *very* poor. Sixty-four percent of poor families (N = 1,009) were very poor. And 73 percent of all poor unrelated individuals (N = 3,056) were very poor. The patterns were much the same for Lafayette and West Lafayette.

Using calculations very similar to these, Potters (1975) divided Indiana counties into three categories: those with "mild," "average," and "acute" poverty. Twenty-four percent of all counties were labeled "mild"; 52 percent were "average"; and 23 pecent were "acute." Tippecanoe County's poverty was "acute." The county had one of the most severe concentrations of extreme poverty in the state.[3]

Table 1
POVERTY IN TIPPECANOE COUNTY, 1970[a]
(Using "Official" Definition)

	Total County	Lafayette	West Lafayette
Total Persons			
1. Number of Poor Persons	9,389	3,470	2,494
% of all Persons	9.6	7.8	15.5
2. Number of Black Poor Persons	181	81	36
% of all Black Persons	19.7	13.6	35.6
3. Number of Spanish-speaking Poor Persons	90	40	9
% of all Spanish-speaking Persons	9.1	9.1	3.9
Families			
1. Number of Poor Families	1,575	584	169
% of all Families	6.1	5.0	4.5
% of Poor Family Heads in Labor Force	68.9	87.0	79.3
Mean Income for Poor Families	$1,737	$1,936	$1,844
% Receiving Public Assistance	8.1	14.0	—
2. Number of Black Poor Families	23	15	—
% of all Black Families	11.9	11.0	—
3. Number of Spanish-speaking Poor Families	17	5	—
% of all Spanish-speaking Families	7.8	—	—
Unrelated Individuals			
1. Number of Poor Unrelated Individuals	4,184	1,408	1,951
% of all Unrelated Individuals	40.3	33.6	46.6
Mean Income of Poor Unrelated Individuals	$972	$986	$959
% Receiving Public Assistance	2.0	3.6	.8
2. Number of Black Poor Unrelated Individuals	114	33	36
% of all Black Unrelated Individuals	45.8	—	—
3. Number of Spanish-speaking Poor Unrelated Individuals	24	15	9
% of all Spanish-speaking Unrelated Individuals	—	—	—

[a]Source: U.S. Department of Commerce, *General Social and Economic Characteristics-Indiana.*

Table 2
SELECTED CHARACTERISTICS OF GREATER LAFAYETTE AREA: 1970[a]

Characteristics	Total County (N = 109,378)	Lafayette (N = 44,955)	West Lafayette (N = 19,157)
Education			
Median School Years Completed	12.5	12.3	16.5
% 4 Years of High School or More	67.7	60.6	92.3
Employment			
% Unemployed	3.4	3.6	2.7
% White Collar	53.8	49.3	77.1
% Government workers	27.5	17.4	48.0
Occupations (Persons ≥ 16 years)			
% Professional	23.7	14.9	54.1
% Managers	7.3	8.0	8.6
% Sales	6.3	7.8	4.6
% Clerical	16.4	18.6	12.8
% Crafts	11.9	15.6	2.8
% Operatives	12.4	15.7	4.4
% Service	14.4	14.4	10.3
% Laborers	3.3	3.2	2.7
% Farmers	1.5	.1	.7
% Farm Laborers	1.2	.2	1.1
% Private Household	1.1	1.4	.8
Income			
% Families ≥ $15,000	20.2	16.4	41.4
% $5,000-$14,999	64.0	69.7	47.7
% < $5,000	15.8	13.9	10.9
Racial Composition			
Blacks			
N	1,082	607	126
%	.9	1.3	.7
Spanish-Speaking			
N	1,109	440	280
%	1.0	1.0	1.5
Asians			
N	766	22	429
%	.7	.05	2.2

[a]Sources: U.S. Department of Commerce, *General Social and Economic Conditions-Indiana* and *Metropolitan Housing Characteristics* (HC [2]-106).

Table 3
AMOUNT OF POVERTY USING RELATIVE APPROACH

	County	Lafayette	West Lafayette
Total Families	25,759	11,760	3,725
Median Family Income	$10,120	$10,181	$13,231
50% of Median	5,060	5,090	6,615
Number of Families Under $5,000	4,064	1,633	407
Percent of Families Under $5,000	15.8	13.9	10.9
Mean Family Size	3.38	3.44	3.21
Estimated Number of Persons in Families with Incomes Below 50% of Median Family Income	13,736	5,617	1,306
Number of Unrelated Individuals Below 125 Percent of Poverty	5,106	1,718	2,360
Estimated Number of Persons in Poverty Using Relative Approach[a]	18,842	7,335	3,666

[a]Combines persons in families below 50 percent of median family income and unrelated individuals below 125 percent of poverty line.

Table 4
NUMBER AND PERCENT OF PEOPLE WITH INCOMES LESS THAN 75 PERCENT OF POVERTY[a]

	Total County	Lafayette	West Lafayette
Number of Persons	6,399	2,349	1,796
% of All Poor Persons	68	68	72
% of All Persons	6.6	5.3	9.4
Number of Families	1,009	388	99
% of All Poor Families	64	66	59
% of All Families	3.9	3.3	2.7
Number of Unrelated Individuals	3,056	962	1,445
% of All Poor Unrelated Individuals	73	68	74
% of All Unrelated Individuals	29.4	23.0	34.5

[a]Source: U.S. Department of Commerce, *General Social and Economic Characteristics-Indiana.*

To what extent were Lafayette area churches involved in social concerns, especially the problem of poverty? Newspaper columns in the 1960s and early 1970s revealed few signs of church involvement in social concerns. In one article (November 13, 1971:A-6), writer Byron Parvis asked: "Should the churches be involved in social action in the community, should they become involved in political activities, and should they be concerned about a multitude of non-church concerns?" He answered by observing that "Ordinarily, most churches refrain from getting too involved, leaving social activities to others." Interviews with religious and community leaders concerning ecumenical activity in the county produced no mention of church involvement in social issues (except for references to LUM). Personal conversations with local clergy indicated their churches were not active in the social concerns of the 1960s. Finally, Rev. Elly said most people he talked with between 1966 and 1971 accepted the idea that local churches were not actively involved in issues relating to poverty. Hope Chapel's decision not to sponsor the Neighborhood Development Project reflected this general pattern.

Cooperation. If a reform group's potential support groups have a history of cooperating in such efforts, or are willing to do so at the moment, they can share their resources and sponsor an urban ministry group. If they have not had such cooperative experiences, they are likely to be jealous of their own resources and distrustful of one another's intentions—conditions that would make support of an ecumenical group like LUM unlikely.

Historically, ecumenism had been a low-priority item for churches in the Lafayette area (Davidson, 1980a). But, there was a surge of interfaith activity during the 1950s and 1960s. The most concrete expression of this ecumenical spirit was the Tippecanoe County Federation of Churches, which began in 1945-46. By the early 1950s, it was receiving support from 22 mainline Protestant congregations. This support continued into the 1960s as the Federation conducted numerous ecumenical programs which were quite well attended by local churchgoers (e.g., summer vesper services at a public park, Union Thanksgiving and Holy Week services, and a leadership training workshop).

Thus, a number of liberal Protestant congregations had worked together for 10-15 years prior to the 1962-1971 period when NDP was evolving into LUM. This history of interfaith cooperation suggested the churches might be willing to support Rev. Elly's efforts to create an ecumenical urban ministry.

Competition. An ecumenical urban ministry would have a difficult time getting started in a community where there already were several similar organizations and where it would have to compete with these organizations for legitimacy and resources. On the other hand, *if there were no other organizations pursuing similar goals (i.e., if the new group could be "the only show in town"), then its chances of being formed would be significantly greater.*

During the late 1960s, the Tippecanoe County Federation of Churches was the only other ecumenical group in the Lafayette area with any interest in social concerns. Between 1964-65 and 1970-71, the Federation drifted away from its traditional focus on interfaith understanding and worship and toward more involvement in social issues. It endorsed an interracial program called Project Commitment and the Big Brothers—Big Sisters program, had a representative on the Lafayette Human Relations Council, studied the matter of temporary housing, opposed pari-mutuel gambling, and conducted a panel on student activism.

However, there were limits to the Federation's involvement in social concerns. Because such involvement was not an extension of the Federation's traditional goals, there was considerable disagreement about its legitimacy. And because the Federation had a small budget and no paid staff, it could not become very deeply involved in any of these issues.

Thus, NDP emerged into LUM partly because there were no other ecumenical groups addressing social issues with both legitimacy and a full-time staff.

Resources: Secular Realm

Community Size. Large, urban populations are more conducive to the formation of groups like LUM than small rural populations are. Though the Lafayette area is not the largest metropolitan area in the state, it clearly is urban (see Table 2). In 1970, the population was 109,378 for the county as a whole: 44,955 for Lafayette; 19,157 for West Lafayette; and 45,266 for the more rural area outside of the two cities.[4]

The population included more racial and ethnic minorities than surrounding counties had, people with rather high levels of education (especially in West Lafayette), and people employed in such diverse areas as industry, agriculture, and higher education (see Table 2).

The Greater Lafayette area performs a central place function for the surrounding area. It is located about two hours southeast of Gary, an hour northwest of Indianapolis, an hour and a half east of Champaign-Urbana (Illinois), and an hour west of Kokomo. Thus, it is the largest city within 60 to 75 miles in all directions. People from the seven rural counties (Benton, Cass, Carroll, Clinton, Montgomery, Warren, and White) in the surrounding area come to Lafayette for a variety of services ranging from work, shopping, and hospitals to sporting events such as state sectional basketball tournaments.

Thus, the Lafayette area had the resources I thought would be conducive to the formation of groups like LUM.

Resources: Religious Sphere

Potential Support Groups. For a group like LUM to get started, there must be a sizable number of Roman Catholic and liberal Protestant churches in the local area. In the late 1960s and early 1970s, there were just over 100 churches in Tippecanoe County. Roman Catholic and liberal Protestant groups comprised about half of all local churches and one-half to two-thirds of all church members.[5] Thus, there was a sizable pool of potential church support for a group like LUM.

Resources in Potential Support Groups. My theoretical framework suggested that the *Roman Catholic and liberal Protestant churches in the area also must have the resources needed to support a new group like LUM.* These resources would include large and affluent memberships. Roman Catholic and liberal Protestant churches also have church agencies at the synod, presbytery, and diocesan levels which have additional resources to support local ministries. As other research has shown (Greenwood, 1967; Johnson, 1980), these church agencies can be important sources of support for new church programs.

The six Roman Catholic churches were quite large, averaging 3,023 adherents. Liberal Protestant congregations averaged about 530 adherents. Conservative Protestant congregations were the smallest of the three groups, averaging 365 adherents (Johnson, Picard, and Quinn, 1974).

It is more difficult to estimate the average wealth of the churches in the 1960s. However, national education, occupation, and income data for the 1960s (Roof, 1979;

Greeley, 1976; Burkey, 1978) indicate that Catholics and liberal Protestants were quite well-off (better off, for example, than members of conservative Protestant groups). Second, it is widely known that several of the largest Catholic and liberal Protestant churches in the Lafayette area include large numbers of well-to-do members from old-line families. My examination of the membership rolls for these churches confirmed this impression. Third, these churches also contain large numbers of highly educated Purdue faculty, their highly educated spouses, and many dual-career families.

Finally, the Catholic diocese had recently formed a Campaign for Human Development committee which had money to support local programs dealing with poverty. The presbytery of Crawfordsville had a Committee on National Missions which also could support urban mission groups like LUM. And, the northern conference of the United Methodist church had a Fund for Reconciliation to support social action projects.

Organizational Factors

I hypothesized that four factors pertaining more directly to LUM also would affect its formation. These were Rev. Elly's leadership, lay support, clergy support, and economic resources.

Leadership. The leader of a new group like LUM must have at least two qualities if the group is to be formed: dedication (commitment) and a sense of direction (competence).

People who worked with Rev. Elly were so impressed with his commitment to a community-oriented ministry, they often spoke admiringly of his energy and willingness to work long hours. Some of the people who worked with him in the formation of LUM have continued to work with the group and have told me how much Rev. Elly's drive inspired them.

It also seemed to inspire people outside of LUM. For example, minutes of the Tippecanoe County Federation of Churches' spring assembly in 1972 included a report from the Community Action and Service Committee urging support of LUM. The report specifically refers to Rev. Elly's leadership qualities: "I am sure all [Federation] members feel we are most fortunate to have a man of Ron Elly's ability and dedication providing a very vital service in this community."

Rev. Elly's experience with New Albany's Downtown Neighborhood Council contributed greatly to the competence component of his leadership abilities. That experience gave him chances to think about the theological dimensions of church involvement in social concerns, learn about the social forces involved in urban life, observe how others conducted a community-oriented ministry, and explore his own ideas. These opportunities and experiences gave him visions of urban ministry and ideas about specific issues which others in the Lafayette community did not have.

Lay Support. A reform group like LUM needs to attract lay volunteers from its potential support groups if it is to be formed. Lay volunteers are likely to be: recruited along lines of existing activity; highly educated; in professional occupations or married to people who are; and of the opinion that churches ought to be involved in social concerns.[6]

The data in Table 5 indicate that seven Presbyterian congregations produced 85 percent of NDP's lay support and 87 percent of its most active supporters. The largest single source of lay support was Covenant Presbyterian Church, a relatively large and growing congregation in West Lafayette. Covenant provided about one-third of all NDP participants and half of all its most active supporters (N = 18). Hope Chapel produced the second largest number of supporters (N = 16). However, as the narrative in Chapter 4 suggested, a majority of these people provided only limited support. Rev. Elly ranked only five of the 16 Hope Chapel people among NPD's most active members. Other local congregations produced fewer supporters, but the ones they produced tended to be very active.

Table 5
SOURCES OF NDP'S MOST ACTIVE LAY SUPPORT

Source of Support	Total Supporters N	Total Supporters %	Most Supportive N	Most Supportive %	Contacted N	Contacted %
Presbyterian Congregations						
Covenant	22	33	18	50	12	67
Hope Chapel	16	24	5	14	4	22
Bethany	9	14	5	14	1	5
University	5	7	1	3	-	-
Central	2	3	1	3	-	-
Faith	2	3	-	-	-	-
Memorial (Dayton)	1	1	1	3	-	-
Other Congregations						
Church of the Good Shepherd	1	1	1	3	1	5
Trinity United Methodist	1	1	1	3	-	-
First Christian	1	1	1	3	-	-
Church of Brethren	1	1	1	3	-	-
Redeemer Lutheran	1	1	1	3	-	-
Other Sources						
Purdue University	4	6	-	-		
Totals	(66)	(99)	(36)	(102)	(18)	(99)

These data point to the importance of social networks as sources of support for groups such as LUM. Additional evidence of the important role networks played in lay support for LUM came from the telephone interviews with the more active supporters (see Table 6).

NDP's most active supporters tended to be highly educated (see Table 7). Eighty-four percent had at least some college education. Twenty-eight percent were Ph.Ds. Over 80 percent were in professional occupations (39 percent) or were married to people in professional occupations (44 percent).

Finally, I asked the more active supporters to describe their religious values, beliefs, and interests as "conservative" (e.g., oriented toward saving souls and personal salvation) or "liberal" (e.g., stressing the importance of church involvement in social concerns), and the extent to which their involvement in NDP was either an extension of these values, beliefs, and interests or a reflection of more secular concerns. About one-third said they were theologically liberal. These people said personal faith was not enough; people of faith needed to act; and the church as a whole should provide ways

Table 6
HOW MOST ACTIVE SUPPORTERS BECAME INVOLVED

How People Became Involved	N	%
Members of other congregations drawn into NDP activities through relationship with people already involved	9	50
Member of Hope Chapel drawn into NDP activities through relationships with others in the church	4	22
Asked by local congregation to participate at Hope Chapel; learned of NDP as a result	3	17
Asked by local congregation to participate in NDP; responded to church appeal for NDP volunteers	2	11
Total	(18)	(100)

Table 7
EDUCATIONAL AND OCCUPATIONAL STATUS OF NDP'S MOST ACTIVE SUPPORTERS

Characteristic	N	%
Occupational Status		
Professional	7	39
Other white collar	-	-
Blue collar	1	5
Homemaker		
A. Married to professional	8	44
B. Married to "other"	-	-
University student	2	11
Total	(18)	(99)
Education		
Ph.D.	5	28
College graduate; Master's; some graduate school	5	28
Some college	5	28
High school graduate	2	11
Some high school or less	1	5
Total	(18)	(100)

for people to express their concern for others. Another 61 percent said they were moderates. Only 5 percent said they were conservative.

When asked why they personally became involved in NDP, half said it was mainly an expression of their religious beliefs and/or their belief that the church should be involved in social action and service to others. Another 27 percent said it was a combination of their religious views and their interest in working with young people. For example, some people had had previous experience with Girl Scouts and Campfire Girls and felt they had something to contribute to NDP. Finally, 22 percent indicated their involvement was mainly a function of their general desire to be involved in the community and NDP provided one way.

Clergy Support. A new group like LUM needs some support from local clergy. Clergy have experience in running religious organizations which lay people tend to lack. They also can provide the new group's leader with collegial, moral support in ways which lay people cannot. I expected young, Presbyterian clergy with some denominational (i.e., hierarchical) responsibilities and/or responsibilities in specialized ministries to be more supportive than pastors of local churches. I also expected the clergy to be more liberal than conservative in their theology; more community-oriented than congregationally-oriented in their conceptions of their ministerial role; more colleague-oriented than congregation-oriented in their professional identities; more liberal than conservative in their political attitudes; and more likely to view their support of LUM as being in their self-interest than as being contrary to their self-interest.[7]

I was able to identify eleven clergy who supported LUM's formation in one way or another (e.g., offering Rev. Elly personal-moral support or getting their churches to support LUM financially).[8] I asked Rev. Elly to rate clergy support of NDP on a scale from 1 (limited support; contributed in one or two specific ways but not a leading supporter) to 10 (an active supporter without whom LUM might not have been formed). Rev. Elly rated four of the eleven ≤ 5 on the 10-point scale, indicating their support was somewhat limited. He ranked the other seven ≥ 6, indicating they were his most active supporters among area clergy.

Six of Rev. Elly's seven most active clergy supporters were Presbyterians. The other belonged to the Church of the Brethren, a denomination with a long-standing emphasis on social concerns. Five were pastors, one was an associate pastor at a campus ministry, and one was a general presbyter. All had had experience working in denominational offices and/or specialized ministries. Five were under 40 years of age; the other two were in their late fifties.

Rev. Elly also rated each man from 1-10 on each of three scales: theological belief—from conservative (score 1) to liberal (score 10); his conception of their ministerial role as relating mainly to their congregations (score 1) or to the community as a whole (score 10); and political beliefs—from conservative (score 1) to liberal (score 10).

Theologically, the clergy tended to be moderates. They belonged to mainline denominations, but Rev. Elly did not view them as especially liberal ($\bar{X} = 6.0$). He scored five of them ≥ 6, but these scores were distributed as follows: $6(N=1)$, $7(N=3)$, $8(N=1)$. As evidence of their moderate-liberalism, Rev. Elly pointed to sermons they had given on social consciousness, their involvement in mission work, and their denominational affiliations. He described two of the clergy as theological conservatives.

In terms of the congregational (pastoral) or community (prophetic) orientations of their ministries, Rev. Elly felt three of the clergy were quite prophetic and gave them scores of 7, 8, and 9. He pointed to their involvement in United Way and school board issues as well as their efforts to increase their parishioners' involvement in local issues. But, he felt the other four clergy were more oriented toward pastoral work within their congregations.

Rev. Elly felt three of the clergy were political liberals and gave them scores of 7. As evidence for these scores, he pointed to their opposition to racism and the Vietnam War and their concern about poverty. He felt the other four clergy were more moderate to conservative in their political outlooks.

Next, I asked Rev. Elly about the clergy's tendency to define their professional identities in terms of their local congregations or their professional colleagues. He said five of the seven were oriented toward their colleagues ($\triangleq 6$ on this dimension). As evidence, he pointed to their involvement in synod activities, national mission committee work, and the Tippecanoe County Federation of Churches. He felt two clergy tended to use their congregations as their reference group.

Finally, I asked Rev. Elly to what extent *he* felt the *clergy* felt it was (or was not) in their professional self-interest to support NDP. He reported that five of them probably saw support of NDP as being consistent with their professional interests. He felt support of NDP gave most of them a chance to live up to *denominational* expectations concerning *some* community dimension to ministry. He also felt it gave some of them a chance to keep in touch with professional colleagues. One pastor had a relatively liberal congregation and needed to be somewhat involved in social concerns (though Rev. Elly felt he probably would have been anyway). Another's church was near a relatively poor downtown area and, though the congregation was not eager to be involved in neighborhood concerns, the pastor felt the church was willing to support NDP as a modest expression of concern. In the other two cases, Rev. Elly felt the clergy did not see support of NDP as being in their best interest. One was pastor of a small struggling church which wanted him to devote his time to church growth. The other felt it was in his interest to tend to pastoral-congregational needs because his colleague was more oriented toward a prophetic role (on campus but not in the community). For these men, support of LUM was riskier.

Thus, a profile of the clergy who supported LUM indicates they were relatively young pastors of mainline (Presbyterian) churches who also were active in hierarchical church work. They tended to be theologically moderate, more pastoral than prophetic in outlook, more colleague- than congregationally-oriented, and moderate to conservative politically. They also tended to view support of LUM as being in their professional self-interest.[9]

Conceivably, this group could have been quite similar to, or quite different from, other clergy on these criteria. I have no way of knowing for sure. But, to obtain at least some evidence on this question, I asked Rev. Elly to compare these clergy with others he knew. He felt they probably were somewhat younger than average, somewhat more community-oriented, somewhat more liberal politically, and somewhat more likely to feel that support of NDP was in their professional self-interest. On the other hand, he felt they were about average in their theological beliefs—neither more liberal nor more conservative than other clergy.

Economic Resources. LUM secured the economic resources it needed to get started. Figures for 1970 show NDP got $4,500 (almost half of its budget) from the presbytery of Crawfordsville Committee on National Missions. Local Presbyterian congregations contributed another $1,500 (about 17 percent of the budget). Other mainline denominations and congregations (especially the United Methodists) contributed just over $2,000 (about 25 percent of NDP's budget). The rest of NDP's resources came from community groups such as the local Hunger Hike, civic associations, fraternities, and sororities.

Conclusion

This chapter indicates considerable support for the structural conduciveness and resource mobilization approaches comprising my open system approach (see Table 8). All seven of the period factors were important. These included three structural conditions (rapid social change, ferment within the religious sphere, and an ecumenical spirit among denominations), and four resource factors (economic prosperity, an abundance of resources in the religious sphere, theological justification for social reform, and the availability of religious personnel to lead in the formation of ecumenical urban ministries).

Table 8
SUMMARY OF ENVIRONMENTAL FACTORS AFFECTING LUM'S FORMATION

	Period		Place		
	Structural Conditions	Resources	Structural Conditions	Resources	
Secular	1 of 1	1 of 1	0 of 1	1 of 1	(3 of 4)
Religious	2 of 2 (3 of 3)	3 of 3 (4 of 4)	3 of 3 (3 of 4)	2 of 2 (3 of 3)	(10 of 10)

Six of seven place factors also were conducive to LUM's formation. These included three structural conditions (the existence of a problem, a willingness among potential support groups to participate in an ecumenical venture, and a lack of competition with similar ecumenical groups), and three resource factors (an urban population, a core group of Roman Catholic and liberal Protestant churches in the area, and an abundance of human and economic resources in these churches). One structural place factor was not important: the conservative political climate in the Lafayette area.

Organizational factors also were important. LUM recruited a committed and competent leader in Rev. Elly. It also received support from highly educated professional people who felt their churches ought to be involved in social concerns, and from clergy who tended to be young Presbyterians with some denominational responsibilities, colleague-orientations, and reasons to believe their support of LUM was in their professional self-interest. (They were not as theologically liberal, not as community oriented in their ministerial roles, and not as politically liberal as I expected.) LUM also succeeded in obtaining the economic resources it needed from two denominations, several local congregations, and other community organizations.

CHAPTER 6

DESCRIPTION OF LUM'S INSTITUTIONALIZATION:

A VOLATILE, CURVILINEAR PROCESS

During the ten years following its formation, LUM struggled to survive and become a viable organization. This struggle involved all 15 of the structural and process dimensions outlined in Chapter 1. Compared to 1972, LUM in 1981 had:
1. a clearer sense of purpose
2. membership policies which more accurately reflected its purpose
3. grown in the size of its membership without increasing the size of its staff
4. achieved a greater degree of financial stability
5. formalized its record keeping
6. experienced gradual differentiation among its committees and greater differentiation among its programs
7. developed a bureaucratic tendency of putting organizational needs ahead of individual needs and treating all employees according to a standard set of personnel policies
8. developed a pattern of decentralized decision making
9. survived the crisis of replacing its original leader
10. more effective staff and board leadership
11. greater stability among its member churches and their representatives, though considerable turnover among its staff
12. a general tendency toward relatively fixed programs, though some degree of flexibility
13. a more productive staff
14. more positive relationships among members of the board and staff
15. generally more positive relationships with other groups which are most important to it (member churches, denominational funding agencies, and low-income groups)

But the process of institutionalizing LUM was neither easy nor linear. It was a volatile, curvilinear process (see Figure 1). After a period of buoyancy and growth (1972-74), LUM went into a period of uncertainty and decline (1975-77), before regaining its stride and expanding again (1978-81).

Figure 1
THE CURVILINEAR PATTERN OF LUM'S INSTITUTIONALIZATION

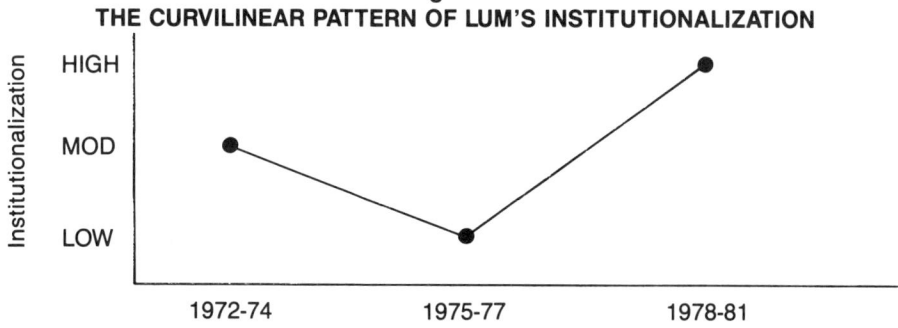

This chapter uses the 15 dimensions listed above to describe the curvilinearity of LUM's institutionalization. Chapter 7 will try to explain it.

Structural Components

Purpose

Between 1972 and 1976, LUM used and coordinated the resources of local churches to address the needs of low-income people living in downtown neighborhoods (see arrow A in Figure 2). LUM did not work directly with local congregations to increase *their* involvement in social concerns; it used their resources to develop programs of *its* own which church members could participate in. However, LUM hoped that by sensitizing local churchgoers to the needs of Lafayette's low-income people, it might be a leavening influence within local churches (see broken arrow B).

Arrow C indicates that LUM's goals were to "identify with the downtown neighborhoods of Lafayette, using their expertise to develop a strategy (or strategies) for meeting the social needs of that group." LUM wanted "to identify problems, implement and coordinate solutions, and serve as community advocates in the larger social structure." According to its "Statement of Mission—1973," LUM wanted to be "a bridge between persons with limited opportunities and persons with many available opportunities"; "to help solve or alleviate disturbing community problems"; and "to stand with those who lack opportunity . . . assisting their speaking and encouraging their persistence in developing their potential as human beings in the family of God." Broken arrow D indicates that LUM also wanted to involve "downtown neighborhood representatives on [its] board."

Arrows E and F indicate that LUM also felt some reciprocal relationship with human service agencies. On the one hand, LUM also wanted to use and coordinate their resources, but LUM's "Statement of Mission—1973" also said the programs it creates "eventually [would be] released to appropriate responsible community social service agencies when and where possible."

By 1977-81, LUM's purpose had changed somewhat (see Figure 3). Arrow A indicates that by 1977-81, LUM viewed itself as being in a *reciprocal* relationship with local churches. It would continue to use and coordinate local church resources, but a new goal was "to increase church involvement in social concerns, especially those affecting low-income people." LUM conceived of this task as involving four issues: increasing the number and quality of social concerns programs within local congregations; elevating social concerns among church members' parish priorities; fostering more compassionate attitudes toward the poor; and integrating church members' vertical beliefs (about God, Christ, and life after death) with their horizontal beliefs (about loving one's neighbor and doing good for others).

Arrow B indicates that LUM also wanted a reciprocal relationship with low-income people. It wanted to involve low-income people in its activities because their ideas and help would contribute to LUM's programs. LUM also wanted to perform four functions with and on behalf of low-income groups: address structural conditions which perpetuate poverty; foster community development among low-income groups, so they would be able to care for their own needs; increase the educational, economic, social, and political resources within low-income groups; and respond to the emergency needs of low-income individuals and families.

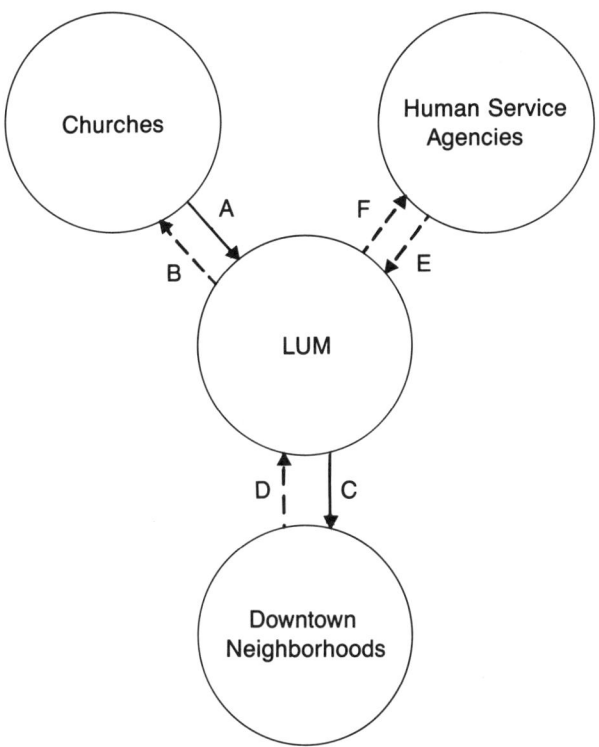

Figure 2
LUM'S PURPOSE: 1972-76

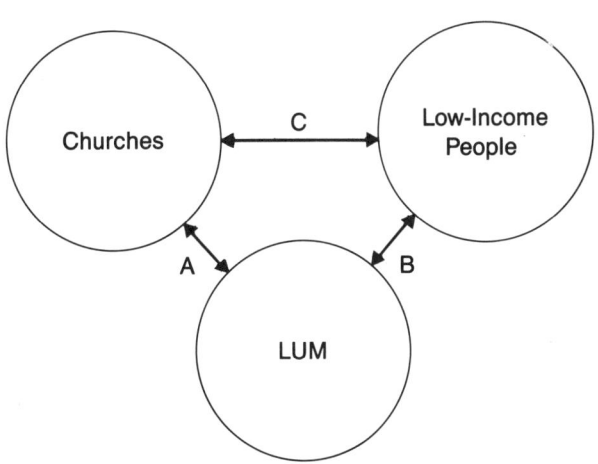

Figure 3
LUM'S PURPOSE: 1977-81

Arrow C indicates that LUM sought to "foster closer relationships between churches and low-income people" *through* its other activities.

By 1977-81, LUM no longer considered human service agencies part of its purpose.

Thus, between 1972-76 and 1977-81, LUM dropped its emphasis on human service agencies, increased its emphasis on working with local churches to enhance their involvement in social concerns, retained its emphasis on addressing the causes and consequences of poverty, and reaffirmed its emphasis on fostering closer ties between churches and low-income groups.

Membership

The NDP proposal for LUM said three groups would be eligible for membership in LUM: low-income, downtown neighborhoods; local churches; and "connectional judicatories." The proposal also indicated that "at least 50-51 percent of the Board [should] come from the areas of the community being served and involved, that is the downtown, or low-income communities." Local congregations and denominational judicatories presumably would comprise the other half of LUM's membership.

However, LUM's actual membership at the beginning of 1972 consisted of nine local congregations (mostly Presbyterian) and one clergyman who was listed as a representative of the presbytery of Wabash Valley, but whose involvement was more personal. Thus, there was a substantial gap between what LUM wanted its membership to be and what it actually was. Local congregations comprised a disproportionate share of the members and low-income groups and downtown neighborhoods were underrepresented on the board.

By the mid 1970s, LUM had become an ecumenical organization which included 19 local congregations and three individual members. The local congregations were all mainline Protestant. Two of the individual members were at-large Presbyterians; the other was a representative of the black community.

In early 1977, LUM's board considered a proposal that the board be comprised of two groups: local churches and low-income groups (dropping the group's earlier interest in judicatory officials and human service agencies and focusing more attention on low-income groups).

The motion with regard to local churches assumed their importance on the board and urged that more local congregations be recruited. The motion passed unanimously.

There were two motions with regard to low-income groups: (1) to create positions on the board for the five groups in the Lafayette area which were over-represented among the poor (low-income white adults, Spanish-speaking adults, the aged, black adults, and youth), and (2) to have two voting seats for each of these groups.[1] The first motion passed 4 to 3 and the second carried 5 to 2.

The bylaws were revised in 1980. A stipulation that member churches should pay 10 cents per member was deleted. And a stipulation was added that at-large members would be included "as the board deems appropriate up to, but not exceeding, 20 percent of the church board membership. The members at large shall be elected annually by the members of the board and shall not serve for more than three consecutive terms."

By 1981, LUM's membership consisted of 29 local congregations and three at-large representatives (see Table 1). Twenty-five of the congregations (90 percent) were Protestant; three (10 percent) were Roman Catholic. The three at-large members were Rosetta Martinez, Ron Chinn, and Jim Davidson.

Table 1
LUM'S MEMBERSHIP: 1981

Member Churches
- United Methodist (N = 8): St. Andrew, First, Christ, Dayton, Trinity, Stidham, Stockwell, and Grace
- Presbyterian (N = 5): Central, Faith, Memorial of Dayton, Bethany, and Elston
- Roman Catholic (N = 3): St. Thomas Aquinas, Blessed Sacrament, and St. Boniface
- Lutheran (N = 2): Our Saviour and University Lutheran
- Episcopal (N = 2): St. John's and Good Shepherd
- American Baptist (N = 1): First
- Disciples of Christ (N = 1): First
- American Baptist and Disciples of Christ (N = 1): Federated
- United Church of Christ (N = 1): Immanuel
- Society of Friends (N = 1): Lafayette Friends
- Mennonite (N = 1): Mennonite Fellowship
- Brethren (N = 1): Church of the Brethren
- Unitarian (N = 1): Unitarian Fellowship
- Inter-denominational (N = 1): University

At-Large Members
- Rosetta Martinez
- Ron Chinn
- Jim Davidson

Size

LUM's membership more than doubled between 1972 and 1981, passing through three stages: growth (1972-75), no growth (1976-77), and growth (1978-1981). LUM grew from 13 members at the end of 1972 to 24 by the end of 1975. Membership was 22 in 1976 and 24 in 1977, then rose from 25 in 1978 to 36 in 1981.

LUM employed 4.0 to 4.5 staff people each year between 1972 and 1978. Staff size dropped from 4.5 in 1978 to 3.0 in 1979, but rose again to 4.0 in 1980-81. The staffing pattern also changed between 1977 and 1981, with the number of full-time staff declining from four to two, and the number of part-time staff increasing from one to four.

As a result, the ratio of staff members to board members grew from one staff person to every 3.2 board members in 1972 to one staff person for every nine board members in 1981.

Economic Resources

Four denominational agencies (presbytery of Wabash Valley, northern conference of the United Methodist church, United Episcopal Charities, and the Indiana-Kentucky conference of the United Church of Christ) have been the largest source of LUM's financial support since its formation in 1972 (see Table 2). In terms of absolute dollars, their support rose rather steadily from $14,535.26 in 1972 to $35,650.00 in 1981. In terms of real dollars (i.e., with inflation taken into account), denominational support in 1981 was at about the same level it was in 1973-74. In percentage terms, denominational support ranged from a high of 56 percent in 1972 to a low of 38 percent in 1981.

Table 2
SOURCES OF INCOME: 1972-1981

	Denominations	Member Churches	Other[a]	Total
1972	$14,535.26	$ 4,840.00	$ 6,325.08	$25,700.34
	56%	19%	25%	100%
1973	$17,749.82	$ 7,699.37	$14,497.97	$39,947.16
	44%	19%	36%	99%
1974	$19,493.04	$ 9,669.04	$15,585.09	$44.747.17
	44%	22%	35%	99%
1975	$25,754.15	$10,852.41	$14,057.36	$50,663.92
	51%	21%	28%	100%
1976	$26,417.21	$15,078.50	$ 8,445.39	$49,941.10
	53%	30%	17%	100%
1977	$27,357.50	$15,107.04	$14,464.04	$56,928.58
	48%	26%	25%	99%
1978	$31,312.50	$14,983.72	$18,853.75	$65,149.97
	48%	23%	29%	100%
1979	$31,100.00	$15,210.04	$29,508.99	$75,818.03
	41%	20%	39%	100%
1980	$33,650.00	$21,340.74	$25,869.87	$80,860.61
	42%	26%	32%	100%
1981	$35,650.00	$26,567.60	$30,997.77	$93,215.37
	38%	29%	33%	100%

[a]Includes: other local churches, civic organizations, individual donors.

A second source of support has been LUM's local congregations. In terms of absolute dollars, their support rose steadily from $4,840 in 1972 to $15,078.50 in 1976 then leveled off at about $15,000 until 1980 when it jumped to $21,340.74 and 1981 when it rose to $26,567.60. Church support exceeded inflation between 1972 and 1976, failed to keep up with inflation from 1977 to 1979, but exceeded inflation again in 1980-81. As a result, in terms of real dollars, local church support in 1981 was at the highest level it ever had been (almost twice what it was in 1972-73). In percentage terms, local church support rose from 19 percent in 1972-73 to 30 percent in 1976, then dropped steadily to 20 percent in 1979, before it rose to 26 percent in 1980 and 29 percent in 1981.

The third source of LUM's support has been "other" groups and individuals (e.g., women's groups with member churches, non-member churches, individuals with an interest in particular LUM programs, Title III and Title XX funds, and the Lilly grants).[2] These "other" sources contributed $6,000-$15,000 (25-36 percent of LUM's total annual income) between 1972 and 1975; they declined sharply to only $8,445.39 (17 percent) in 1976, but then increased rapidly until they reached $29,508.99 (39 percent) in 1979. They dipped somewhat to $25,869.87 (32 percent) in 1980 before rising to $30,997.77 (33 percent) in 1981. Relative to inflation, "other" contributions declined between 1972 and 1976 but rebounded between 1977 and 1981. In terms of real dollars, then, "other" contributions in 1981 were at about the same level they were at in 1973-74.

Table 3
INCOME, EXPENSES, AND RESERVES: 1972-81

	New Income[a]	Expenses	Year-end Balance[b]	Reserves General[c] Investments, Savings	Specified Accounts
1972	$25,700.34	$25,479.20	$ +221.14	-	-
1973	39,947.16	37,670.53	+4,926.88	-	-
1974	44,747.17	47,598.77	+2,073.68	-	-
1975	50,663.92	51,386.23	+245.57	-	-
1976	49,941.10	48,871.12	+1,315.55	-	-
1977	56,928.58	55,087.13	+3,149.94	-	-
1978	65,149.97	55,587.87	+7,939.31	$6,247.84	$3,003.46
1979	75,818.03	67,170.22	+6,687.19	12,758.73	6,412.08
1980	80,860.61	77,742.54	+2,991.25	8,474.93	10,256.12
1981	93,215.37	93,356.20	+1,850.42	13,860.89	9,579.23

[a]New income; not counting the balance from previous year.
[b]Refers to the difference between the balance at beginning of year and the balance at the end of the year.
[c]Includes interest from all reserves.

LUM's income exceeded its expenses in 1972 and 1973, leaving a total balance of $4,926.88 at the end of 1973 (see Table 3). However, expenses exceeded income in 1974 and 1975. To meet expenses, LUM drew upon its reserves, reducing them to only $245.57 at the end of 1975. Between 1976 and 1981, LUM's income exceeded its expenses. In 1981, LUM raised $93,215 and had reserves of $23,440.12.

Formalization

LUM has been quite formal since its formation. It was incorporated as the Neighborhood Development Project in 1969. Bylaws for the Lafayette Urban Ministry were created in 1973 and have been revised on occasion.

LUM also has been rather formal in terms of minutes of board and Executive Committee meetings. In fact, the amount of paper used for staff reports, committee reports, and minutes of meetings has been something of a standing joke within the group.

LUM also has been very formal with regard to financial records since its earliest years. I was able to locate records of annual income and expenses (real and projected) for every year LUM has existed.

The one area where LUM became noticeably more formal concerned its incorporation papers. When a representative from the Unitarian Fellowship inquired about the papers in 1976, staff and board members were unable to recall when the papers were filed or where they might be. The situation could have threatened the existence of the group if the papers were not found and LUM had to pay federal taxes back to 1972 (or earlier). After considerable board concern and staff time, it was learned that the incorporation papers applied to the Neighborhood Development Project (not LUM) and, therefore, needed to be reprocessed through the federal government. Reprocessing was completed in 1978.

Complexity

LUM experienced virtually no vertical differentiation between 1972 and 1981. Its staff attended conferences in other communities (e.g., SCUPE's Urban Congresses in Chicago, 1978 and 1980) and made occasional presentations about LUM in other communities (usually within 100 miles of Lafayette), but LUM did not develop any programs to deal with issues outside of Lafayette.[3]

However, LUM experienced considerable horizontal differentiation. In 1972, LUM had no formal committees. By 1973, two committees had emerged: Finance and Funding, and Volunteering Recruitment and Relations (later changed to Membership Recruitment and Relations). In 1975, two other committees emerged: Personnel Policies and Salary Review, and Long Range Planning (later changed to Program and Planning). In 1980, LUM added a Public Policy Committee.

Table 4
LUM PROGRAMS: 1972-81, BY YEAR BEGUN

1972

    Volunteer Transportation (1972-   )
    Centralized Emergency Fund (1972-   )
    Summer Camp (1972-   )
    Adventure Clubs (1972-77)
    Good Friends Visitation (1972-77)
    Christmas Project (1972-   )
    Adult Basic Education (1972)
    Integrated Hands (1972-74)
    Teen Leadership Development (1972-77)

1973
- Council on Aging (1973-74)
- Fuel Crisis Task Force (1973-74)
- Spanish-Speaking Persons Task Force (1973-75)

1974
- Human Development Coalition (1974-77)
- Revenue Sharing Task Force (1974-75)

1975
- Community Infant Care Center (1975)
- Pastoral Counseling Center (1975-77)

1976
- None

1977
- None

1978
- Advocates (1978-)
- Shamrock Park (1978)

1979
- Jubilee Christmas (1979-)
- Mothers' Group (1979)
- Newsletter (1979-)
- Public Policy (1979-)
- Seeds of Vision (1979-)
- Survey of Churches (1979-80)

1980
- Repairs on Wheels (1979-)
- Grow-a-Row (1979-)

1981
- Food Buying Club (1981-)

The pattern of differentiation with regard to programs has been somewhat different (see Table 4). Between 1972 and 1981, LUM sponsored 27 different local programs. There was a rapid increase in new programs between 1972 and 1974. Fifty-two percent of all LUM programs were operational within the first three years. During the next three years (1975-77), LUM's attention turned to more organizational issues and there was a lull in new program development. Between 1978 and 1981, 11 programs were begun (41 percent of all LUM programs). Two were begun in 1978, six in 1979, two in 1980, and one in 1981.

Bureaucratization

In its first five to six years, LUM had some sense of organization, but was not very bureaucratic in its behavior. It conceived of a position called urban minister, but it was created for and identified with one man: Rev. Elly. As his job description indicates, the urban ministry was the urban minister and whatever activities he became involved in:

JOB DESCRIPTION FOR THE LAFAYETTE URBAN MINISTER (1972)

It is the sincere desire of this committee to keep this job description as flexible as possible. We have no desire to tie the Urban Minister down to certain jobs even if these jobs become obsolete during the course of the year.

As we see it, the most difficult task of the Urban Minister will be to become accepted by the downtown neighborhood of Lafayette in which he will work. This means that the people of the area must *trust* the minister.

We feel that the Urban Minister has a real ministry of reconciliation within the downtown community, reconciliation between those with limited opportunities and those with many available opportunities and to the church of Christ.

1. *COORDINATION* — The Urban Minister must coordinate the available community resources with the church resources in discovering and meeting the needs of the urban community in which he serves.

2. *ADVOCACY* — In the name of Jesus Christ the Urban Minister shall stand for and with the poor in the structures (political, social, and economic) of the community, *always* with the support and knowledge of the Board of Directors of the Lafayette Urban Ministry.

3. *PROGRAM* — The Urban Minister will be in charge of planning and implementing such programs as summer camping experiences, adventure clubs, senior citizens activities and such other programs as the minister feels the need arise in the community.

4. *INTERPRETATION* — We feel that the Urban Minister will naturally want to accept certain speaking engagements in order to interpret his mission to the participating churches and civic groups. However, his main task will be to work with the downtown community.

5. *ADMINISTRATION* — The Urban Minister will be the administrative head of the program, responsible for any additional staff hired subsequent to this job description.

6. *SALARY* — The salary of the Urban Minister is negotiable. The Lafayette Urban Ministry will pay 15 percent pension, 25 percent of salary for housing, allow a one month vacation and a two-week study leave. Along with this, in November of each year the Board of Directors will establish a review committee to review, with the minister, both the minister's salary and this job description.

7. *RESPONSIBILITY* — The Urban Minister is responsible to the Board of Directors of the Lafayette Urban Ministry. He will be a non-voting member of the Board, he will present and report both his success and all failures, his joys and his problems.

In the areas of youth and transportation, the staff and programs also existed before the positions (which were created for specific people). The youth coordinator position (later combined with the teen leadership coordinator position) was an extension of NDP's camp and crafts programs and, thus, existed prior to 1972 when a new person was hired for the program. A job description was created at that time.

A transportation-senior citizen coordinator position was created in 1972 because LUM wanted to hire a particular person and absorb the project which she already was coordinating out of the basement of Bethany Presbyterian church.

A secretary was recruited without a written job description. Minutes of the board meeting in April 1977 are the first indication of a job description for a secretary.

LUM also operated in a rather informal, non-bureaucratic manner regarding personnel policies. Staff meetings during Fall 1975 revealed that LUM was torn between its historic emphasis on the individual and an emerging bureaucratic approach to staffing. One staff member complained that her job involved incompatible expectations that some of her work would take her out of the LUM office *and* that she would manage the transportation office (including resolving scheduling problems involving drivers and people in need of rides). Proposed solutions gave higher priority to the staff member's personal well-being than LUM's organizational and program interests. Potential solutions included: a cutback in LUM's transportation service, transferring the transportation service to some other agency, redistributing the work load among staff (e.g., for Rev. Elly to do some of the staff member's work), and adding staff or volunteers to the transportation area.

The decision to add personnel precipitated another struggle. The staff member felt a blind volunteer who answered the phone in the transportation office should be moved into a staff position, claiming she "cares about people" and has experience with the program. Rev. Elly took a more bureaucratic approach. He said, "Too often we have built jobs around people" (using his own job as an example): "It is time," he said, "for LUM to separate job from person." He favored writing a new job description, advertising the job, and letting anyone apply (including the blind volunteer). The other staff members agreed, viewing the issue as a choice between "feelings about a person" and "how the job is done."

The issue was resolved with two actions indicating LUM was not ready to make a decisive move in the direction of a bureaucratic approach to staffing (though it was tending in that direction). The staff member went from three-quarter time to full-time and Rev. Elly agreed to see whether the local vocational rehabilitation office had funds to train handicapped people.

During the 1977-81 period, LUM handled its staffing and personnel policies in a more bureaucratic manner. When someone left the staff, the staff and board considered the organization's needs, prepared a job description for the tasks that needed to be done, and recruited individuals to fill those positions. For example, when Rev. Elly resigned as urban minister, his position was redefined as administrative officer, with the following job description (see Appendix A for a detailed list of duties and qualifications):

> The Administrative Officer (A/O) of the Lafayette Urban Ministry (LUM) is responsible to the Board of Directors of the Lafayette Urban Ministry for discovering, planning, and implementing programs which are consistent with the goals of the Lafayette Urban Ministry; will promote and seek to coordinate available resources both human and financial within the community, its churches and agencies, both public and private, in the support and financing of the Lafayette Urban Ministry;

will be responsible for directly supervising the paid and volunteer staff of the Lafayette Urban Ministry except where the supervisory responsibility is specifically delegated and for providing resources for the Board of Directors and its committees. This position combines two areas of responsibility which ultimately may be separated.

When the transportation coordinator resigned in 1978, that position was redefined as program coordinator and a new person was hired. When that person resigned only a few months later, essentially the same job description was used to hire a replacement. When the secretary resigned in 1979, her position was redefined as office manager and a minister was recruited to fill it.

LUM's personnel policies also became more bureaucratic. The first mention of personnel policies and benefits came in October 1974 when Rev. Elly "requested for the rest of staff, salary review, possible health insurance benefits, and personnel policies and practices (i.e., maternity)." By February 1975, the staff had made arrangements for major-medical insurance. In March 1975, the Personnel Policies and Salary Review Committee recommended personnel policies governing leaves of absence, vacation time, and medical insurance.

In early to mid 1976, one staff member became pregnant and wanted to do more of her work at home. Rev. Elly contended that her work required her to be in the office. Faced with this emotional choice between giving priority to personal needs or LUM's program, the board decided to suspend the staff member for six months without pay. She felt the board's actions were unfair and refused to come back to work. In October 1976, the board hired someone to replace her.

Also between 1977-1981, a staff evaluation form was created so the annual salary review could be based on a standardized set of criteria; staff members prepared updated job descriptions; and in September 1977, the board approved a document outlining fringe benefits and working conditions.

The final chapter in LUM's struggle to develop a more bureaucratic approach to personnel issues involved LUM's handling of a former secretary's request for $439.28. In 1975, three of LUM's four members requested major-medical coverage. The secretary did not. During 1976, she requested that LUM pay her cash in lieu of the money it would have put into major-medical on her behalf. While some staff and board members informally indicated support for her request, the board never approved it (due to the budget crunch it faced at that time). In February 1979 (one month after she resigned), she sent a letter to LUM indicating she felt LUM still owed her the amount it would have spent had she wanted coverage.

LUM's Personnel Policies and Salary Review Committee undertook a thorough (16 page) review of all records pertaining to personnel policies in general and medical insurance in particular. On the basis of that review, LUM's board concluded in May 1979 that it "has no legal obligation to pay the claimed fringe benefit" and that "a letter be sent to [the staff member] explaining this decision."

Thus, between 1977 and 1981, LUM established a pattern of putting positions before people and, in this sense, became more institutionalized.

However, it also retained its awareness of itself as a social movement organization oriented toward change and did not want to become too bureaucratic in its job descriptions. In April 1980, the chair of the Personnel Policies and Salary Review Committee expressed the view that "LUM is not a highly organized bureaucracy; its mission deals with change and it needs to change to keep on top of things." LUM's new director responded in agreement: "LUM shouldn't have rigid job descriptions, keeping people separate, doing separate things." He said, "LUM needs to take advantage of the 'gifts' people bring to LUM and find ways for them to contribute; we must be flexible."

Distribution of Authority

Authority has been divided among five groups: the board as a whole, the Executive Committee, the officers, chairs of standing committees, and the staff.

In the early 1970s, LUM had an advisory board, which served Rev. Elly and the rest of the staff. By the mid 1970s, it had developed into a board of directors which met monthly to discuss and decide on issues relating to matters brought to it by the Executive Committee, officers, committee chairs, and the staff.[4]

In LUM's first year, there was no Executive Committee. But, by 1973 and 1974, an Executive Committee was evolving. By 1975, it was meeting monthly, two weeks before the board meeting. Its members consist of the officers, the immediate past president, the chairs of all standing committees, and the director. According to the bylaws, the Executive Committee "shall have the power to act as the board of directors when the board of directors is not in session. These actions are to be reported to the board of directors, at the next meeting of said board." In addition to acting on behalf of the board, the Executive Committee also identifies issues that need to be brought to the board's attention or sent to committees; reviews the issues which the committees want the board to act on; and sets the agenda for the board meeting.

In 1972, LUM had only three officers: a chairman, vice-chairman, and secretary-treasurer. By 1974, the secretary-treasurer's position had been split into two. Now LUM has four officers: a president, vice-president, secretary, and treasurer.

In 1972, LUM had no standing committees. By 1973, it had two, and by 1975, it had four. By 1981, LUM had five standing committees: Finance and Funding; Membership Recruitment and Relations; Program and Planning; Personnel Policies and Salary Review; and Public Policy.

Finally, the staff consists of a director, a program coordinator, and several interns. The director is the head of staff. In the area of administration, he is responsible for the execution of board policies; communication with member churches and other significant groups LUM relates to; hiring, supervising, and firing all other staff; and preparing all documents and proposals pertaining to LUM's economic resources. In the area of program, he is responsible for developing ideas relating to possible or on-going programs, implementing programs the board has approved, and working with the Program and Planning Committee to evaluate LUM's programs.[5]

The program coordinator is a full-time employee who ultimately is responsible to the director but directly responsible for one or more programs. The program coordinator is responsible for LUM's larger, on-going projects (e.g., Advocates). Interns are responsible for more specific, short-term projects (e.g., the Seeds of Vision conference or the Grow-a-Row project).

Though all board and staff members participate in the formulation of LUM's policies at least to the extent of membership on some committee and the right to vote at board meetings, the central positions and people are the officers, the chairs of standing committees and the director. These positions and people, more than others, have the authority to affect which issues are raised for discussion (and which ones are not) and how they are resolved.

Thus, one can determine the extent to which authority is highly centralized or decentralized if one knows what proportion these positions/people are of the total number of board and staff people (i.e., what the ratio is between these positions/people and all other board and staff people). The smaller the proportion (the larger the ratio), the more authority is concentrated in the hands of a few. The larger the proportion (the smaller the ratio), the more decentralized authority is.

At the very beginning, authority was quite highly centralized in the hands of only four people: Rev. Elly and the three officers. These people constituted about 23 percent of all board and staff members. There was one key policy maker for every 4.2 members of the board and staff.

Authority become more decentralized during the next four years. Between 1973 and 1976, key policy-making positions/people constituted 31 percent of board and staff members. The ratio of key policy-makers to all other board and staff members shrank from 1:4.2 in 1972 to 1:2.9 in 1976.

Between 1977 and 1981, the overall pattern of decentralized authority continued. Key policy-making positions/people comprised 28 percent of all of LUM members, and the ratio of key policy-making positions to members averaged 1:3.6.

Process Components

Administrative Succession

The process by which Rev. Elly resigned as pastor-director of LUM and Rev. Dolphin succeeded him as director took three years, starting in early 1975 and ending in early 1978.

Rev. Elly had an interest in pastoral counseling which dated back to the early 1970s. In fact, he was taking courses in pastoral counseling in Indianapolis once a week, thinking that someday he might like to move into that area of ministry.

Records show that in October 1974 "Ron Elly detailed the need for expanded counseling services in our jail, nursing homes and other agencies including the Family Service Agency where there is a need for skilled pastoral counselors to help ease their counseling case load." In September 1975, a letter was sent to all clergymen in Tippecanoe County inviting them to a meeting "to hear about and to share in a proposed new service to our community . . . a Pastoral Counseling Center. . . ."

In the next 12 months, Rev. Elly began counseling more and more people. In September 1976, the Program and Planning Committee's evaluation of LUM noted that: "Ron Elly's counseling with the Institutional Ministry and Pastoral Care Center should focus on low-income people or else be viewed as a role which competes with his responsibilities to LUM." Rev. Elly submitted a report to LUM's Personnel Policies and Salary Review Committee which included his proposal to: "move to 3/4 of my work time in the staff position as pastor-director of LUM and 1/4 of my work time in the staff position of pastoral counselor in the Lafayette Counseling Center (in which LUM is a participant)." LUM approved his proposal at its meeting in November 1976. By December 1976, "the Service Site Committee with the Indiana Counseling and Pastoral Care Center [had] approved the extension of a call for 10 hours a week (1/4 time) and passed that on to [the] Wabash Valley Presbytery for approval."

The pace of change quickened in 1977. By February 1977, the Pastoral Counseling Center was described as "very active." In May 1977, a member of the Pastoral Counseling Center's Service Site Committee met with LUM to discuss three areas of potential conflict between LUM and the Pastoral Counseling Center: competition for local church dollars, the higher priority local pastors might give to a Pastoral Counseling Center compared to a social action group like LUM, and competition for Rev. Elly's time and attention. This meeting marked the first time Rev. Elly publicly told the whole LUM board he was interested in becoming a full-time pastoral counselor.

By mid 1977, the LUM board was responding to the Program and Planning Committee's 1976 evaluation by redefining staff roles, including changing the pastor-director's job description. In June 1977, Rev. Elly's report to the LUM board included the following discussion of his future with LUM:

> I want to clarify any confusion concerning my future in the Lafayette Urban Ministry. This statement is precipitated by events at the last monthly Board meeting, and by my own concerns professionally and personally.
>
> First, regarding the potential adoption of the whole LUM evaluation via the recommendations yet to be voted in regard to staffing of LUM, I will not be a candidate or applicant for any one of the three new positions. It is my conclusion that should LUM hire a new Financial Officer or Administrative person and I remain on staff, the change would be on paper only as I would still be "pastor-director" by tradition, history and community custom.
>
> Second, regarding the potential retaining of the present LUM staffing arrangement, i.e., Pastor-Director with program staff under that, I will not long be your person. I am tired. I have also trained professionally and function presently anywhere from quarter-time (as contracted) to half-time (not so) in that job now as pastoral counselor. To continue very long split in roles and functions is too wearing for me personally and drains me of any sense of substantive contribution to either urban ministry—social concerns or pastoral counseling.
>
> Thirdly, I am pointing toward my resignation but not announcing one. Any call to become a pastoral counselor or clinician operating in the field of counseling will be negotiated with the Personnel Committee and Executive Council to balance my own needs against the best interests and needs of LUM to make a healthy transition. I will, through both groups, keep you posted on this matter.

Also in June 1977, LUM's board approved the recommended changes in staff roles, agreeing to create a new position called administrative officer (or director).

By July 1977, attention shifted from the Program and Planning Committee's evaluation to the Personnel Committee. That committee developed a job description for the director and was preparing to search for someone to fill the position. Meanwhile, the Service Site Committee "with the Indiana Counseling and Pastoral Care Center [in Indianapolis] was considering a document 'Proposed Income for Pastoral Counselor' and developing a call for the services of a full-time pastoral counselor."

The job description for the director (see Appendix A) was approved by LUM's board in August 1977.

There were several important developments in September 1977. The Pastoral Counseling Center Service Site Committee voted to employ Rev. Elly and open the center full-time starting October 1, 1977 (contingent upon approval from the Ministerial Relations Committee of the presbytery of Wabash Valley, which was granted). Rev. Elly resigned as pastor-director of LUM. Rev. Kurt Kremlick (who had served as chair of the Personnel Policies and Salary Review Committee) was made interim head of staff while LUM searched for Rev. Ell's replacement. And, LUM began advertising for a new director.

At this point, Rev. Elly was told the presbytery's Mission and Support Committee (which was providing about one-third of LUM's total income) might cut its support of LUM in 1978.[6] Rev. Elly, Rev. Kremlick, Rev. Kenneth McCullen (pastor of Central

Presbyterian Church), Rev. David Hancock (chair of LUM's Finance and Funding Committee), and I went to the committee's September meeting to respond to questions and plead for continued support of LUM.[7] The Mission and Support Committee voted to increase the amount of its support for 1978.

Forty-three people applied for the job of director by October 1977. Members of the Personnel Policies and Salary Review Committee reviewed all the applications. The four top candidates were invited to Lafayette and interviewed by the people who had read the resumes. After these visits, the committee decided that two candidates were more acceptable than the other two. The two less acceptable candidates were notified that they were no longer in the running.

The Personnel Policies and Salary Review Committee then met to determine which of the two more acceptable candidates would be its first choice. The group agreed to seek a consensus rather than live with a vote that might be very close. The discussion which followed was described by virtually all participants as "painful" because they liked both candidates so much they did not want to say "yes" to one and "no" to the other. In fact, some participants wished they could make one of the candidates the director and give the other man another position in the organization. But, not being able to do that, all the members of groups shared their evaluations of the candidates in terms of the job description and any other considerations they felt were relevant. After two hours, a consensus emerged. The committee would recommend Rev. Judson Dolphin to the board as its first choice.[8]

On January 11, 1978, LUM's board and pastors of member churches met Rev. Dolphin and his wife Mary Jane and voted to "call" him as LUM's new director. On January 15, 1978, a reception was held in honor of Rev. Elly's work with NDP and LUM. Rev. Dolphin took over in March 1978. His installation was held in June 1978.

Leadership

Staff. Rev. Elly and Rev. Dolphin's leadership styles have been very similar in many respects, but also different in several important ways.

A focused approach to leadership emerged in the late 1960s, was formalized in Rev. Elly's job description in 1972, and became a virtually irreversible part of his leadership style.[9] Though he strove for a more distributed style, the group viewed *the* ministry as *his* ministry and depended on him for nearly all aspects of the group's life.

Rev. Elly also became involved in many different activities relating to local churches, human service agencies, and low-income groups. If that were not enough, he also was cultivating his growing interest in counseling.[10]

Rev. Elly's own style stressed "initiation of structures." He led in the formation of an Adult Basic Education program (1972), the Spanish-Speaking Persons Task Force (1974-1977), the Revenue Sharing Task Force (1974-1975), and the Community Infant Care (1975, the only one of the projects which never materialized). However, his emphasis with regard to *other* staff members was the management and execution of programs (though they also were expected to do all they could to improve these programs). Rev. Elly urged staff members to fulfill these expectations, but exhibited a great deal of "consideration" (i.e., support) when they were unable or unwilling to do so.

Finally, Rev. Elly tended to operate personally in terms of normative incentives. He was LUM's only urban minister and he often referred to his own work as a calling or ministry. As a result, he extended himself far beyond the time and energy one would expect from someone who viewed his work only as a job and/or was motivated only by money. But, he did not expect other members of the staff to view their work in the same way. They were not called urban ministers and Rev. Elly seldom, if ever, referred to their work as a calling. He treated them with consideration, but relied on monetary incentives and rewards. And they tended to respond in kind. When they complained, it was in terms of their work loads and the inadequacy of remuneration.

Rev. Dolphin has a more distributed style of leadership. He assumes he is a source of leadership in the organization, but not the *only* source. His behavior reflects a view that LUM contains many people with different gifts which must be cultivated.

Rev. Dolphin has tended to concentrate his attention on LUM and its two main constituent groups: local churches and low-income groups. He relates to human service agencies insofar as they pertain to LUM's role in the community, but he does not relate to them as constituent groups. For example, shortly after he arrived in Lafayette, the Human Development Coalition (which Rev. Elly chaired) asked Rev. Dolphin if he would serve as its chairperson. He said he could not.

Like Rev. Elly, Rev. Dolphin exhibits a personal interest creating structures which respond to community and individual needs. But, he also expects other staff member to have a similar approach to their work. He expects them to execute existing programs, but he is not satisfied if that is all they do. He responds least positively to staff and board members who are satisfied with the status quo and most positively to those who share his interest in "making things better."

Finally, like Rev. Elly, Rev. Dolphin views his work as a ministry, but he expects other staff members to view their work in the same way. He frequently uses the terms "mission," "ministry," and "calling" to refer to the staff's work with LUM. He is overtly theological-scriptural in his approach to them and the programs they are responsible for. He also has sought staff members who share his view that working with LUM is a calling and its work must be theologically-scripturally grounded.

Board. The board's leadership has been curvilinear: moderate during 1972-74, weak in 1975-77, and strong since 1978.

In 1972-74, the board relied heavily on Rev. Elly. It expected him to raise the funds and (along with other staff members) run the programs. There were ad hoc committees, but they tended to meet only when Rev. Elly convened them. Phil Carpenter, the representative from St. Andrew United Methodist church, was asked to be president in successive years (1973-74)—a fact which, without disparaging his abilities, indicates that the board did not include enough other leaders to elect someone else president in 1974. During this period, church members attended 73 percent of all board meetings and occupied almost all offices and committee chairs (see Table 5 and 6).

The board's leadership became increasingly problematic in 1975-77. Church representatives attended meetings less often and occupied barely half of all offices and committee chairs.

The year 1975 was particularly difficult. In February, a special board meeting was called to address a financial crisis. All staff members attended, but only eight of sixteen board members showed up. Rev. Donald Nead (campus pastor at University Church) was asked to attend the meeting as an organizational consultant. In his report on the meeting and LUM's general situation at that time, Rev. Nead noted:

> . . . there is strong indication of some organizational pathology, some of which may be reflected in the following:
> a. Low level of commitment to LUM on the part of local churches and/or on the part of the person designated as LUM Board member.

    b. Inadequate communication systems in order to keep Board informed of meetings, time and location, as well as fully informed as to all of the issues before LUM through its staff and Board.
    c. Inability to stabilize Board membership so that it can be developed as a functioning unit; turnover is too rapid to develop any group awareness and/or commitment to the tasks at hand.

He also indicated there was a lack of "working members of the Board . . . who have specific skills."

Table 5
BOARD MEMBER ATTENDANCE: 1972, 1975, 1979

	1972	1975	1979
Total	66%	52%	72%
	(N = 14)	(N = 21)	(N = 27)
Church Representatives	73%	55%	69%
	(N = 11)	(N = 18)	(N = 22)
At-Large Members	41%	35%	85%
	(N = 3)	(N = 3)	(N = 5)

My notes on board meetings during fall 1975 indicate that I too felt the board was not exhibiting great leadership. For example, at the September 1975 meeting, almost all the questions were addressed to Rev. Elly; board members seldom asked questions of themselves or held themselves accountable for actions. Phil Roberts (a church representative) described the situation well when he said: "the staff is supposed to serve the board, but the board needs [to exercise more] leadership." At the October 1975 board meeting, Roberts noted the "uneven participation of board members on committees." My notes indicate: "Board members don't bring anything to the meeting; active roles = Ron Elly, two staff members, and three board members; others sit and approve or ask minor questions." In December, my notes indicate: "³/₄ of an hour [has] passed and [the board is] still horsing around with minor issues while a couple of important motions still have to be dealt with."

In 1976 and 1977, LUM turned increasingly to at-large members for leadership. And their efforts stimulated board activity. In 1976, President Tom Hull formalized the committee structure and made sure all board members were assigned to a committee. During the first half of 1977, the board approved the Program and Planning Committee's recommendations to recruit additional member churches and two board members from each of five groups which are disproportionately poor; promote more social concerns programs within member churches; and adopt a new staffing arrangement. In the second half of 1977, attention shifted to the Personnel Policy and Salary Review Committee which accomplished two major tasks: the codification of personnel policies and

Table 6
PERCENTAGE OF CHURCH REPRESENTATIVES AND AT-LARGE MEMBERS AMONG OFFICERS AND COMMITTEE CHAIRS: 1972-74, 1975-77, 1978-81

	1972-74			1975-77			1978-81		
	Officers	Com Chairs	Total	Officers	Com Chairs	Total	Officers	Com Chairs	Total
Church Representatives	100 (N=12)	75 (N=3)	95 (N=15)	61 (N=8)	42 (N=5)	52 (N=13)	100 (N=16)	59 (N=10)	79 (N=26)
At-Large Members	- (N=0)	25 (N=1)	6 (N=1)	38 (N=5)	58 (N=7)	48 (N=12)	- (N=0)	41 (N=7)	21 (N=7)

the selection of a nominee to replace Rev. Elly. The Finance and Funding Committee and other members of the board also sought to increase LUM's income and limit its expenses.

However, the board still struggled with its leadership role. It seemed unsure of itself as it acted on the important issues of the year. And while some board committees and individual members were quite active, others were not. In March, members of the Membership Recruitment, and Relations Committee said they did not feel they knew enough about LUM to go out and persuade other local churches to join. A membership list published in May showed that six member churches did not have representatives. Less than 60 percent of board members voted on the issues of board membership and staffing arrangements. In July, only three officers and one staff member attended the Executive Committee meeting. In September, the vice-president resigned. In November, Tom Hull consented to be president again in 1978 because there was a lack of other willing candidates; and attendance at board meetings was so problematic the Executive Committee agreed that the minutes should list the names of those who failed to attend.

Between 1978 and 1981, the board exercised more leadership. Attendance by church representatives increased, as did their role as officers and committee chairs. At the board meeting in May 1978, Ned Helmuth, who had been on the board since 1975, "expressed his appreciation of the active interest the younger board members [were] taking in LUM." In September 1978, Rev. Dolphin said that, compared to other church boards he had known, LUM's board was an unusually active group: "You don't just sit back like zombies," he told the group. In December 1979, Rev. Dolphin thanked the officers for their "dedication and enthusiasm. They have been strong officers who enabled much to develop this past year."

Stability

Thirty-two local congregations had joined LUM at one time or another through 1981. Four of these dropped their memberships and one renewed its membership in 1981. Thus, LUM has had a record of considerable stability insofar as retention of its member churches is concerned (91 percent).

Stability prevailed between 1972 and 1975, when only one church dropped out. From 1976 to 1978, LUM experienced some instability as three churches dropped out. Between 1979 and 1981, stability returned: no churches dropped their memberships and one which dropped out earlier rejoined.

LUM's experience with church representatives has been one of considerable turnover. On the average, member churches have changed representatives about every two years.

The turnover rate was a considerable problem from 1972 to 1976, when churches changed representatives about every two years or less. LUM was smaller then and turnover among board members had very disruptive consequences. The 1976 evaluation noted that "LUM now lacks continuity, particularly on the Board," and recommended that "all LUM Board members should serve for at least three years." The turnover rate between 1976 and 1981 slowed somewhat, but not a great deal. Member churches still appointed new representatives every 2.5 years. However, with LUM's larger board, the impact of the turnover was not as great.[11]

LUM also has had twelve at-large members. On the average, these members have participated on the board for nearly twice as long as the representatives from the member churches.

Finally, I ascertained the month and year each staff member joined LUM and—if they resigned or were fired—when they left. Between 1972 and December 1981, LUM had a total of 20 employees. Six people served two years or more; four people for nearly two years; and ten people for less than one year. Thus, LUM has had a mixed record in full-time positions where one would hope for stable employment patterns.

Flexibility

Over the 10-year span from 1972-81, about one-third of LUM's program decisions involved additions to or deletions from the previous year's program.

In LUM's first year, 44 percent of its programs were new, indicating LUM was quite flexible at that stage (the rest of the programs were carried over from NDP).

From 1973 to 1977, LUM continued to exhibit some flexibility (developing seven new programs while dropping seven others), but overall, its program became more fixed, culminating with no changes in 1977.

Between 1978 and 1981 LUM exhibited renewed flexibility. In those four years, eight old programs were dropped and eleven new ones were added.

Productivity

Over the 10-year period between 1972 and 1981, LUM averaged 2.3 programs and activities per staff member. LUM's productivity was somewhat below that average in all but one year between 1973 and 1978. The number of staff members increased from four in 1972-73 to 4.5 through 1978, but the number of programs and activities dwindled from nine in 1972 to only six in 1978 (the period when LUM was focusing more attention on internal, organizational concerns).

With organizational matters more under control, productivity jumped sharply to its highest point ever from 1979 to 1981. The number of staff shrank to three in 1979 and four in 1980 to 1981, but the number of programs and activities jumped from only six in 1978 to twelve in 1981.

Intra-Organizational Relations

The climate within LUM has varied over the years (see Figure 4). In 1972-73, it was quite positive. From 1974 to 1977, the climate was more negative. Between 1978 and 1981, the climate improved dramatically.

1972-73. During the first couple of years, the staff and the board were buoyant and optimistic. Staff members were mainly involved in executing programs LUM had inherited from NDP, exploring new program ideas, and developing an organizational and financial base for the group. Relations between staff and board members were friendly and mutually supportive.

There were no serious frictions between the board and the staff during this period, but by 1973, some concerns were surfacing. There was some underlying concern about the viability of such a new group, but the group had grown between 1962 and 1971 and the board felt relatively confident about Rev. Elly's ability as a fund raiser. The staff, on the other hand, felt its main responsibilities were in the area of programs and that board members should be more aggressive in pressing their congregations for more financial support and seeing to it that church pledges were paid.

1974-77. The climate within LUM during the mid 1970s was decidedly more negative.

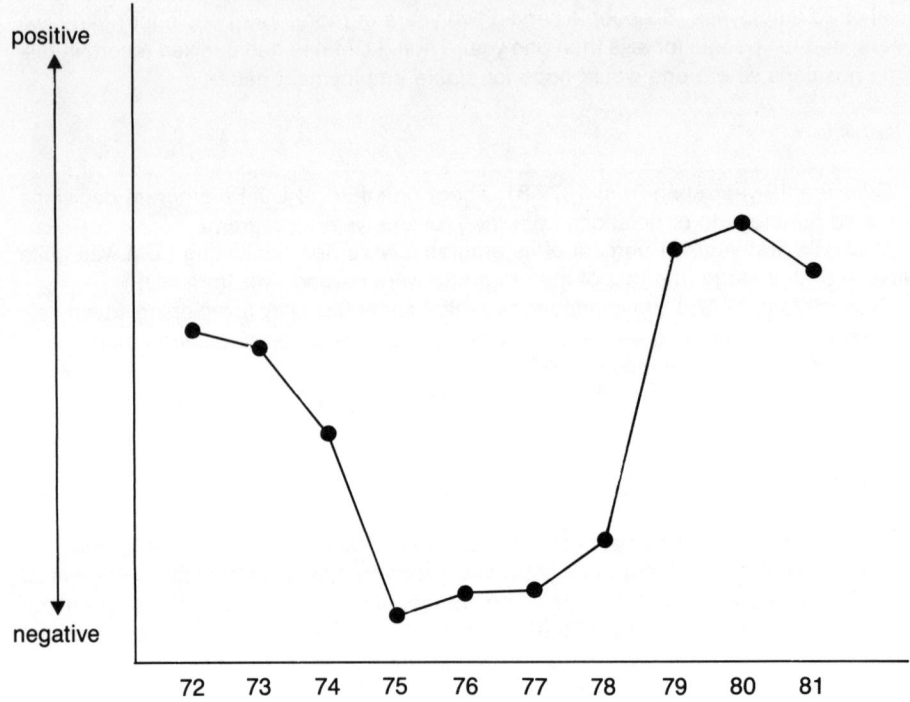

Figure 4
INTRA-ORGANIZATIONAL RELATIONS, 1972-1981

It was most negative in 1975. On January 29, 1975, there was no money to buy gas for the transportation service mini-bus; letters for camp could not be sent out; there was no mailing for Adventure Club leaders; and the hiring of a mini-bus driver could not take place. A special meeting of the board was called for February 8.

All of the staff was present, but only eight representatives were there. The following excerpts from the minutes indicate the substantive and emotional issues that were discussed at the meeting:

> The issue was not just payroll but the fact that L.U.M. could not serve its clients without resources. Ron felt "abandoned." It was felt that the sixteen member churches were using L.U.M. to carry on a "Charade" ministry to the downtown area. It was simply a "miserable way to live" for Ron and the entire staff. Virginia Boncy added that it was quite uncomfortable "not knowing what is happening" and that she felt quite "insecure." Linda Mulvey pointed to the January board meeting where there was no quorum. She continued that she was "upset and confused."

Rev. Elly again expressed his concern about the board's lack of activity at its meetings in April and May. In May, he told the board:

> I am discouraged by several things—the negatives off my chest first.

1. The financial picture of L.U.M. for the remainder of 1975 and into 1976 remains cloudy and feels as if L.U.M. is running on the bad side of a deficit.

I feel, and in some cases, know, progress on these issues has been again left with staff, or no progress has been made.

2. The system of member church representation and link-up by a director chosen from a member church is not working: Some directors we do not see; some churches change directors so quickly the Board and staff keeps introducing itself to one another at each meeting; member churches do not seem to be on the whole planning through their "director" in-put into L.U.M. program nor asking (wanting) L.U.M. in-put into their programming. I am not placing blame as much as sharing my observation/frustration.

These two, financial struggle and Board representation, put together yield a feeling that at times I am (we are) doing something few people really are committed to, or the commitment is not spelled out in tangible ways other than money and little of that from local member churches. To get volunteers is a constant hassle which jeopardizes programs.

The end result of all of this is low Pastor-Director morale, the nagging sense that I am not doing something right and too often work alone, the temptation to throw up my hands and to leave for a better job where I will be able to do things I enjoy with a collegiality and without insecurity as to Board or money. I want some specific changes in the present state of affairs or I have considered a move to a new job as of January 1, 1976 where the benefits and enjoyment are more fulfilling and the persistent hassles and insecurities are less emotionally taxing. I have said what is going on with me . . . *I presently do not know how to shift from what we have been and gotten into; I want the chance for us to talk seriously about out common ministry before I grow so dissatisfied I am disillusioned and angry and that is not healthy for me, the rest of the staff nor the Board and our 17 churches, let alone our volunteers and neighbors with whom we discover God's caring love. That is the negative side.*

Staff meetings during fall 1975 revealed a number of strains among staff and between staff and board. Among staff, there were increasing concerns about the viability of some long-standing programs (Adventure Clubs) and the execution of others (Volunteer Transportation and Good Friends). There also were substantial disagreements among staff over how to fill a vacant position (this issue was discussed in the section on bureaucratization), the way in which the transportation program was being managed, and the possibility of cutbacks in staff time and/or salaries.

Staff members also harbored many doubts about the board's commitment and leadership. One staff member felt the board member who headed her committee was not doing her job. Another said she felt "alone"; that board members were not actively involved in LUM's programs; and that they did not know much about what was going on. She also felt it was a burden for her to educate the board so it could make informed decisions she felt she could make more efficiently. Comparing LUM with the local Head Start board, she said the local Head Start board is "younger, blacker, and . . . more interesting." Staff members frequently joked about their need to manipulate the board to get anything done.

Another special board meeting was held in December 1975 to discuss the 1976 budget. The staff brought in a proposed budget of $61,604 ($8,438 more than 1975's eventual expenses of $53,266). The board voted for the principle of a balanced budget and then approved a budget of only $48,810 ($12,794 less than the staff proposed).

Staff salaries were frozen and the board agreed to "establish goals for new monies and . . . methods to raise it for 1976."

These problems persisted in 1976 and 1977, but the climate within LUM improved somewhat. There was more trust, cooperation, and optimism as the staff and board searched for solutions to the problems they had identified in 1975.

1978-81. The climate within LUM was distinctly more positive between 1978 and 1981. The shift toward more positive relations within the group was especially dramatic in 1978.

Staff and board members worked together on the superordinate goals for enhancing LUM's programs and resources. The staff was suggesting a variety of new program directions and new projects. Board committees responded enthusiastically to these efforts. Committees were active in specific tasks related to programs and/or were developing new functions in relation to emerging directions (e.g., the Program and Planning Committee which had spent more time on planning in 1976 and 1977 was now spending more time on program development).

Signs of trust, cooperation, and optimism were numerous. Rev. Dolphin told the Program and Planning Committee "The staff hasn't felt isolated from the board. There is a feeling of mutual respect." Also in September, board member Dennis Sorge said he was "sold on LUM and always will be because Iv'e been a part of it and seen how it works." Also in September, another relatively new board member, Gary Henriott, told a group of United Methodists that LUM "is the most impressive organization I have ever been involved in."

In November and December, LUM's first social concerns conference was a success; church pledges to LUM for 1980 increased; a solicitation for the Centralized Emergency Fund produced over $3,000; and churches and individuals donated over $4,000 in gifts for the first Jubilee Christmas Shop. The spirit within LUM was at an all-time high. The board rewarded the staff with merit increases in salary. Staff member Rev. Roger Callahan praised the board for its participation. And Rev. Dolphin concluded his report with the following:

> There is a sense of excitement about what is happening through the Urban Ministry. The support from member churches and individuals is gaining as we prepare to take new efforts in ministry. I know that I speak for the entire staff when I say thank you for the support, confidence and willingness to assist that you continually offer. You are a strong board, united in purpose. More than anything else you are making a difference in what is able to be accomplished.

In 1980 and 1981, the climate within LUM continued to be quite positive, though it tended to be more subdued. In contrast to the excitement over the successful experiences of 1979, the board and staff seemed to assume their confidence in one another and went about their business.

Inter-Organizational Relations

This section describes LUM's relationships with member churches, denominational funding agencies, low-income people, and other groups.

Member Churches. Between 1972 and 1974, LUM's board and staff viewed their relationships with local churches as mainly financial. The churches were a source of money which could be used to do social concerns on their behalf. Churches also were a source of volunteers for LUM programs. In return for their support, the pastor-director would "interpret" its activities to the member churches. But, LUM did not conceive of itself as having any other substantive input into the churches.

Between 1975 and 1977, relationships with member churches grew increasingly problematic. In February 1975, Rev. Donald Nead indicated there was a problem in "the inter-face relationship between LUM and the local churches supporting it." He suggested local churches were not sending LUM very competent or highly motivated representatives; local churches were not very aware of what LUM was doing and did not feel much "ownership" of it; there was a gap between LUM's staff and staff members in local churches; and the financial relationship was not well understood or organized.

Three member churches withdrew their memberships from LUM between 1975 and 1978. While other circumstances having nothing to do with LUM also were involved, the fact that these withdrawals all occurred during a time in which LUM was struggling organizationally suggests they were at least partly indications of poor relations with LUM at the time.

In April 1978, Rev. Dolphin met with Tom Hull, Rev. Kenneth McCullen, Rev. Ron Liechty (pastor of St. Andrew United Methodist), Mary Jo Hipshire (a staff member at St. Thomas Aquinas Church), and Joyce White (the representative from Federated Church) to discuss LUM's relationships with its member churches. The meeting indicated that (a) member churches were not convinced that support of LUM was in their best interest; (b) LUM did not provide member churches with enough "opportunities for its participating congregations to recognize and celebrate their united commitment to mission"; (c) LUM did not reach enough people in the churches with educational material that would explain what LUM is all about; (d) there was not enough "personal contact" between LUM and its member churches; and (e) the process LUM used to raise funds from member churches did not always converge with the churches' budget processes.

Between 1979 and 1981, relations with member churches improved considerably. LUM sponsored several programs designed to serve its member churches. These included a Seeds of Vision conference, a monthly newsletter, a free survey of church members' attitudes about a wide variety of subjects, the Grow-a-Row project, the Jubilee Christmas Shop, and the Repairs on Wheels program.

In September 1979, Rev. Dolphin told the board LUM is "doing a lot of things with churches, perhaps not as quickly as we need to, but we're making progress." He said he "senses widening arenas of support." In March 1980, he told the board that "LUM has greatly strengthened its roots in local churches . . . they have confidence in us."[12]

In 1981, LUM's board discussed its future directions, one of which was to increase efforts to work more closely with local churches to increase the number and quality of social concerns programs they could sponsor on their own or with LUM's assistance.

Denominational Agencies. Relationships with denominational funding agencies were quite positive from 1972 through 1976, somewhat negative in 1977 and 1978, and quite positive again in 1979-81.

As I showed in Chapter 4, the presbytery of the Wabash Valley was the first important source of outside funds for the Neighborhood Development Project. It continued its support of LUM between 1972 and 1976. The northern conference of the United Methodist church became the second largest source of support in 1972 and increased its support steadily throughout the 1972-76 period. By 1975, the Episcopal diocese of Indianapolis also was contributing to LUM. These groups required proposals which requested routine information which they used to evaluate LUM's application and to decide (a) whether they would continue to support LUM and (b) if so, to what extent. There was no indication of distrust, conflict, or concern on the part of these denominational agencies between 1972 and 1976.

Relations with denominational agencies became more problematic during 1977 and 1978. In mid 1977, the presbytery of the Wabash Valley indicated it might cut back its support of LUM if Rev. Elly was replaced by someone other than a Presbyterian. This was the first time that presbytery had ever indicated it might reduce its support, and given the extent of presbytery's support, the LUM board became very concerned. A significant cutback by presbytery could have been devastating in its own right, but also could have caused other groups to become suspicious and possibly reduce their support. The team of people LUM sent to talk with the presbytery's Mission Committee was successful in convincing the committee to continue its support of LUM in 1978.

Also in 1977 and 1978, the northern conference of the United Methodist church raised questions about its support of LUM. Some of these questions were related to LUM's own behavior at the time (e.g., who it would select as its new director and its plans to cultivate more programs within local congregations). Other questions had more to do with other issues within the denomination which might affect some reallocation of its resources (i.e., shifting some of the money it had given to LUM into other United Methodist projects). In the end, the denomination did not reallocate its resources and after Rev. Dolphin met with United Methodist officials to explain what LUM was doing and to reassure them that LUM was not "simply going to turn all of its programs over to the churches," the northern conference's support was reaffirmed.

Between 1978 and 1981, LUM's relations with denominational agencies were quite positive. There was no indication of suspicion, distrust, or major cutbacks. Support from the Episcopal diocese of Indianapolis increased and the United Church of Christ became LUM's fourth source of denominational support.

Low-Income Groups. LUM has always identified itself with the poor. And it has always said that it would like low-income people to play a significant role in its deliberations and programs.

LUM has related to low-income groups as clients through seventeen programs. Eight (47 percent) of these programs have been intended for the poor in general, regardless of age, race, or other considerations; four (24 percent) have emphasized youth; three (18 percent) have been geared to the aged; and two (12 percent) have been oriented toward racial minorities.

The extent of LUM's programming for low-income people has varied over the years. Between 1972 and 1975, LUM was involved in 9 to 10 programs each year which were designed to serve one or more low-income groups.

Between 1976 and 1979, LUM's overall involvement in low-income programs declined. LUM completed or discontinued its involvement in seven programs, while adding only three.

When the board met with Rev. Dolphin in January 1978, it told him that it expected "more outward program emphasis now that the group had made some hard decisions about internal affairs," and "more involvement on the part of low-income groups." By June 1979, Rev. Dolphin reported that the staff's personal contact with low-income people was increasing as the Advocates program expanded and more and more low-income people were needing to use the Centralized Emergency Fund. In 1980, LUM added the Repairs on Wheels and the Grow-a-Row programs. And in 1981, the board pledged itself to becoming more directly involved with low-income groups in community development and addressing social policies and practices that foster poverty. The Food Buying Club was one expression of this emphasis.

However, low-income people have played almost no role at all on LUM's board. Only three low-income representatives have ever served on the board.

Other Groups. LUM also has had relationships with several other groups, the most important of which have been human service agencies, township trustee offices, and the Tippecanoe County Federation of Churches.

As its early purpose statements indicated, LUM wanted to develop positive relationships with local human service agencies. In 1974, an evaluation LUM submitted to the presbytery of Wabash Valley listed 71 "social service agencies and community groups . . . we have coordinated with and continue to combine services with or provide information, supervision and direction to in implementing their concerns and avoiding duplication of church resources with theirs." It is not surprising, then, that one criticism from local churches was that LUM "is just another social service agency."

By 1976-77, LUM was planning to focus more attention on churches and low-income groups and less on human services agencies. By 1978, LUM's programs no longer related directly to agencies.[13]

LUM's relationships with township trustee office of poor relief began in the mid 1970s. Rev. Elly ran for a seat on the advisory board of the Fairfield township trustee, who is responsible for poor relief in Lafayette (the Wabash township trustee is responsible for poor relief in West Lafayette). Rev. Elly served in that capacity for one term but, feeling ineffectual in that role, he decided not to run again.

When LUM adopted the Advocates program in 1978, its contacts with the Fairfield and Wabash township trustees increased. The Advocates have found themselves in an adversary relationship with township trustees. The trustees want to limit low-income people's dependence on public funds. The Advocates want to help low-income people obtain whatever relief they are entitled to. The result has been increased friction between LUM and trustees' offices and a tendency for both groups to develop more jaundiced views of each other. LUM has openly criticized the trustee system of poor relief at its board meetings and in late 1981 formed a task force to explore ways in which the system might be changed. One township trustee was instrumental in having his church withdraw its membership from LUM. At least one other has tried.

In the early 1970s, when LUM was being formed, the Tippecanoe County Federation of Churches supported LUM's formation and encouraged local churches to do the same. By the mid 1970s, the Federation had all but eliminated its involvement in social concerns and struggled to regain its earlier interests in interfaith understanding—leaving social concerns to LUM. Thus, the groups divided the ecumenical turf and reduced the potential friction between them (though they remained conscious of their competition for financial support from local churches).

In 1978, the Federation suggested a liaison person serve on the two boards to increase communication between the groups. LUM agreed, but the link lasted only a year; when the liaison person left town, neither group felt compelled to find a replacement.

In 1979, the two groups were brought together when the Indiana Council of Churches sponsored a program for evaluating ecumenical groups throughout the state. LUM and the Federation pooled their resources and obtained about $6,000 in support from the Indiana Council of Churches to conduct separate evaluations of the two groups. The evaluations made the two ecumenical groups more aware of their common reliance on local churches but their different emphases on ecumenism (the Federation) and social concerns (LUM), and their different organizational styles (LUM being much larger and more highly structured).

Conclusion

Examination of 15 dimensions of LUM's institutionalization between 1972 and 1981 points to two conclusions. First, LUM was more highly institutionalized in 1981 than at any point in its 10-year history. It not only survived; it grew and matured. Second, LUM's institutionalization was a curvilinear process. After a brief period of buoyancy (1972 to 1974), LUM declined (1975-77), before regaining its stride (1978 to 1981). This curvilinear pattern was most apparent with regard to ten dimensions (seven of which pertain to process components): size, resources, complexity, administrative succession, leadership, stability, flexibility, productivity, intra-organizational relations, and inter-organizational relations. LUM's progress toward institutionalization was more gradual along five other dimensions (all of which pertain to structural components): purpose, membership, formalization, bureaucratization, and distribution of authority. Appendix B updates LUM's institutionalization through 1984.

Chapter 7 offers some explanations for LUM's curvilinear pattern of institutionalization.

CHAPTER 7
ANALYSIS OF LUM'S INSTITUTIONALIZATION: MOBILIZING THE RESOURCES

This chapter explains the curvilinear pattern of institutionalization described in Chapter 6. I will consider structural and resource factors at the societal and local levels, the role that a half dozen dimensions of institutionalization played, and finally, the impact of LUM's effectiveness on its institutionalization.

Societal ("Period") Factors

Structural Conditions: Secular Realm

Social Conditions. I hypothesized that a *societal interest in social change would facilitate the institutionalization of a group like LUM; the reaffirmation of traditional values would not.*

From 1972 to 1974, the social change of the 1960s persisted along certain lines. The women's movement was growing in size and strength, as evidenced by the growth of the National Organization of Women. The Senate passed the Equal Rights Amendment (ERA) in 1972 and sent it to the states for ratification. In the same year, the White House held a conference on aging which gave impetus to an emerging movement to alter societal policies and practices excluding older Americans from full participation in the American way of life. The courts continued to call for busing to foster racial balance in public schools. And members of the American Indian Movement (AIM) occupied Wounded Knee to protest white domination of tribal government.

The persistence of some interest in social change was conducive to LUM's institutionalization. LUM's involvement in the formation of the Tippecanoe County Council on Aging, Older Citizens Visitation (later Good Friends), and Volunteer Transportation can be traced to the nation's growing awareness that older Americans do not have as much access as other people do to the goods and services they need. LUM's support of a Community Infant Care Center also can be traced to the expanding role of women in the labor force and the need for day care services for infants so women could work.

However, there also were important signs that the nation was tired of the protest and change of the 1960s and wanted to reaffirm some of its traditional commitments. Conservative Richard Nixon soundly defeated liberal George McGovern for president in 1972. Nixon opposed federally-supported social programs, calling for more investigations of welfare fraud and more local control through Revenue Sharing (whereby the government would return funds to the state and local levels so local officials could determine how the funds would be spent). Racial and ethnic minorities accused the federal government of lagging in its enforcement of federal policies to enhance minority participation. And after quick adoption of the Equal Rights Amendment by several states, "Unexpected opposition slowed ratification of the (ERA)" by 1973 and 1974 (*Encyclopedia Americana*, 1974:654).

By the mid 1970s, the nation's interest in social order clearly superseded its interest in social change. There were "no dramatic changes in women's political, economic, and social status" in 1976 (*Encyclopedia Americana*, 1977:553). There was no progress in ratification of ERA. Public and judicial support for busing waned. Minority issues such as affirmative action were called into question as the nation's economy soured and business tried to cut costs. President Ford expressed his disapproval of federal social programs and stressed the need for more state responsibility in social welfare. The courts exhibited an increased interest in "restructuring the rights of criminal defendants, reinforcing states' rights, and curtailing access to the federal courts" (*Encyclopedia Americana*, 1977:166). Between 1972 and 1975, 33 states "passed new capital punishment laws reinstating the death penalty for certain crimes" (*Encyclopedia Americana*, 1976:193).

In 1976, the nation chose as president a white, male, Baptist from the South whose image was designed to appeal to nation's traditional emphasis on small business and church-going families in small towns. And, although President Carter was "committed to racial justice, human rights, open government, and fairness in the courts, 1977 was a year in which civil liberties and minority rights lost more than they gained at the hands of the federal government" (*Encyclopedia Americana*, 1978:156). Proposition 13 signified a tax revolt which reduced the possibility of increased federal involvement in health and social programs.

The nation's conservative mood was very conducive to the candidacy of Ronald Reagan in 1980. His landslide victory over Jimmy Carter was the culmination of the nation's desire to return to traditional social and economic values. He articulated his commitment to a strong defense and his belief that, if the nation's economy were allowed to operate according to the principles of free enterprise, the private sector would be revitalized and would produce social benefits for all Americans, including minorities and the poor. Within his first two years in office, President Reagan increased defense spending, reduced federal regulations on business, provided tax incentives for the private sector, reduced taxes (especially for people in the upper tax brackets), and reduced federal spending on social programs. He also launched his "new federalism" program calling for more state and local control over social welfare programs.

Contrary to my expectation that the growing conservatism of the 1970s and early 1980s would have a negative effect on LUM's institutionalization, LUM became *more* highly institutionalized, not less.

Structural Conditions: Religious Sphere

Religious Policies and Practices. Chapter 2 argued that *ferment within the religious sphere would be conducive to the institutionalization of a group like LUM* and that the lack of change within the sphere would inhibit its institutionalization.

The decline of religious liberalism and the ascendancy of religious conservatism were clear patterns by 1972 and 1973 (*Encyclopedia Americana*, 1973:500). Expo '72 attracted thousands of young people who were part of "the Jesus movement." Also in 1972, thousands of Roman Catholics attended a gathering of people involved in "the charismatic movement." And Key '73 mounted a large and expensive effort to "call our continent to Christ."

By 1974 and 1975, major conflicts were occurring between religious liberals and conservatives within several denominations, most dramatically among Lutherans as conservatives sought to purge liberals from seminaries, and among Episcopalians over the ordination of women and a new Book of Common Prayer. The National Council of

Churches and the World Council of Churches experienced substantial cutbacks in financial support. And in 1975, a group of religious leaders meeting at Hartford Seminary issued an "Appeal for Theological Affirmation," in which they denounced the religious liberalism of the 1960s and called for a return to more traditional Christian tenets.

Religious conservatism clearly held the upper hand by the later 1970s. The "electronic church" brought conservative Protestantism into American homes. The Episcopal and Presbyterian churches took conservative positions on the ordination of homosexuals. The Roman Catholic church declared its opposition to the ordination of women.

The most visible evidence of religious conservatism in the early 1980s was the "moral majority." Through several organizations and leaders (the Rev. Jerry Falwell in particular), the moral majority "claimed that liberals, humanists, and leftists in religion and politics had conspired to take God out of the public schools, to teach evolution as an alternative religion, and to create a climate on television and in popular culture that was unfavorable to traditional American values" (Marty, 1981:605). In the elections of 1980, the moral majority played an important role in the unseating of several liberal Congressmen and the election of conservative Ronald Reagan as president.

These conditions may have contributed to the demise of some ecumenical urban ministries during the 1970s, but not LUM. LUM survived in spite of the growing religious conservatism of the 1970s and early 1980s.

Ecumenism. Chapter 2 suggested *a spirit of interfaith cooperation is needed for a group like LUM to be institutionalized.*

But, interest in ecumenism peaked in the late 1960s. Johnson (1980:336-342) described the reduction in support of many ecumenical ideas and organizations during the 1970s, including many urban ministries (also see Vander Werf, 1976). Kelly (1979:191) found that "few clergy reported membership in an interfaith group and most said that in an average year they read less than one book and only about one scholarly article about other faiths." According to Hogan (1982:1), "Christians really made an effort to get to know one another during the 1960s, but now they seem to be struggling just to maintain simple relationships with one another." Johnstone (1975:264) agreed, saying that "enthusiasm and commitment in theory for ecumenism have not been enough to affect much notable success since 1968." Garrett (1980:346, 348) used phrases like "recent frustrations," "the slackening of participatory support," and "the ecumenical quandary" to describe interfaith relations in the late 1970s.

This situation clearly was not conducive to the institutionalization of LUM. It may help explain LUM's struggles to survive between 1972 and about 1977, but it does not explain why LUM became more institutionalized after 1977. LUM's institutionalization occurred in spite of the declining interest in ecumenism at the national level.

Resources: Secular Realm

Economic Conditions. I expected that *economic prosperity would be conducive to the institutionalization of LUM* and that a weak economy would inhibit its institutionalization.

The nation's economy sputtered during the 1970s and early 1980s. The Gross National Product, personal income, and personal disposable income were higher in 1981 than in 1971, but they did not maintain the rates of growth they experienced during the 1960s. After jumping 245 points between 1962 and 1971, the Dow Jones Industrial average was only 48 points higher in 1981 than it was in 1971 (932.76 vs. 884.76). Personal savings did not keep up with inflation, and the unemployment rate during the

1970s was about twice as high as it had been during the 1960s. Thus, in contrast to the very strong economy of the 1960s (which contributed to LUM's formation), indications are that LUM survived in spite of weak economic conditions in the 1970s.

Resources: Religious Sphere

Resources. Chapter 2 argued that *expanding resources within a sphere would be conducive to the institutionalization of groups like LUM,* and that declining resources would have negative effects on their institutionalization.

Resources within the sphere of religion declined during the early to mid 1970s. There were about 400,000 *fewer* church members in 1975 than there were in 1972. Church membership as a percentage of the total population also declined from 62.4 in 1972 to 60.7 in 1976 (reversing the post-World War II trend toward increased church membership). The value of new church construction also declined sharply between 1972 and 1975. Finally, per-capita contributions to the church (which had risen rapidly during the 1950s and 1960s) also declined (Jacquet, 1980:248). While contributions had risen from $77.01 per capita in 1961 to $85.69 in 1971 (an 11.3 percent increase), they declined from $88.02 in 1972 to $85.94 in 1975 (a 2.3 percent decrease).

However, these declines were reversed during the late 1970s and religious resources increased again. Church membership increased by 6,500,000 between 1976 and 1981, though church members as a percent of the total population continued to decline (58.7 percent in 1981). The value of new church construction increased somewhat between 1976 and 1981 (Jacquet, 1984:272). And per capita contributions to the church increased from $85.94 in 1975 to $88 in 1981.

In short, religious resources at the national level experienced the same curvilinear pattern LUM experienced. When national resources declined during the early 1970s, LUM struggled; when they increased again in the late 1970s, LUM experienced rather rapid institutionalization.

Justification. For a social movement organization like LUM to be institutionalized within a sphere such as religion, that sphere must include some ideological justification of social reform. The absence of such a theme would make the institutionalization of a reform group difficult, if not impossible.

Christianity's prophetic tradition persisted through the 1970s, though it was not as pronounced as it had been in the 1960s. Within Catholicism, one of the most significant expressions of this prophetic heritage was the 1976 "Call to Action"—a national assembly of over 1,300 Catholic clergy and lay people which took place in Detroit. The delegates considered "key issues affecting the life and future of the American people, particularly those issues relating to justice in the church and in American society" (Egan, Roach, and Murnion, 1979:287).

In 1981, the United States Catholic Conference also published a book (*Quest for Justice*, edited by Benestad and Butler) containing letters from American bishops expressing the church's prophetic position on a number of key issues, including poverty. This volume summarized the theological principles underlying the Catholic church's record as an advocate for justice and equality.

Within Protestantism, the prophetic tradition was kept alive by leaders of the World Council of Churches and National Council of Churches and a growing number of leaders within Protestantism's more conservative evangelical wing. For example, in November 1981, United Methodist Bishop James Armstrong, president of the National Council of Churches, argued that "the church must unashamedly identify with the poor and the hungry . . . (the church) belongs to Jesus Christ and must be free to bring judgments of God to bear upon every political and economic system" (*Journal-Courier*, November 9, 1981).

However, Christianity's prophetic tradition was not as dominant a theme as it had been in the 1960s when the NDP was emerging into LUM. It was still heard, but increasingly overwhelmed by voices calling for a return to more personal-spiritual emphases.

Personnel. For a group like LUM to be institutionalized, there has to be a pool of personnel to run it.

The number of Catholic seminarians, priests, nuns, and brothers declined sharply during the 1970s (Kim, 1980). However, among Protestants, "the demographic situation, the feminist movement, the overall job market, and the present religious ferment . . . combined to increase the number of current seminarians and entering clergy" during the late 1970s (Carroll and Wilson, 1980). There was a similar pattern in the number of seminary graduates between 1972 and 1975. The total number of seminary graduates hovered between 3,100 and 3,200. Between 1975 and 1979, it jumped from 3,145 to 4,213 (a 33 percent increase). During the late 1970s, the demand for clergy dwindled while the supply grew. As the demand for clergy to fill parish and non-parish positions shrank, there was a growing number of clergy who were "not functioning in a church-related ministry position but still retain(ed) their credentials as clergy" (Carroll and Wilson, 1980:39).

This situation was conducive to the institutionalization of urban ministry groups like LUM. When Rev. Elly resigned, 74 percent of the applications LUM received were from ordained clergy and candidates for the ministry. Thus, the over-supply of Protestant clergy contributed to LUM's success in the process of administrative succession which, in turn, affected several other dimensions of LUM's institutionalization (as I will explain later in this chapter).

Local ("Place") Factors

Structural Conditions: Secular Realm

Political Climate. A liberal political climate should contribute to the institutionalization of a group like LUM, while a conservative climate should stifle it. But Indiana's conservative political climate grew during the 1970s. In the presidential elections of 1972, 1976, and 1980, the state voted very enthusiastically for the three Republican candidates—Richard Nixon, Gerald Ford, and Ronald Reagan. The state's three governors (Edgar Whitcomb, Otis Bowen, and Robert Orr) were Republicans. Republicans held a majority of state Senate and House seats in eight of the 10 years between 1972 and 1981. State taxes remained the lowest of all 50 states (declining by 10 percent between 1970 and 1980) and Indiana remained last in federal dollars received per capita (*Statistical Abstracts*, 1985:34).

A Republican was mayor of West Lafayette from 1972 to 1979. And, at least 10—and usually 11 or 12—of the 13 township trustees were Republicans. A Democrat was mayor of Lafayette, but had to work with a predominantly Republican city council. A Democrat became mayor of West Lafayette but her city council also had more Republicans on it than Democrats.

The Lafayette area's conservatism also was reflected in the editorials in the *Journal-Courier* embracing President Reagan's budget cuts and his new federalism program. It also was evident in two episodes in which the local United Way pitted the needs of low-income people off against the needs of middle-income people and sided with the middle class.[1]

Thus, the conservative political climate in the Lafayette area was not conducive to LUM's institutionalization. LUM survived in spite of it, not because of it.

Structural Conditions: Religious Sphere

Persistence of the Problem. The persistence of the problem (in this case the lack of local church involvement in issues relating to poverty) should contribute to the institutionalization of a group like LUM. If there were no problem (i.e., churches were socially active and there were no poverty), there would be no need for an ecumenical urban ministry.

Chapter 5 showed that poverty was a real problem in Lafayette and local churches were not actively involved in social concerns at the time LUM was formed in 1971. Both of these problems persisted through the 1970s.

In 1979, median family income in Tippecanoe County was $20,544. Half of the median was $10,273.50. Twenty-eight percent of all families had incomes of $10,000 or less (up sharply from the 15.8 percent of families which were below half of the median in 1969).

The government's "official" statistics (c.f., *County and City Data Book*, 1983) indicate there were 11,700 poor persons in Tippecanoe County in 1979 (compared to 9,389 in 1970). The poor comprised 11.1 percent of the population (compared to 9.6 percent in 1970). Thus, even using the government's more conservative estimates, there was more poverty in the Lafayette area in 1979 than there was a decade earlier.

Evidence from the 30 church survey in 1979 also indicates that local churches were not actively involved in social concerns during the 1970s.

Respondents were given a list of church programs and activities and asked to rank the ones they had been most involved in personally (see Table 1). Most parishioners were involved in programs and activities related to the inner-workings of the congregation (i.e., administrative-financial business churches need to take care of, and groups dealing with members' needs). Only about 5 percent of churchgoers were involved in programs relating to social and community issues. This overall pattern appeared in all categories of churches, suggesting it is an widespread characteristic of church life, especially among white Christians.[2]

Respondents also were asked to rate 23 aspects of church life from "very unimportant; lowest priority" (score 1) to "very important; highest priority" (score 6). The areas parishioners gave the highest priority pertained to personal faith and fellowship among church members (see Table 2). Next came a cluster of items which generally had to do with personal morality and helping needy individuals. The items receiving the lowest priority were outreach items involving social reform and closer relationships with other social and religious groups.[3] Thus, churchgoers' priorities generally corresponded with prevailing church programs and activities.

Table 1
CHURCH PROGRAMS
(Percent)

Program	Most Involved In	Second Most Involved In	Third Most Involved In
None/Other	27	44	69
Church Business	16	9	3
Youth Programs	16	6	3
Choir	10	6	2
Men's/Women's Groups	8	9	6
Adult Religious Education	7	4	2
Family Activities	4	5	4
Food	3	5	3
Local Mission/Social Concerns	2	2	1
Evangelism	2	3	1
Church Office (Volunteer)	2	2	1
Planning Worship	1	1	1
Publicity	1	2	1
Foreign Missions	1	1	1
Represent Church	1	1	2

Table 2
PARISH PRIORITIES
(Means and Percent "Very" or "Quite" Important)

	%	X[a]
1. Provide religious education for children and youth.	90	5.4
2. Provide for guidance and growth of individual members.	91	5.4
3. Preach the Gospel in worship services.	86	5.3
4. Make the church a strong fellowship in which members of all classes and races feel unity and mutual support.	80	5.1
5. Make competent pastoral counseling available to all persons.	80	5.1
6. Develop a special youth ministry.	70	4.9
7. Develop understanding between youth and older generations.	65	4.8
8. Celebrate frequently the Lord's Supper.	66	4.8
9. Maintain Christian moral standards among members in the areas of alcoholism, gambling, sexual conduct, and related matters.	65	4.7
10. Encourage individual members to carry out acts of charity to needy persons.	58	4.6
11. Assist all members in reflecting on questions of personal morality.	57	4.5
12. Support and organize local church programs for aiding needy persons.	52	4.5

13. Work with other faiths to bring religion to shut-ins and the unchurched.	52	4.4
14. Study social issues in the light of Biblical teachings.	52	4.4
15. Work for the unity of all Christian believers.	52	4.4
16. Support mission efforts to preach the Gospel in all lands.	51	4.4
17. Open avenues of communication between people of differing social groups.	41	4.2
18. Encourage more understanding of other religious faiths.	36	4.1
19. Provide worship which makes free use of music and the arts.	38	4.0
20. Engage in personal evangelism locally.	35	3.9
21. Provide church support for the poor and oppressed in organizing for their rights.	31	3.8
22. Provide opportunities for worship with people from other faiths or denominations.	24	3.8
23. Encourage individual members to support social reform.	24	3.7

[a]Items are ranked by mean scores, not percentages: means could range from 1 (lowest priority) to 6 (highest priority).

To explore parishioners' social attitudes, I asked people to explain why there was poverty in Tippecanoe County. The top five reasons given stressed alleged deficiencies among low-income people. These were: lack of thrift (56 percent); sickness and physical handicaps (53 percent); loose morals and drunkenness (53 percent); lack of effort (52 percent); and lack of ability (37 percent). Another alleged deficiency mentioned quite often (31 percent) was lack of religious faith.

The respondents did not attach as much importance to structural sources of poverty. The five structural items tended to rank toward the bottom of the list: low wages (37 percent); prejudice and discrimination (25 percent); failure of society to provide enough good schools (22 percent); lack of jobs (16 percent); and "being taken advantage of by rich people" (16 percent).[4]

I also examined church members' vertical and horizontal beliefs (see Table 3). Members of all churches scored quite high on vertical beliefs about a life after death, the existence of a personal God, and the divinity of Christ. There was less consensus on the horizontal belief items. About two-thirds of the respondents "strongly agreed" that "To love God means caring for others in need; faith without works is dead." However, only 30 percent "strongly agreed" that "The way I treat my fellow man will determine my fate in the hereafter." Two separate analyses have revealed no significant relationship between these spheres of belief (Myers and Davidson, 1984; Davidson and Roberts, 1984).

Table 3
VERTICAL AND HORIZONTAL BELIEFS
(Percent)

	%
Vertical Beliefs	
I know there is a personal God and I have no doubts about it.	
Strongly Agree	83
Agree Somewhat	10
Uncertain/Disagree	6
Jesus is the Divine Son of God and I have no doubts about it.	
Strongly Agree	88
Agree Somewhat	7
Uncertain/Disagree	5
I am sure there is a life after death.	
Strongly Agree	71
Agree Somewhat	14
Uncertain/Disagree	15
Horizontal Beliefs	
To love God means caring for others in need: faith without good works is dead.	
Strongly Agree	65
Agree Somewhat	27
Uncertain/Disagree	8
Churches should not concern themselves with social and economic issues.	
Strongly Agree	37
Agree Somewhat	31
Uncertain/Disagree	32
The way I treat my fellow man will determine my fate in the hereafter.	
Strongly Agree	30
Agree Somewhat	37
Uncertain/Disagree	33
Helping one's fellow man in need is more important than any personal religious belief or practice.	
Strongly Agree	23
Agree Somewhat	34
Uncertain/Disagree	43

In short, as many as 28 percent of the area's families experienced real economic hardship; Lafayette churchgoers were not involved in social concerns programs; social concerns (especially social reform) ranked low in parishioners' priorities for their congregations; church members believed that poverty is rooted in the "deficiencies" of low-income people; and vertical and horizontal beliefs were quite separate dimensions of faith for most parishioners.

The persistence of these problems allowed LUM to develop programs (e.g., Advocates) oriented toward the causes and consequences of poverty and programs to cultivate social concern within local churches (e.g., Seeds of Vision).

Ecumenism. I assumed that *potential support groups also would need to have favorable attitudes about cooperating with one another for LUM to become institutionalized.* If they harbored hostilities toward one another and/or had negative ecumenical experiences, LUM's chances of being institutionalized would be limited.

In 1971, Rev. John Buchanan told members of the Tippecanoe County Federation of Churches that local churches were placing more emphasis on "internal problems" and the "ecumenical fervor of the early 1960s has dissipated."

The survey of 30 churches indicated there still was interest in interfaith issues and activities, but parishioners preferred some types of ecumenical activity over others. In the previous three years, about three-quarters of church members had been involved in behaviors expressing general interest in other religious groups: reading, attending a lecture, and attending worship services in another denomination. About half had attended an ecumenical worship service, participated in an interfaith group, or participated in an activity sponsored by several churches. Finally, about one-quarter of the respondents had volunteered to represent their church in some interfaith activity (Myers and Davidson, 1984).

But, when parishioners were asked where ecumenism ranked among their parish priorities, they said 13, 15, 18, and 22 out of 23 items (see Table 2). They attached more importance to "work[ing] with other faiths to bring religion to shut-ins and the unchurched" and "work[ing] for the unity of all Christian believers" (52 percent) than to "understanding other religions faiths" (36 percent) or having "opportunities for worship with people from other faiths and denominations" (24 percent). Thus, people were most willing to engage in practical forms of ecumenism which brought religion to others and least interested in theological forms of ecumenism which involved reflection on or changes in their own religious views.

Overall, then, there was only modest interest in ecumenism, but some willingness to work together on projects of mutual interest. This situation permitted, but probably did not stimulate, LUM's institutionalization.

Competition. The more groups like LUM have to compete with similar groups, the more of their time and energy they will spend competing for turf and resources and the more difficulty they will have becoming institutionalized. The less competition they have, the more they will be able to put their time and energy into activities more directly related to becoming viable community organizations.

There was only one other ecumenical group competing with LUM for turf and local church support at the time LUM was formed: the Federation of Churches. The Federation entered the 1970s somewhat confused by the events of the 1960s, changes in its own programming, and the decline in ecumenical interest at the national level. Discussion of the Federation's goals increased. Committees did not produce programs and activities as much as they had in the past. The Federation's Food Pantry was turned over to Church Women United in 1973. The number of churches in the Federation dropped to 15. And the Federation struggled to locate and retain leaders.

Between 1974-75 and 1981, the Federation shifted away from some of the social action it had become involved in during the late 1960s and early 1970s. In 1979, it reaffirmed its traditional emphasis on ecumenism. It also faced another choice: whether to become a program sponsoring agency (the model it had operated on in the growth years of the late 1950s and early 1960s) or to become a "catalyst and clearinghouse" for interfaith activities (the model it was tending to follow by the mid to late 1970s). The Federation chose to be a catalyst and clearinghouse.

Thus, between 1972 and 1981, the Federation dwindled in size and—to quote one person—"got out of the social concerns business." As a result, there was less competition between LUM and the Federation in 1981 than there was in 1972. While the two groups solicited funds from many of the same local churches, they needed very different amounts for very different purposes. For all practical purposes, they were no longer competitors.[5]

Resources: Secular Realm

Community Size. A large, urban population should contribute to the institutionalization of a group like LUM.

The population of Tippecanoe County grew from 109,378 in 1970 to 121,702 in 1980.[6] The city's social, educational, and occupational resources remained basically the same. The Lafayette area also continued to preform its central place function for the surrounding area. Purdue University's faculty and student enrollments continued to grow during the 1970s. Caterpillar Company built a large plant, producing several hundred new jobs. And Lafayette remained a center for the distribution of services. When the federal government's support of the Legal Services program was reduced in 1981, Legal Services offices in surrounding counties were closed and the responsibilities of the Lafayette office were increased from four counties to nine. These urban characteristics contributed to LUM's institutionalization.

Resources: Religious Sphere

Potential Support Groups. I assumed that *a core group of Roman Catholic and liberal Protestant churches would be conducive to the institutionalization of a group like LUM.* Roman Catholic and liberal Protestant churches comprise about half of all area churches and an even larger proportion of LUM's member churches (see Table 4). In 1972, Roman Catholic and liberal Protestant congregations comprised 91 percent of all of LUM's member churches; in 1977, 84 percent; and in 1981, 83 percent. These

Table 4
TYPES OF CONGREGATIONS WHICH SUPPORT LUM
(Percent)

	Estimated % of all Christian Churches	LUM Member Churches		
		1972	1976	1981
Roman Catholic and Liberal Protestant[a]	50	91 (N = 10)	84 (N = 16)	83 (N = 24)
Conservative Protestant[b]	50	9 (N = 1)	16 (N = 3)	17 (N = 5)

[a]Includes: Roman Catholic, Episcopal, Presbyterian, United Methodist, Church of the Brethren, United Church of Christ, Society of Friends, Mennonite, Unitarian, and interdenominational.
[b]Includes: Lutheran, Baptist, and Disciples of Christ

churches also have provided the majority of LUM's leaders and resources. Thus, they have had a substantial impact on the institutionalization of LUM.

Resources in Potential Support Groups. If potential support groups are large and affluent, LUM's prospects for institutionalization should increase. If potential support groups were small and relatively poor, their lack of human and economic resources would limit LUM's prospects for institutionalization.

LUM's member churches have tended to be large. In 1981, they averaged 714 members per church. Ten congregations (46 percent) had over 800 members (six of *these* had memberships of 1,000 or more). On the average, LUM's member churches were larger than the six non-member churches which participated in the 1979 survey.

LUM's member churches also were quite affluent. On the average, 48 percent of their members were college graduates, 34 percent were in professional occupations, and 35 percent had family incomes of $25,000 or more. These congregations were considerably higher in socio-economic status than the six other congregations included in the survey. They also were more affluent than the U.S. population as a whole—only 16.4 percent of which had completed college, only 15.5 percent of which were professionals, and 34.7 percent of which had family incomes of $25,000 or more (*Statistical Abstracts*, 1980:149, 418, 450).

Clearly, LUM's member churches had abundant human and economic resources, a condition which was very conducive to LUM's institutionalization.

Organizational Factors

Chapter 2 argued that conditions within LUM also would affect its institutionalization. Specifically, some dimensions of institutionalization should be more important than others, and LUM's effectiveness in achieving its goals should enhance its organizational viability.

Key Dimensions of Institutionalization

My theoretical framework assumed that six dimensions would be most important: *purpose, economic resources, administrative succession, leadership, intra-organizational relations, and inter-organizational relations.*

The evidence in Table 5 indicates what actually happened. Leadership was the most important dimension, affecting all 14 of the other dimensions. It was followed by purpose (which affected six other dimensions), administrative succession (five other dimensions), and economic resources (three other dimensions). Complexity, stability, and productivity each had some effect on two other dimensions. Six other dimensions affected one dimension, and two dimensions had no appreciable effects on any other dimensions.

Thus, I correctly anticipated the importance of four dimensions, over-estimated the importance of two dimensions, and under-estimated the importance of two others.

Table 5
EFFECTS OF KEY DIMENSIONS OF INSTITUTIONALIZATION

Dimension	Number of Dimensions It Affected	Dimensions It Affected
Leadership	14	Purpose, Membership, Size, Resources, Formalization, Complexity, Bureaucratization, Distribution of Authority, Administrative Succession, Stability, Flexibility, Productivity, Intra-organizational relations, and Inter-organizational relations
Purpose	6	Membership, Resources, Complexity, Flexibility, Intra-organizational relations, and Inter-organizational relations
Administrative Succession	5	Complexity, Leadership, Flexibility, and Intra-organizational relations, and Inter-organizational relations
Economic Resources	3	Complexity, Administrative Succession, and Intra-organizational relations
Complexity	2	Distribution of Authority and Inter-organizational relations
Stability	2	Resources and Intra-organizational relations
Productivity	2	Stability and Inter-organizational relations
Size	1	Resources
Bureaucratization	1	Intra-organizational relations
Inter-organizational relations	1	Size
Distribution of Authority	1	Intra-organizational relations
Intra-organizational relations	1	Productivity
Membership	1	Intra-organizational relations
Formalization	0	--------
Flexibility	0	--------

Leadership. Staff leadership affected eight other dimensions of institutionalization; board leadership affected ten.

Staff leadership affected LUM's size. In the early 1970s, when Rev. Elly was most enthusiastic about LUM and devoting most of his time to it, LUM grew (from nine member churches at the beginning of 1972 to 19 by the end of 1975) and from one staff member (himself) to 4.5.

As Rev. Elly's attention turned to organizational matters within LUM and the development of Pastoral Counseling Center, LUM leveled off in size. Stidham United Methodist—a small outlying church—joined LUM, but Covenant Presbyterian—a large, West Lafayette church which had contributed many leaders and substantial funds—withdrew. Staff size also remained about the same.

After Rev. Dolphin joined LUM, several new churches joined LUM. The number of new churches increased by 53 percent between 1977 and 1981. Rev. Dolphin also reduced staff size and rearranged LUM's staffing pattern (with fewer full-time and more part-time employees).

Staff leadership had essentially the same effects on LUM's economic resources. LUM's income increased rapidly in the earliest years of Rev. Elly's leadership, but leveled off during the years he was making the transition into pastoral counseling. "Other" income actually declined and denominational support failed to keep up with inflation. After Rev. Dolphin became director, LUM's income increased sharply, especially from the member churches and "other" contributions.

Staff leadership also affected LUM's complexity. Under Rev. Elly's leadership, LUM's programs expanded between 1972 and 1974. From 1975 to 1977, several programs were dropped and the only new one was the Pastoral Counseling Center Rev. Elly started. Under Rev. Dolphin's leadership, the program expanded quite rapidly. His influence was evident in the fact that several of the new programs LUM sponsored in the late 1970s (e.g., Repairs on Wheels, Grow-a-Row) were adaptations of programs he had developed while in Pittsburgh.

Staff leadership also affected the process of administrative succession. As Rev. Elly became more aware that he wanted to move into pastoral counseling full time, he took steps to insure LUM's survival. The main thing he did was to recruit at-large members he felt would increase board leadership. He urged Tom Hull, an at-large board member, to serve as president in 1976 and Dee Tritschler, another at-large member, to be president in 1977. He also asked Rev. David Hancock, an associate pastor at Trinity United Methodist Church, to serve as chair of the Finance and Funding Committee in 1977. He recruited Rev. Kurt Kremlick, pastor of Memorial Presbyterian Church in nearby Dayton, Indiana, to head up the Personnel Policies and Salary Review Committee. And he willingly embraced my proposal to evaluate LUM.

These at-large members played crucial roles in the process of administrative succession. Tom Hull's professional expertise in industrial supervision promoted improved working relations among staff and board members. Dee Tritschler's positive outlook and long-standing commitment to LUM provided hope when things were roughest. The evaluation resulted in numerous organizational changes, including a revised conception of the director's role. Rev. Kremlick's experience with ministerial job searches contributed to the smooth handling of that task. He also became LUM's interim-director, being responsible for LUM's operations between Rev. Elly's departure in mid 1977 and Rev. Dolphin's arrival in February 1978. Rev. Hancock's fiscal policies helped conserve the funds LUM needed during this volatile period.

Staff leadership also has affected LUM's stability. LUM's church membership was quite stable during the early years of Rev. Elly's leadership. However, between 1974 and 1978, three congregations withdrew from LUM. Two of these withdrawals involved differences with parish leaders over the church's role in society. The Unitarian Fellowship's withdrawal had little or nothing to do with LUM. Stability was restored under Rev. Dolphin's leadership. Nine new congregations joined LUM between 1978 and 1981, the Unitarian Fellowship reactivated its membership, and no churches dropped out of LUM.

The pattern with regard to staff stability has been different. There was more stability among the staff under Rev. Elly's leadership than there has been under Rev. Dolphin's. Four of the six staff members who have worked for more than two years served under Rev. Elly; two have worked under Rev. Dolphin. Of the 10 people who have worked for less than one year, seven have served under Rev. Dolphin and only three under Rev. Elly.

Staff leadership also has affected productivity. Rev. Elly stressed the "initiation of structures" in his own work, but expected the rest of LUM's staff to manage the programs they were responsible for. Rev. Dolphin also has stressed "initiation of structures" in his own work, but also has expected the rest of the staff to create new programs and share in their implementation. As a result, LUM's productivity ratio has been higher under Rev. Dolphin's leadership than Rev. Elly's.

Staff leadership also has had a direct effect on intra-organizational relations. During the early years of Rev. Elly's leadership (1972-74), relationships among board and staff members were quite positive. As his attention increasingly turned toward pastoral counseling in 1975-77, relationships within LUM deteriorated. Intra-organizational relations have improved under Rev. Dolphin.

Finally, staff leadership has had some effect on inter-organizational relations. Rev. Elly's frustration trying to integrate social concerns into parish life at Hope Chapel resulted in an assumption that local congregations were not interested in social outreach. This assumption lead to his tendency to pay relatively little attention to congregations (except as sources of financial support) and to concentrate on "doing social concerns on their behalf." The effect was a style of leadership which limited LUM's relationships with local churches (indeed, fostered considerable isolation).

Rev. Dolphin had had more successful experiences introducing social concerns into church programs—experiences which fostered an assumption that it *is* possible to enhance the quantity and quality of social programs within local congregations. This assumption (along with other factors pertaining to LUM's purpose, which I will discuss shortly) caused Rev. Dolphin to seek closer relationships with local congregations. His efforts have paid off.

Both directors have been able to get along well with low-income people. This ability has allowed LUM to maintain open lines of communication with low-income groups. But, their differing leadership styles have produced different types of contacts between LUM and low-income people. Under Rev. Elly's leadership, he and other members of the staff had personal contact with smaller numbers of low-income people through programs such as Adult Basic Education and Adventure Clubs which took place outside the LUM office and apart from the board. Under Rev. Dolphin's leadership, members of the staff have had personal contact with larger numbers of low-income people through programs such as Advocates and Jubilee Christmas Shops which take place in LUM's facilities or local churches and which foster more contact between board members and low-income people.

Staff leadership has had no appreciable effect on LUM's relationships with denominational agencies. Both directors have done what the agencies require insofar as grant applications are concerned. And, despite the two men's different leadership styles, relations with denominational agencies have not changed much over the years.

Finally, the two men's leadership styles have produced different relationships between LUM and local human service agencies. Rev. Elly's style was to be very active in local agencies. The attention he gave agencies tended to reaffirm their sense of worth and his style of expressing "consideration" engendered positive feelings toward him and LUM. Rev. Dolphin's more focused style of leadership has resulted in less activity with agencies and his tendency to challenge people and groups to build more effective programs has contributed to the friction with the Southside Community Center and some township trustees.

Board leadership has also played a key role in LUM's institutionalization. The board was primarily responsible for the clarification of LUM's purpose which took place during the mid 1970s. The Long Range Planning Committee (later Program and Planning) developed a model for urban ministry as part of the 1975-76 evaluation. The model was used a a framework for evaluating where LUM stood at the time and the changes it needed to make to become more like the model.[7]

LUM's board discussed this model at special meetings in September and October 1976. At the end of the October meeting, the board voted "to accept the report and move toward putting the model into effect with the understanding that each recommendation is to be voted on specifically by the Board of Directors."

LUM's purpose was specified further in 1980 during the Program and Planning Committee's evaluation of LUM's programs.[8]

The Program and Planning Committee also addressed the matter of membership. The model indicated that "[each local] church which joins LUM should have a seat on LUM's administrative board." Ideally, the person filling that seat could be elected by, and accountable to, a social concerns committee within his/her church. The model also explained that low-income groups should have seats on LUM's board.

A motion was made at the December 1976 meeting to recruit additional congregations. There was considerable discussion—especially related to theological differences between mainline and conservative Protestants, strategies for recruiting Catholic congregations, and the implications of recruiting Jewish congregations into a group which had a Christian background. Without resolving all of these issues, the board voted unanimously to broaden its base within local churches.[9]

A second motion was made to recruit representatives from five community groups which were disproportionately poor (young people; black, white, and Spanish-speaking adults; and older people). Several arguments were made why low-income people should be on the board,[10] and why there should be two representatives from each of the five low-income groups.[11] Discussion of these issues took place over the course of three monthly board meetings and ended with a 4 to 3 vote in favor of having low-income people on the board and a 5 to 2 vote for having two representatives from each of five groups. The board had approved the motion, but with mixed feelings.

In 1980, the board modified its position on membership of low-income people, voting to accept at-large members (including low-income representatives) "as the board deems appropriate up to, but not exceeding, 20 percent of the church board membership."

Board leadership also has affected LUM's size. During the early to mid 1970s, LUM's board left the recruitment of member churches and low-income people to Rev. Elly. In the late 1970s, the board assumed more responsibility for recruitment of new members and its efforts (along with those of the staff) paid off.

Board leadership also has had direct effects on LUM's economic resources. Board member Dennis Sorge of St. John's Episcopal Church was instrumental in convincing United Episcopal Charities to increase its support of LUM. Gary Henriott, of Immanuel United Church of Christ, also persuaded the Indiana-Kentucky conference of the United Church of Christ to contribute to LUM. And individual board members have been more aggressive in their efforts to secure pledges from their congregations.

Board leadership also has affected LUM's formalization. Though Rev. Elly had made sure LUM had bylaws and incorporation papers, detailed minutes of meetings, and financial records, the board's leadership was responsible for significant improvements in several of these areas during the late 1970s. The Unitarian Fellowship's representative raised the question concerning the whereabouts and contents of LUM's incorporation papers—an episode which caused considerable stress, but resulted in the formalization of LUM's relationship with the Internal Revenue Service. Rev. Hancock, Joyce White, Dennis Sorge, and Gary Henriott played major roles in the formalization of LUM's policies in the area of finance and funding between 1977 and 1980.

The board also has developed specific roles within LUM and codified personnel policies for people occupying these roles (bureaucratization). When he was president in 1976, Tom Hull was instrumental in defining committee functions and board members' responsibilities for committee work. The Program and Planning Committee called for numerous changes, including a redefinition of the director's role and the responsibilities of other staff members. And Rev. Kurt Kremlick—interim director of LUM between Rev. Elly and Rev. Dolphin and chair of the Personnel Policy and Salary Review Committee from 1977 to 1979—was a major force in the preparation of a new job description for the director, LUM's personnel policies document, and the detailed report which resolved the issue concerning a former secretary's fringe benefits.

The board also played a role in the decentralization of authority which took place from the mid 1970s through the early 1980s. Rev. Elly had great control and the board had little. During the mid 1970s, at-large board members assumed more responsibility. Their leadership during this period, and the success they had bringing LUM through the crisis period, produced a decentralization of authority. Rev. Dolphin would still have considerable authority, but he would have to deal with a board that had grown more accustomed to formulating ideas and expected to play a major (not just an advisory) role in important decisions.

The board's leadership was a key factor during the process of administrative succession. At-large members were especially important in the process—more so than representatives of member churches. At-large members were LUM's presidents in 1976 (Hull), 1977 (Tritschler), and 1978 (Hull again). The chairs of the Finance and Funding Committee in 1977 (Hancock), the Membership Recruitment and Relations Committee in 1978 (Tritschler), the Personnel and Policies and Salary Review Committee in 1977 and 1978 (Kremlick), and the Program and Planning Committee in 1976 through 1978 (Davidson) were all at-large members. They, along with other officers and committee chair people, shouldered much of the responsibility for finding a new director.[12]

Board leadership also contributed to improved intra-organizational relations during the late 1970s. Board members shared an experience of successfully leading LUM through the traumatic process of administrative succession. That experience fostered confidence within the group. The growth of board leadership during the late 1970s further contributed to board members' self-confidence and trust in one another.

Finally, the board leadership played a role in LUM's relations with other groups. Board members such as Phil Roberts, Tee Montford, Ned Helmuth, Mike Mecklenburg, Dorothy Olsen, Louise Jewell, Dan Dykhuizen, Mike Presti, Sue Axtell, Dennis Sorge, and Gary Henriott (to name only a few) have solidified LUM's relations with their local congregations. Dennis Sorge and Gary Henriott have said publicly that the leadership of LUM's board has been a key factor in their excitement about LUM and their efforts to enhance their denominations' support of LUM. Board leadership has had little or no bearing on LUM's relationships with low-income groups.

To summarize, staff and board leadership have had quite different implications for the institutionalization of LUM, with staff leadership having more effect on process dimensions, and board leadership having more effect on structural dimensions. Staff leadership has affected three structural dimensions (size, resources, and complexity) and five process dimensions (administrative succession, stability, productivity, inter-organizational relations, and intra-organizational relations). Board leadership has affected all but one of the seven structural dimensions (complexity) and three process dimensions (administrative succession, intra-organizational relations, and inter-organizational relations).

Purpose. The second most important dimension of institutionalization has been LUM's sense of purpose. It has had observable effects on six other dimensions (3 structural and 3 process).

During the early 1970s, LUM's purpose was to be "a means for the local church member to demonstrate his or her outreach to the less fortunate." In doing so, it would work most closely with low-income people in downtown neighborhoods and human service agencies.

However, LUM's membership criteria were not closely related to this sense of purpose. At least half of LUM's board was to be comprised of low-income people (that did not happen). Each local congregation which joined was to have a representative (that did happen). Finally, though human service agencies were part of LUM's purpose, they were not represented on its board.

When LUM clarified and changed its purpose in 1976-77, it also changed its membership criteria. Its new purpose focused LUM's attention on two groups: local churches and low-income people. Both groups were to have representatives on the board.

The change in LUM's purpose also affected its financial resources. As LUM's interest in working *with* local churches increased, so did its reliance on churches for financial support. In 1981, two-thirds of LUM's resources came from denominational agencies and local congregations; the other one-third came from individuals and other community groups. As LUM's interest in human service agencies declined, so did its interest in federal funds supporting many agency programs. Evidence of this was LUM's decision in 1978 not to accept federal funds to expand its involvement in transportation for the elderly.[13]

LUM's change of purpose also affected its complexity. The new purpose LUM adopted in 1976-77 assumed that local congregations *should* be involved in social concerns and that part of LUM's reason for existing was to help them become more involved. As a result, LUM developed numerous programs (e.g., a monthly newsletter called *The Seed*, Jubilee Christmas, the Seeds of Vision conferences, and Grow-a-Row) to increase local churches' own involvement in social concerns.

LUM's purpose also has affected its flexibility. LUM always had been willing to create experimental programs, then turn them over to other groups. And LUM made some efforts in this direction during the 1970s with regard to the camp program and Adventure Clubs.

However, LUM's programs became increasingly fixed over time. The evaluation of LUM in 1975-76 called attention to several undesirable consequences of accumulating programs without turning any of them over to other groups (e.g., the budget would not permit it in the long run and it tended to isolate LUM from local churches). At its meeting in June 1977, LUM's board approved a recommendation from the evaluation that LUM "continue to provide needed services to churches and low-income groups . . . [but also put] more emphasis on program development and evaluation in the churches and low-income community." This decision (along with factors related to leadership and administrative succession) contributed to the increased flexibility in LUM's programs during the late 1970s. By the end of 1981, several of the programs which had been cornerstones for LUM in the early 1970s (e.g., Adventure Clubs, Teen Leadership Development, and Good Friends) had been dropped, turned over to other groups, or were being shared with other groups. LUM's effort to share responsibility for the camp program with the Southside Center failed, resulting in LUM's continued sponsorship of that program.

The clarification of LUM's purpose has contributed to more positive relations within the organization. On several occasions, Rev. Dolphin has stated that the decisions LUM's board made as a result of the evaluation in 1975-76 produced a consensus which solidified the group. The sharpening of LUM's focus on two constituencies (local churches and low-income groups) allowed board and staff members to conceptualize their efforts in terms of biblical and church teachings related to justice and equality. It allowed them to relate to one another in terms of these common religious concerns (rather than potentially divisive grounds related to partisan politics or secular-economic theories). Thus, board members with different political affiliations and economic theories have worked closely together.

Finally, LUM's sense of purpose has affected its inter-organizational relations. During the early 1970s, relations with congregations were strained. After LUM decided in 1976-77 that one of its two main goals was to work *with* local churches to increase *their* involvement in social concerns, relations with the congregations improved.[14]

LUM's decision to reduce its emphasis on human service agencies has reduced the amount of time and energy LUM staff members spend on agency concerns. The result has been greater social distance between LUM and local agencies.

The change in LUM's sense of purpose has had no appreciable effects on its relationships with denominational agencies or low-income people.

Administrative Succession. The process of administrative succession affected five other dimensions of LUM's institutionalization: one structural dimension (complexity) and four process dimensions (leadership, flexibility, intra-organizational relations, and inter-organizational relations).

The process of administrative succession produced *more* differentiation in LUM's committee structure (the Personnel Policies and Salary Review Committee was formed in 1975 to deal with policy and salary issues affecting all staff; the Long Range Planning Committee also was formed in 1975 to conduct the 1975-76 evaluation), but *less* differentiation in the area of program (LUM's only new programs in the 1975-77 period were to support the formation of a Community Infant Care Center—which failed—and lead in the formation of the Lafayette Pastoral Counseling Center—which Rev. Elly expected to direct as soon as it was established).

The process of administrative succession also affected leadership within LUM. As Rev. Elly devoted more of his energy to the formation of the Pastoral Counseling Center, and other staff members were occupied with their program responsibilities, leadership by at-large board members increased. The Long Range Planning Committee pressed the board to make decisions on the recommendations from the 1976 evaluation. The Finance and Funding Committee was busier than usual trying to anticipate the financial impact of the board's decisions and to limit LUM's expenses. Once those decisions were made, the Personnel Policies and Salary Review Committee moved into the forefront, preparing personnel policies documents, job descriptions, and procedures for searching for a new director.

The process of administrative succession also reduced LUM's flexibility. As concentration on organizational matters increased, programs became more fixed. Between 1975 and 1977, the board and staff chose to continue on-going programs as much as possible, to add only two new programs (the Community Infant Care Center and the Lafayette Pastoral Counseling Center), and to drop three programs (the Revenue Sharing Task Force, the Spanish-Speaking Persons Task Force, and the Community Infant Care Center).

Administrative succession had a mixed influence on relations among board and staff members. It produced some friction and anxiety among staff members who were not sure what might happen to their jobs and/or their programs. Some church representatives also tended to become less regular in their attendance, suggesting they were not eager to take part in the time-consuming and emotional activities involved in keeping the organization afloat while at the same time trying to change its course for the future. But, other board members—especially at-large members—tended to "rally around the cause." They were open, honest, and trusted one another as they pursued the superordinate goal of replacing Rev. Elly and implementing the new model.

Finally, the process of replacing Rev. Elly strained LUM's relationships with some churches. Some United Methodist clergy and lay people indicated their unhappiness with some aspects of the new model (especially the idea of turning programs over to local churches), some of the procedures used to select a new director (they perceived an under-representation of United Methodists in the search process), and the results of the search (that a United Methodist was not chosen). They expressed the possibility that some or all of the United Methodist churches in the area might pull out of LUM (though none ever did).

There also were some strains in LUM's relationship with the presbytery of the Wabash Valley, principally over the question of whether it would continue its support of LUM at the same level. However, these tensions receded when the presbytery pledged its continued support.

The process of administrative succession had no direct or observable effects on LUM's relationships with human service agencies or low-income people.

Economic Resources. LUM's economic resources have had important implications for its complexity, the process of administrative succession, and intra-organizational relations.

The rapid expansion of LUM's income during the 1972-74 period allowed LUM's programs to improve. For example, the transportation program expanded to include a van, two station wagons, and paid drivers. The contraction of funds during the mid 1970s also contributed to the decline in new programs in 1976 and 1977. And Rev. Dave Hancock and the Finance and Funding Committee stridently enforced a policy of fiscal conservatism which would not permit the expenditure of money which LUM did not have. Finally, as revenues increased again in the late 1970s, new programs were started. Lilly Endowment's support permitted the 1979-80 survey and consultation with 30 local churches. Local church support was directly responsible for the creation of the Jubilee Christmas Shops and the Seeds of Vision conferences. Thus, the curvilinear pattern of funding contributed to the curvilinear pattern of program development.

LUM's economic resources also contributed to its success in replacing Rev. Elly. Local church support leveled off during this period, but provided $14,000 to $15,000 which LUM needed. LUM might not have been able to survive without it. Indeed, there was considerable concern about LUM's survival when Covenant Presbyterian Church withdrew its membership and its annual pledge of about $1,500 (the second largest pledge at the time). If one or two other large donors had pulled out at the same time,

LUM might not have survived. Denominational support also persisted when LUM needed it the most. The reason LUM was so nervous about the support from the presbytery of the Wabash Valley and the northern conference of the United Methodist church was that if either one—and especially if both—of these groups had withdrawn their support in 1977 or 1978, LUM almost certainly would have folded. The existence of these economic resources allowed LUM to conceptualize a position of full-time director and to offer a salary that would be attractive to a competent person.

Finally, LUM's economic resources in the 1972-75 period allowed for staff salary increases and provided the materials the staff needed to do their jobs with personal satisfaction and interpersonal harmony. As economic resources began to level off in late 1974 and 1975, negativism became more common. The board felt it did not have the money to provide the salary increases and the supplies the staff felt it needed. Staff members felt their efforts were not being rewarded. Moreover, staff members began to test one another and the board in their competition for LUM's limited economic resources. The result was unhappiness on all sides. Neither the staff nor the board looked forward to board meetings. Bad news outweighed the good. As income expanded during the late 1970s, the board was able to provide cost-of-living (and some merit) increases for the staff. The board felt better about its role, and the staff felt good about being rewarded for its efforts. Their relationships were more cooperative and less conflictual. Both groups began to look forward to board meetings again. Good news now outweighed the bad.

Complexity. LUM's increased complexity has affected two other dimensions: the distribution of authority and inter-organizational relations. In 1972, LUM was almost totally dependent on Rev. Elly; to a considerable extent, LUM *was* Rev. Elly. And though the director retains a great deal of authority and remains the dominant force within the organization, the formation of standing committees in 1973, 1975, and 1980 and the expansion of the Executive Committee's role over time have increased the board's involvement in decision-making and diminished LUM's reliance on its director (a situation which Rev. Elly constantly struggled to achieve and which helped to save the organization he founded).

The development of new programs also has affected LUM's relationships with other groups. When LUM sponsored almost no programs *for* local congregations, its relationships with the church were poorest. Local congregations were not sure what LUM was all about and what it was doing with their money. As the number of programs oriented toward local congregations increased, LUM's relationships with member churches also improved.

The reverse has been true with regard to local human service agencies. During the early to mid 1970s, when LUM sponsored several programs which benefited agencies, LUM's relations with agencies were very positive. As LUM reduced its involvement with local agencies, relations with the agencies cooled.

Finally, LUM's sponsorship of the Advocate program has produced negative relationships with some township trustees and one of LUM's member churches. LUM's practice of taking low-income people to trustees' offices and advocating their case increased LUM's belief that the trustee system is not an effective way to handle poor relief. This view led to the formation of a task force to make the community more aware of the problem and to seek ways of changing it. LUM's advocacy on behalf of low-income people also has fostered resentment among some trustees. One trustee was instrumental in persuading his church to withdraw its membership from LUM. In September 1981, another trustee had her lawyer request copies of LUM's charter and/or bylaws in an effort "to ascertain whether this organization is meeting the needs of the poor of my township as stated in their charter and/or bylaws, since it appears to me that they are no longer advocates of the poor, but rather adversaries of the township trustee." LUM responded by sending her a copy of its bylaws and inviting her to meet with LUM's staff and/or board. She did not respond to that invitation.

Stability. The stability of LUM's church memberships during the early 1970s contributed to the adequacy of its financial resources during that period. Between 1972 and 1976, LUM could count on pledges from most of its member churches. However, when Covenant Presbyterian Church withdrew in 1976, it also took away its annual pledge, which was 14 percent of all congregational contributions and 3 percent of LUM's total income in 1975. When Holy Trinity Lutheran and the Unitarian Fellowship withdrew in 1978, LUM lost another $300 in contributions from member churches (2 percent of its congregational contributions and .005 percent of its total income in 1978). With these losses, LUM needed to generate new money just to stay even. As stability returned in the late 1970s and early 1980s (including the return of the Unitarian Fellowship), LUM's resources increased. The addition of new member churches and the increased giving of several old ones produced a real increase in LUM financial resources between 1979 and 1981.

Turnover among board members has had some negative effect on relationships within the organization. When the turnover of board members was most rapid during the early to mid 1970s, intra-organizational relations were most negative. Board members could not count on one another and staff members grew increasingly suspicious of board members' commitment to LUM. As the turnover slowed down in the late 1970s and early 1980s, intra-organizational relations improved. Board members recognized one another, exchanged friendly greetings, and conducted their business on the basis of trust.

Productivity. The deceased productivity of LUM's staff between 1973 and 1978 probably accounted for some of the instability and negative relationships with member churches during that period; the staff's increased productivity between 1978 and 1981 almost certainly has contributed to increased stability and improved relations with member churches. One of the complaints some United Methodist leaders expressed during the mid 1970s was that they were not sure they were getting their money's worth out of LUM. That complaint has not been heard since LUM's productivity has increased.

Size. LUM's size has affected its economic resources. As the number of member churches increased from nine at the beginning of 1972 to 19 at the end of 1975, church contributions rose from $4,840 to $10,852.41. When the number of member churches leveled off at 19 in the mid 1970s, church contributions also leveled off. When the number of new member churches increased again between 1978 and 1981, income from local churches also increased from $14,983.72 in 1978 to $26,567.60 in 1981. New member churches also have had some effects on denominational support. After St. John's Episcopal Church and Immanuel Church of Christ joined LUM, United Episcopal Charities and the Indiana-Kentucky conference of the United Church of Christ support of LUM increased.

The size of LUM's staff also has had some effect on its resources. During the early to mid 1970s, when LUM's staff was largest, its resources were most limited. During this period staff salaries comprised over 70 percent of LUM's budget. As the number of full-time staff members dropped from four in 1977 to two in 1980, LUM was able to save considerable money. The resignations of Rev. Elly (September 1977), Ginny Boncy (October 1977), Veronica Blann (July 1978), and Sharon Shrottenback McCabe (November 1978) produced salary savings which allowed LUM to develop reserves it had never had before.

Bureaucratization. During the early to mid 1970s, when LUM let the needs of individual staff and board members transcend the needs of the organization, LUM also experienced the most negative relations among its board and staff. Staff members invidiously compared their salaries, fringe benefits, office hours, and work loads. The dissension also affected staff members' relationships with the board (as the staff felt a need to manipulate the board) and the board's relationships with the staff (as the board grew increasingly impatient with staff members' concerns about their personal well-being at a time when the organization was struggling to survive).

As LUM developed a clearer set of roles, and a universalistic set of personnel policies, frictions among staff members declined sharply. The increased bureaucratization also led to more harmonious relations between the staff and the board; as the expectations on both sides became clearer, the suspicions and distrust which plagued LUM during the mid-1970s waned.

Inter-organizational Relations. LUM's relationships with local churches have affected its size. During the mid 1970s, when LUM's relationships with local churches were most tenuous, three congregations withdrew their memberships. As LUM's relationships with local churches improved over the years, the number of local churches wanting to belong to LUM increased. In some cases, pastors (or other church members) heard positive things about LUM's work in the community and called LUM to inquire about membership. In other cases, LUM initiated contact with a prospective church and was able to convince the church to join.

Distribution of Authority. The distribution of authority has affected relations within LUM. When authority was most highly centralized around Rev. Elly, relationships among board and staff members tended to be most strained. The decentralization of authority which occurred during the mid 1970s produced a more equitable sharing of responsibility and a greater sense of trust and confidence within the group.

Intra-organizational relations also might have had some bearing on LUM's productivity. Certainly, as relations among the staff and board deteriorated during the mid 1970s, the staff's productivity also deteriorated. However, the complaints of some staff members suggest that low productivity might have been responsible for the negative relations within the group, not vice versa.

Membership. The clarification of who belongs to LUM and who does not might have affected LUM's relationships with other groups, but it is difficult to say for sure. The reaffirmation of LUM's commitment to local churches might have had some beneficial effect on its relationships with them, but I suspect LUM's purpose, the programs it has run for churches, and the increased leadership of the board and staff have had even more effect.

Finally, *formalization* and *flexibility* have had little or no effect on LUM's institutionalization.

Effectiveness

To examine the impact LUM's effectiveness has had on its institutionalization, I needed to determine if there has been any correlation between the two and, if so, demonstrate that effectiveness has been a causal influence on institutionalization.

To do this, I divided LUM's overall pattern of institutionalization into two categories: relatively "low" (1972-77), and relativity "high" (1978-81). I also divided LUM's programs into two groups: those which LUM sponsored between 1972 and 1977, and those which it sponsored between 1978 and 1981. I then computed a mean effectiveness score for all the programs in the two time periods (see Chapter 8 for more details).[15]

The data in Table 6 indicate that as LUM's programs became more effective, the more highly institutionalized LUM became. This pattern prevailed for programs LUM conducted on behalf of local churches and for those which LUM conducted to increase local churches' own involvement in social concerns, but it was especially true for the programs LUM created to foster more social concerns within local churches.

I also can show that effectiveness directly affected five dimensions of institutionalization: size, economic resources, leadership, intra-organizational relations, and inter-organizational relations.

As LUM's effectiveness increased (especially working *with* local churches), the number of local congregations joining LUM also increased. Susan Axtell reported that she was so moved by the first Seeds of Vision conference that she urged her church (Our Saviour Lutheran) to join LUM. However, LUM's effectiveness in programs relating to the causes and consequences of poverty has not had the effect of increasing low-income people's representation on LUM's board.

Table 6
LUM'S INSTITUTIONALIZATION BY ITS EFFECTIVENESS

| | Institutionalization | | |
Effectiveness	LOW (1972-77)	HIGH (1978-81)	DIFF
Overall	2.8	3.3	.5
(a) On Behalf of Churches	2.9	3.3	.4
(b) Within Churches	2.5	3.3	.8

LUM's increased effectiveness also has increased its economic resources, especially support from local churches. Some of this effect is indirect, through size: each new member church has meant increased resources for LUM. But, LUM's effectiveness also has affected its resources directly. Churches which belonged to LUM in 1977 increased their contributions by an average of 66 percent between 1977 and 1981. In five cases, the increases were over 100 percent.

LUM's effectiveness also has contributed to leadership. The more effective LUM's programs have been (especially in the churches), the more member churches have tended to send LUM representatives with real leadership skills.

LUM's effectiveness also has improved relationships within the organization. The success of programs such as the Advocates, Seeds of Vision, and Jubilee Christmas has produced uninhibited joy among staff and board members. Whenever LUM has had some significant accomplishment, board and staff members have responded by expressing their gratitude to one another. Staff members have reaffirmed the importance of the board and its leadership; the board has reaffirmed its confidence and trust in the staff.

Finally, LUM's effectiveness has improved its relations with other groups, especially local churches. Highly visible and popular groups such as Seeds of Vision and Jubilee Christmas have produced a much greater understanding in local churches of what LUM does and how its programs can benefit them. In contrast to the uncertainty and doubt which prevailed during the early and mid 1970s, local churches' leaders now are more likely to express their trust and confidence in LUM. They also are more likely now to call upon LUM for assistance, participate in its programs, and respond with unsolicited letters of commendation.

Conclusion

The purpose of this chapter has been to explain LUM's curvilinear pattern of institutionalization. None of the three structural conditions at the national level had any appreciable effect (see Table 7). Nor did the economic resources in the secular realm. However, all three of the resource factors within the religious sphere played significant roles. Religious resources declined during the early 1970s, but increased again by 1976—right at the time LUM started to rebound. There also was an over-supply of Protestant clergy, which contributed to LUM's success replacing staff. And, though it did not enjoy the primacy it had in the 1970s, Christianity's prophetic heritage persisted, providing continued justification for groups like LUM.

Three of the four structural conditions at the local level had the expected effects: the persistence of the problem, the willingness of churches to work together, and the lack of competition with other groups with similar goals. The area's conservative political climate (a structural factor) had no discernible effect.

All three of the local resource factors were important: Lafayette's urban population, the existence of Roman Catholic and liberal Protestant churches in the area, and the abundance of human and economic resources in these churches.

Table 7
SUMMARY OF ENVIRONMENTAL FACTORS AFFECTING LUM'S INSTITUTIONALIZATION

	Period		Place		
	Structural Conditions	Resources	Structural Conditions	Resources	
Secular	0 of 1	0 of 1	0 of 1	1 of 1	(1 of 4)
Religious	0 of 2 (0 of 3)	3 of 3 (3 of 4)	3 of 3 (3 of 4)	2 of 2 (3 of 3)	(8 of 10)

Organizational factors also played major roles in its institutionalization. Four dimensions of institutionalization were especially important: (1) leadership, which affected every other dimension; (2) LUM's sense of purpose, which affected six other dimensions; (3) the process of administrative succession, which affected five other dimensions; and (4) economic resources, which affected three other dimensions. LUM's increased effectiveness—especially in its efforts to work *with* (not just on behalf of) local churches—also had positive implications for LUM's size, economic resources, leadership, intra-organizational relations, and inter-organizational relations. Thus, LUM contributed to its own institutionalization by mobilizing the resources it needed to survive and become a viable social movement organization.

CHAPTER 8
DESCRIPTION OF LUM'S EFFECTIVENESS:
INCREASING OVER TIME

LUM's official goal has been to increase church involvement in social concerns, especially the causes and consequences of poverty in Tippecanoe County (Chapter 6). LUM has conceived of this goal in two ways. One has been to address the causes and consequences of poverty *on behalf of local churches.* This goal has had four specific components:
1. To address social policies and practices that create and/or perpetuate poverty
2. To cultivate relationships with and among low-income groups
3. To increase the social and economic resources within low-income groups
4. To respond to the emergency needs of low-income families.

LUM's other approach to its official goal has been to *increase local congregations' own involvement* in social concerns. This goal also has four specific components:
1. To increase the quantity and quality of social concerns programs sponsored by local churches
2. To increase the priority church members attach to social concerns as a component of parish life
3. To foster more compassionate attitudes about poverty and low-income people
4. To integrate churchgoers' vertical beliefs about the supernatural and their horizontal beliefs about loving one's neighbor and doing good for others.

There has been a close relationship between LUM's official goals and its operative goals. The board and staff have created 27 programs which are consistent with the group's official goals (see Table 1). And they have sought to conduct these programs in ways which would produce results consistent with these goals.

Table 1
LUM'S PROGRAMS IN RELATION TO ITS GOALS

GOALS	
To address causes and consequences of poverty on behalf of churches	To increase churches own involvement in social concerns
Change Policies and Practices (N = 5) 1. Advocates 2. Fuel Crisis Task Force 3. Human Development Coalition 4. Public Policy 5. Revenue Sharing Task Force	*Increase Sponsorship of Programs (N = 5)* 1. Christmas Project 2. Grow-a-Row 3. Integrated Hands 4. Jubilee Christmas Shop 5. Repairs on Wheels

Organizing the Poor (N = 8)
1. Advocates
2. Christmas Project
3. Food Buying Club
4. Good Friends
5. Integrated Hands
6. Jubilee Christmas
7. Mothers Group
8. Spanish-speaking Task Force

Increase Resources (N = 11)
1. Adult Basic Education
2. Adventure Club
3. Community Infant Care Center
4. County Council on Aging
5. Grow-a-Row
6. Pastoral Counseling Center
7. Repairs on Wheels
8. Shamrock Park
9. Summer Camp
10. Teen Leadership Development
11. Volunteer Transportation

Emergency Relief (N = 2)
1. Advocates
2. Centralized Emergency Fund

Change Priorities, Attitudes, and Beliefs (N = 3)
1. The *Seed*
2. Seeds of Vision
3. Survey/consultation

The purpose of this chapter is to examine the effectiveness of these programs. First, I will examine the programs relating to LUM's goal of addressing the causes and consequences of poverty on behalf of local churches. Then, I will assess the programs relating to its goal of stimulating more social concern within local congregations.

I will describe each program, placing it into one of four categories: (1) counter-productive, (2) little or no effect, (3) somewhat effective, and (4) very effective. A program will be considered: *counter-productive* if it has fostered policies and practices perpetuating poverty, precluded or broken down relationships with and/or among low-income people, prevented resources from developing within low-income groups, or created—rather than responded to—the need for emergency relief, stifled the development of social concerns programs within local congregations, caused church members to attach lower priority to social concerns, fostered less compassionate attitudes about poverty and the poor, and/or contributed to the separation of vertical and horizontal beliefs; *ineffective* if it had no observable effect—either positive or negative; *somewhat effective* if its net effect has been modest progress toward specific goals; and *very effective* if it has had a substantial impact on the problem it was designed to address. Clearly, some subjectivity is involved in assigning any program to one of these categories, but that is an inherent part of evaluation. All I can do is to use the most concrete criteria and evidence available and assure the reader that I have tried to be as impartial as possible.

In the final section, I will compare the effectiveness of programs in operation between 1972 and 1977 and those in operation between 1978 and 1981. In this way, I will be able to determine the extent to which LUM has become more (or less) effective in achieving its goals over time.

*Addressing Causes and Consequences
on Behalf of Local Churches*

Table 2 indicates that, on the average, LUM's programs addressing the causes and consequences of poverty have been somewhat effective (mean score 3.2). LUM has been most effective providing emergency relief (mean score = 4.0); somewhat less effective increasing the resources within low-income groups (mean score = 3.4); and least effective in organizing the poor and altering policies and practices affecting poverty (mean score = 3.0 in both cases).

Table 2
OVERALL EFFECTIVENESS OF LUM'S PROGRAMS
TO ADDRESS THE CAUSES AND CONSEQUENCES
OF POVERTY ON BEHALF OF LOCAL CHURCHES

Programs to:	Counter Productive (X1)	Little or No Effect (X2)	Some Effect (X3)	Very Effective (X4)	Mean Score
Alter social policies and practices					
% = 100		20	60	20	
N = 5	-	1	3	1	3.0
Create relationships with and among the poor					
% = 100	-	25	50	25	
N = 8	-	2	4	2	3.0
Increase resources within low-income groups					
% = 100	-	18	18	64	
N = 11	-	2	2	7	3.4
Provide emergency relief					
% = 100	-	-	-	100	
N = 2	-	-	-	2	4.0

Change Policies and Practices

One program designed to change social policies and practices has been very effective.

Revenue Sharing Task Force. In 1973, federal funding of local programs was changing from an approach which stressed support of projects with specific restrictions laid down by Congress and enforced by federal agencies to a revenue sharing approach where by federal government returned block grants (with few strings attached) to local communities which decided how best to use the money. In response, Rev. Elly called together a Revenue Sharing Task Force, which determined that many other Indiana communities were using revenue sharing funds to support human services agencies, but that "in Tippecanoe County the only expenditure which could be considered to be social services is $20,000 committed by the county government for Wabash Center [a mental health facility]. All other expenditures are primarily capital out lays for one-time capital improvements." The task force's interpretation of the law was that revenue sharing funds *could* be used for human services; its position was that some portion of the funds *should* be used for human services.

The task force invited board and staff members from many local agencies to attend meetings in late 1973 and early 1974 to explore their views on the matter and to determine what steps they might take. They decided "to see that important programs receive a priority rating and hearing, and that order is brought out of the chaos of social services vying with one another in the face of cut-backs and scarce funds." They explored the issue with the mayor of Lafayette and the city council, constructed descriptions of local agencies, developed a screening committee and a set of procedures the committee could use to determine how federal funds could be allocated among the agencies, and made a presentation to the Lafayette city council in March 1974.

The task force persuaded the city council to allot about $30,000 of interest from revenue sharing funds to human service agencies. The city council's decision was noteworthy enough to attract editorial attention in the Lafayette, *Journal-Courier* (October 10, 1974).

In addition to its impact on the use of revenue sharing funds in 1975, the task force's actions have had long-term effects. Local agencies no longer screen and prioritize their own proposals as they did the first year (they found that to be a cumbersome and divisive process). Instead, they submit their proposals to the city council with the knowledge that the council is willing to use revenue sharing and community development funds to support human services. For example, in 1981, Lafayette received $736,000 in community development funds, $80,000 of which was "for the Tippecanoe County Council of Aging, Legal Aid, the Family Service Agency and the health referral service [Community Development] helps fund" (Lafayette *Journal-Courier*, June 25, 1981). Thus, LUM's Revenue Sharing Task Force was instrumental in causing local officials to adopt a policy of allocating federal funds to human services.

Three other programs have had some positive consequences, but have not been quite as effective as the Revenue Sharing Task Force.

Human Development Coalition. In 1974, Rev. Elly led in the formation of a Human Development Coalition which was to be "a citizens' social service planning body in the area of social and health services and tied into the multitude of planning bodies locally and regionally." By 1975, Rev. Elly was the convenor of the Coalition and its members (about 20 individuals and 15 agencies) were "meeting together monthly in Forum to discuss [their concerns about human service], plan together, and coordinate programs."

In February 1976, the Coalition co-sponsored a community workshop with United Way, United Stand for Children and Youth, and the National Association of Social Workers-Central Indiana Chapter. The purposes of the workshop were "to assess major human needs; to set priorities; [and] to work out approaches to solving these problems.[1]

The Coalition also absorbed the Revenue Sharing Task Force's concerns about support of human services and expanded its scope to include other federal funds, particularly community development. In 1976, the Coalition reviewed all the proposals various agencies submitted for Housing and Community Development funds. It, then, reported its assessment to the Lafayette and West Lafayette city councils. It reaffirmed the importance of using community development funds to support human services to people living in community development target areas and ranked the proposals in terms of their priority for funding.

But, the Coalition struggled in its efforts to take root in the agencies and coordinate their activities. Several agencies offered moral support, but the Coalition's membership drive in 1976 had only "poor" results because there was "not enough agency support." In January 1977, Rev. Elly indicated that the Coalition "hasn't really acted as a coordinating vehicle among agencies (for basic operations) . . . Informal meetings attempting to settle inter-agency friction seemed to create stronger antagonisms. Attempts to set up and improve services proved threatening . . . There is a need for self-criticism if services are to expand and/or improve."

In 1978, Rev. Elly resigned as convenor of the Coalition. Shortly after Rev. Dolphin's arrival in Lafayette, he was asked to be convenor, but declined. Since then, it has sputtered and lapsed into inactivity.

Advocates. The Advocates program was started in the mid 1970s by Joan Hawbaker, who had been actively involved in many human service activities over the years. The advocates are middle class volunteers who assist low-income people with problems such as housing; help them fill out applications for federal assistance programs; accompany them to utility companies or the township trustee office; and speak on their behalf when low-income people are confronted with an uncooperative clerk or manager. Another goal of the Advocates program has been to monitor the policies and practices of organizations affecting the poor, especially the township trustee system of poor relief.

By 1976, there were seven advocates, who needed office space. Rev. Elly offered them space in LUM's office. Mrs. Hawbaker then indicated she would like LUM to take more responsibility for the program. LUM's Program and Planning Committee, Executive Committee, and board discussed the pros and cons of adopting the Advocates program for several months, finally adopting the program in August 1978.[2]

Between 1978 and 1981, the advocates were successful in getting township trustees to develop more regular hours and/or ways of being more accessible to low-income people through the use of telephone recording devices. The advocates also monitored the policies and practices of Project SAFE, a state program to assist low-income people with their fuel bills during the winter months. LUM identified a number of weaknesses in the way the program was conducted and explained these weaknesses in a letter to the state's Community Service Administration in February 1981. In August 1981, LUM sent another letter to the state commission with several suggestions for ways of increasing the poor's awareness of and access to the program and its benefits.

Public Policy. The Public Policy Network consists of a group which meets regularly to study issues relating to public policy in general and legislation affecting the poor in particular, and a network of individuals who receive the results of the smaller group's deliberations with the intention of taking some action.

In May 1980, the Public Policy Network determined that Tippecanoe County did not have a special supplemental food program for Women, Infants, and Children (WIC).[3] It then urged the approximately 200 people who received its bulletin "Agenda for Social Concerns" to write to the Visiting Nurse Service, the county medical society, and the county board of health describing the need for WIC and asking them to apply for WIC. It also asked these people to raise the issue within the social concerns committee of their local congregations. At LUM's board meeting in June 1981, Rev. Dolphin announced that the county board of health had recognized the value of WIC and would be making an application for a WIC program in the county.

The Public Policy Network's other major concern was the township trustee system of poor relief. In July 1981, the committee initiated a study of the present system of poor relief and ways of improving the system according to Christian principles of social justice. That study gave rise to the Indiana Task Force on Poor Relief which continues to work toward changing the present system of poor relief (see Appendix B).

One of LUM's efforts to affect social policies and practices relating to poverty was largely ineffective.

Fuel Crisis Task Force. In December 1973, Rev. Elly convened a Fuel Crisis Task Force which "focused on (1) the problem of heat for the schools, particularly the [rural schools covered by the Tippecanoe School Corporation] and (2) the concern that our young people would be out of school with little to do. The task force also was concerned (3) that business at that time was not considering limiting its hours, and (4) that the churches and synagogues had not responded to the crisis." The group's goals were: "to discover what [the] situation is; to promote discussion between all parties involved (i.e. government, business, three school corporations, suppliers, Purdue University); and to make suggestions (i.e., recommendations)."

In March 1974, the task force issued an eight-page report and made several recommendations. However, there is no evidence that the task force achieved its goal of stimulating discussion among major energy suppliers and consumers, or that local churches acted on any of the task force's recommendations.

Relationships with and among the Poor.

Two of LUM's programs to cultivate relationships with and among low-income people have been very successful.

Advocates. The Advocates program has been LUM's chief mechanism for developing closer ties with low-income individuals and families. By 1981, LUM's advocates were working with over 1,000 low-income individuals and families, providing assistance and fostering closer relationships with and among low-income groups in other ways. Invitations to the Jubilee Christmas Shop are sent to people LUM has helped through Advocates. Starting in 1981, LUM's Summer Camp invitations went to children in families which the advocates had helped.

Jubilee Christmas. During a Seeds of Vision conference in November 1979, keynote speaker Rev. Don Bakely asked: "Why at Christmas do Christians want to play hero with someone else's kids? Wouldn't it be better to find ways for those parents to be heroes in the eyes of their own little ones?" The idea moved many of LUM's board and staff members deeply. The organization acted quickly to devise a Jubilee Christmas Shop which would allow low-income parents to select gifts for their own kids. LUM asked individuals and groups within local churches to stock the Christmas Shop with new toys, used clothes, food, gift wrapping, and cash donations. Individual volunteers also helped in the shop, stocking shelves and wrapping gifts. Low-income parents LUM has worked with through the Advocates program were invited to "buy" their Christmas gifts for their children at the shop by donating money and/or time to help others even less fortunate than themselves.

The number of low-income families participating in Jubilee Christmas increased from 49 in 1979 to 121 in 1980 and 190 in 1981. The number of local churches participating in Jubilee also increased. LUM conducted a Jubilee of its own in 1979 through 1981. Over 20 local churches have participated in it each year (for more details, see section on Jubilee Christmas later in this chapter). In 1980, First Christian Church conducted one and Dayton United Methodist Church and Memorial Presbyterian Church of Dayton co-sponsored another. In 1981, these churches were joined by Immanuel United Church of Christ and Christ United Methodist which co-sponsored another Jubilee Shop (*Journal-Courier*, December 21, 1981).

Four other programs have been less effective but have contributed somewhat to the development of better relationships with and within low-income groups.

Spanish-Speaking Persons Task Force. In 1973, Rev. Elly recognized that Spanish-speaking people coming into and living in the Lafayette area encountered problems such as communication and employment. He and several people in the Spanish-speaking community developed the idea of a task force "to help raise standards of living," "[sponsor] Spanish-speaking cultural events," and "better coordinate services with needs in a personal way." In October 1973, LUM's board adopted the Spanish-Speaking Persons Task Force "as an advocacy issue," supporting it "in speaking out to the injustices seen and felt."

Fifteen to 20 Spanish-speaking people participated in the SSPTF between 1973 and 1977. The group heightened local awareness of the difficulties in being a Spanish-speaking person in Lafayette's predominantly anglo environment by distributing information through church bulletins, radio, television, and the local newspaper; assisted Spanish-speaking people who encountered language problems in communicating with anglos in local hospitals and police stations; responded when there were complaints from Spanish-speaking people that they were being stopped for minor traffic violations and detained while local officials checked to see if they were citizens or illegal aliens; met with local police to discuss the issue and was successful in putting an end to the practice; and received a $1,000 grant from the Campaign for Human Development to conduct an Hispanic American Day in 1975.

But, the SSPTF never achieved its goal of becoming a clearinghouse for information on education, job opportunities, social events, musical exchange, health, Spanish classes, and classes on citizenship. Nor was it successful in forming a "recreational center where cultural activities will foster better understanding between [Spanish-speaking people] and the rest of the community."

By late 1975 and early 1976, the SSPTF was not meeting regularly and a small number of individuals were doing the group's work. LUM's evaluation of its 1976 programs indicated that the "Spanish-Speaking Persons Task Force has died. It met through the spring and early summer [of 1976] with declining attendance . . . Until such time as the need arises, the SSPTF will be dormant."

The task force has reconvened twice. In February and March 1979, members of the SSPTF met with LUM's Program and Planning Committee to discuss ways in which LUM might be more responsive to the concerns of Spanish-speaking people. The group identified eight issues.[4] LUM explored the matter of housing in relation to the Advocates program, but did not become more directly involved in that area or any of the other issues discussed at the February and March meetings.

Also in March 1979, the SSPTF met with a Democratic candidate for mayor. Members of the SSPTF complained that the incumbent mayor had ignored the needs of Spanish-speaking residents, and asked that Spanish-speaking people be included in the challenger's administration if he were elected.[5] The incumbent mayor won the primary and the election, and the SSPTF has not been active since.

Good Friends. According to a LUM document in October 1977, the "purpose of [the Good Friends] program is to provide social contacts and development of friendly, ongoing relationships between the volunteer and the [housebound, lonely] person he/she visits."

In 1973-74, about 10 volunteers visited 35-40 older citizens. The program grew in 1975, at which time about 30 volunteers were visiting about 60 people. However, by 1976 Good Friends was struggling. LUM's evaluation of its 1976 programs indicated that Good Friends "had not been an active, responsible service. . . . The number of volunteers has gone down and the number of referrals to [Good Friend] has increased . . . this program has had its problems. There are too few volunteers for all the persons needing visitors and too many limits on the staff person's time as coordinator for two very demanding services to make this program what it should be." The 1977 evaluation indicated that the program continued to struggle. With other staff and program changes in 1978, Good Friends was phased out as an active program.

Christmas Project. In the early 1970s, the Christmas Project was known as the Christmas Cooky Project, indicating its emphasis on volunteers bringing cookies and other small food gifts to isolated and elderly people at Christmas time. As many as 80 volunteers made cookies and/or visited 60 to 70 isolated and elderly people each year between 1972 and 1974.

Between 1975 and 1981, several changes were made. Rather than relying on individual volunteers, the Christmas Project relied more and more on local congregations to provide people to visit isolated and elderly people. The program's name also changed, reflecting a reduced focus on cookies as gifts and an increased focus on building relationships. Finally, though the project name reflects the continuing focus on Christmas, there has been an increased emphasis on building relationships that will last throughout the year.

Several local congregations developed groups of members to visit as many as 100 to 150 people during the Christmas season. However, the project had not succeeded in making very many relationships that lasted beyond the Christmas season. When asked to what extent such relationships are developed, Rev. Dolphin said: "I think it's the rarest exception that it happens . . . There may be two or three visits around the Christmas season, but it doesn't go beyond that."

Food Buying Club. LUM's experience with the Advocates program and the Centralized Emergency Fund (to be discussed later) indicated that the poor use their limited resources to pay utility and other bills, frequently leaving them with little money to purchase food in either the quantity or quality they need. Thus, in fall 1981, LUM's staff devised a program whereby LUM could help low-income people obtain food at a substantial savings while fostering closer ties with and among people in low-income areas. Low-income people would collect food orders from others in their neighborhoods and apartment complexes, LUM's staff would consolidate the orders and purchase the food in quantity, and low-income people would distribute it among those who had placed orders.

Between October 6, 1981, when the first order was placed and March 1982, when the eighth order was placed, 125 different low-income people had participated. Altogether, they have purchased $9,286.55 worth of food. In the average order, 40 to 50 low-income people ordered $600 to $900 worth of food.

Two other programs have not succeeded in fostering closer relationships with and within low-income groups.

Integrated Hands. In January 1972, Rev. Elly met with an inter-racial group called Integrated Hands, asking whether churches on the near Northside could become more involved in recreation programs for teenagers, "tolerant adults" could be organized to chaperone teenage recreation programs in the evenings at the Lincoln Community Center on the near Northside, and the community as a whole could "provide more for teenagers to do that is constructively supervised, particularly on the weekends." He explored these issues with members of several of LUM's member churches on the near Northside of Lafayette. In April 1972, he reported that involving the local churches "looks like a lengthy process in my personal opinion." In fact, local churches never became involved (though many black and white church members did participate in other inter-racial programs such as Project Commitment and Project Equality).

Mothers' Group. By 1979, LUM's staff realized that many low-income women face similar problems. The staff felt that women might be able to handle these problems better if they talked them over with other women. There also was some discussion of including a few middle-class women from member churches in the group. However, LUM's staff never fully took charge of the program and adequate leadership failed to emerge from the women who participated in some preliminary meetings.

Increase Resources Within Low-Income Groups

Seven of LUM's programs to increase resources within low-income groups have been very successful.

Summer Camp. Mrs. Hanstra and some other volunteers with the Neighborhood Development Project felt that low-income youngsters in the area around Hope Chapel did not have a chance to go to camp as many children in the church did. So, they started a camp program. By the time NDP evolved into LUM, LUM was providing two camping programs: a day camp for 5 to 8 year olds and a week-long over-night camp for 9 to 13 year olds. The day camp was mainly for youngsters who were involved in the Adventure Club program.

The over-night camp was for older kids. The day camp program was turned over to the Greater Lafayette (Southside) Community Center in 1977. In 1976, LUM unsuccessfully tried to integrate the over-night camp into the larger camping program sponsored by Pine Creek United Methodist Camp. From 1977 to 1980, LUM co-sponsored the overnight with the Southside Community Center. Because of the frictions which developed between LUM and the Southside Center over the camp program, LUM once again sponsored its own over-night camp in 1981.

Since that time, LUM has invited youngsters in families LUM has worked with through the Advocates program. Also in 1981, the youngsters' parents were invited to attend a "parents night" at the camp. The response was so positive that LUM staff experimented with a "family camp" program in fall 1981. Its purpose was to make camp an extension of family life and an experience that might strengthen bonds among family members. Thus, by 1981 camp was becoming a more effective means of building relationships with and among low-income people.

As a rule, 50 to 75 children participated in the day camp each year. One hundred to 125 youngsters have participated in the over-night camp each year.

Response to the program has been very positive, indicating it is a service which middle- and low-income groups are willing to support. People who know about the camp, have visited it, or worked as volunteer counselors have attested to its quality.[6] In 1980, the Lafayette *Journal-Courier* carried a feature article highlighting the program, saying the camp "is one of those 'good' stories that just plain brings out the best that is in us as a community."

Volunteer Transportation Service. This program originally was intended to provide a service to elderly and other low-income people who needed transportation to and from places such as the doctor, dentist, and grocery store. The concept of the program expanded in 1973, when—as part of a grant to form the Tippecanoe County Council on Aging—LUM received money to support a mini-bus to provide rides to and from the Senior Center. The transportation service consisted of the mini-bus and volunteer drivers until 1978 and 1979, when LUM made several decisions which changed its approach to transportation.

In 1977 and 1978, LUM participated in a Special Transportation Committee to explore the transportation needs of human service agencies, the elderly, and low-income people. The committee determined that the agencies wanted a more coordinated transportation service for their clients and that a more coordinated system could improve transportation service to elderly and low-income people for whom the community bus system was costly and/or inconvenient. It also learned that the Area IV Council on Aging could provide two new ideas through a federal, Urban Mass Transportation (UMPTA) grant.

In July 1978, a transportation broker proposed that LUM take responsibility for the two UMPTA vehicles and expand its service to local agencies and their clients. The question for LUM was whether to become the provider of transportation for local human service agencies? In August 1978, LUM's board voted *not* to accept the two UMPTA vans.[7]

LUM's decision not to expand its role in transportation precipitated action within local agencies. They did not develop a comprehensive transportation program to serve all of their needs, but several developed transportation systems for their own clients. For example, the Tippecanoe County Council on Aging has used the two UMPTA vans (called "Care-a-vans") and a station wagon to transport elderly people to and from the Senior Center and to doctors, dentists, grocery shopping—things LUM used to do with the mini-bus. LUM returned to its original purpose of finding volunteer drivers to help low-income individuals with special transportation problems.

Records showing the exact number of rides provided and riders served between 1972 and 1975 are not available. However, figures in various documents indicate volunteers and the mini-bus were providing about 600 rides to 100 to 125 people each year during this period.

The records between 1976 and 1981 are much better. With increased reliance on the mini-bus and station wagon and reduced utilization of volunteer drivers, the numbers increased to over 10,000 rides for about 425 people in 1978. After turning the mini-bus and the station wagon over to the Tippecanoe Council on Aging in 1979, LUM relied exclusively on volunteer drivers to meet the transportation needs of low-income people under 60 years of age who called for help. In the last half of 1979, the volunteer drivers averaged about 23 riders per month; in 1980, 13 riders; and in 1981, 10 riders.

County Council on Aging. In November 1972, Rev. Elly mentioned the need for more and better services specifically for the aged during a "minute for mission" presentation at Central Presbyterian Church. The minutes of the LUM board's December 1972 described what happened:

> Following the "minute for mission" message given by Rev. Elly at Central Presbyterian Church in November [1972], Rev. Elly was advised by Dr. George Davis, director of the Indiana State Commission on Aging and the Aged, who was in attendance, that some funds were available for the Senior Citizens' Council that LUM, the Family Services Agency, and the Community Centers had recently been initiating.

The funds were related to the Revised Older Americans Act Congress had just passed. Through that act, funds would be sent from the federal level to the states, and within the states to area and county councils on aging. Area councils would coordinate the funding and activities of the county councils which would provide the services. The federal funds were available; the state agency existed; but the area and county councils had not been formed.

Rev. Elly responded quickly, calling a meeting in February 1973 to discuss the formation of the Tippecanoe County Council on Aging. The announcement of the meeting said the purposes of the council were to:

> gather and maintain up-to-date information on public and private resources available for the elderly; . . . provide an information and referral service; . . . identify and assess services presently available and determine the current needs; . . . develop plans to coordinate and utilize the resources of the community effectively; and . . . be especially concerned with providing increased opportunities for employment and voluntary services for older persons who wish to continue active participation in the community. The Council will assist in preparing requests for grants and applications for Title III project funds, and make recommendations concerning approval.

The 35 people in attendance voted to create the council. At LUM's board meeting in March 1973, "Rev. Elly reported the first quarter of the grant from the Council on Aging, $5,143.50, will include a purchase of a mini-bus."

Thus, within a few months, LUM had been instrumental in forming the Tippecanoe County Council on Aging (shortly before the Area IV Council on Aging was formed). The County Council on Aging now operates a Senior Center on Main Street in Lafayette and is seen as a very active and successful agency providing many important services to elderly people.

Pastoral Counseling Center. Chapter 6 described Rev. Elly's role in developing the Lafayette Pastoral Counseling Center between 1974 and 1977. The center was to provide pastoral counseling for people referred to it by local pastors and/or people who wanted to talk about personal matters with a clergyman but did not belong to a local church. Rev. Elly tried to reserve about one-quarter to one-third of his appointment time for low-income people, whom he would serve either without cost or at a cost they could afford. He was the Center's only staff person until 1979, when the work load was so great that another counselor, Rev. Dr. Paul Kitley, was added to the staff. In 1980, Rev. Elly dissolved his relationship with the center in a dispute with the center's parent organization in Indianapolis, transferring his pastoral counseling services to Mascouten Family Institute and Mental Health Clinic in West Lafayette. The Pastoral Counseling Center continues to function. In 1981, Rev. Kitly reported that the center continues to serve "families of all races from all economic and religious backgrounds . . . The fee is set according to the person's ability to pay . . . no one is turned away because of the inability to pay all or even a major part of the fee."

Shamrock Park. In 1978 the Lafayette *Journal-Courier* ran a series of articles on the deterioration of facilities at Columbian Park, a public recreational park frequented by low-income residents. Rev. Dolphin inquired about the possibility of church volunteers contributing their time and talents to help repair the park's facilities. The head of the parks department indicated that LUM could contribute the most by repairing a dilapidated shelter at Shamrock Park in the low-income, Southside area. Rev. Dolphin organized about 15 volunteers from several member churches (especially the Church of the Brethren). The group successfully repaired the shelter during three weekends in August and September 1978.

Repairs on Wheels. Rev. Dolphin viewed the work at Shamrock Park as a pilot project for a more comprehensive Repairs on Wheels program which he said "would be a small group of church members who would go to the homes of elderly and low-income people and help them unclog their drains and fix their roofs."

The program evolved in late 1978 and early 1979. In 1979, volunteers were involved in 68 repair projects; in 1980, 151; and in 1981, 183. Thus, the program is not large enough to have had a major impact on the housing problems of Lafayette's elderly and low-income populations, but it has been successful in mobilizing volunteers to help 402 individuals and families in about three years. The program received some very favorable coverage in a feature article in the March 3, 1980, issue of the Lafayette *Journal-Courier.*

Grow-a-Row. LUM assumed that many church members and other community residents who plant gardens in the summer often over-plant or could easily grow an extra row of corn, beans, peas, or cucumbers which could be distributed to people in low-income neighborhoods. People with extra food could take it to their local churches (which might integrate the program into a worship service), or they could bring it to a storefront on Main Street where LUM would store the food. LUM would organize volunteer drivers and vehicles for bringing the food into four low-income neighborhoods two evenings per week during July and August. LUM also would select leadership families within the four low-income neighborhoods who would help identify needy people in the neighborhood and see that they got a share of the food. Thus, the program also contained a community development component. In 1981, the program was expanded in two ways: increasing the number of neighborhoods served to six, and creating a separate garden which neighborhood youngsters and others could cultivate.

Though it is quite new, indications are that the Grow-a-Row project might become a very effective means for increasing the distribution of food in low-income neighborhoods. Over 2,000 pounds of food were distributed in the four neighborhoods in 1980; over 3,000 pounds were distributed in 1981. And the response within the low-income neighborhoods has been very positive. Leadership families have cooperated with LUM's staff and carried out their responsibilities of seeing that the food gets to needy people within their neighborhoods. Barb Edwards, who headed the project in 1980, told LUM's board that her experiences with the leadership families dispelled myths about the laziness and selfishness of the poor and confirmed their willingness to work and share resources with one another. The Lafayette *Journal-Courier* praised the project in an editorial, July 22, 1981.

Two other programs have been somewhat effective means for increasing resources among the poor.

Adventure Club. The Adventure Club program was an educational and recreational program created by the Neighborhood Development Project. It served as many as 100 low-income youngsters each year during the early 1970s. However, the number of participants dropped to 85 in 1974 and 65 in 1975. In 1976, Ginny Boncy (who was in charge of the program) suggested the decline probably was due to an overall decline in the number of young children (enrollments in nearby elementary schools also were down), the Southside Center's increased emphasis on youth programs, and some movement of low-income families out of the Southside area. That evaluation also indicated that it was "more difficult than in the past to find and retain committed volunteers."

Thus, LUM explored the possibility of running the Adventure Club program in conjunction with the Southside Center. According to Ginny Boncy's evaluation:

> This cooperation with GLCC was agreed upon by GLCC and was implemented in the Spring of 1976. However, when the program resumed in the fall, attendance was low (about 40) and a sufficient number of volunteers was not found in spite of increased efforts, and GLCC made a decision not to assume any responsibilities for the program. Though they were still willing to house it, they are also providing more recreational and field trip activities for this age children than were before, and there was question whether the program is needed at this time. A factor to keep in mind is that GLCC did not exist when the Adventure Clubs were started in that neighborhood.

In February 1977, Ginny recommended that "the [Adventure Club] program be considered temporarily disbanded until such time as it seems needed." The board agreed. The program has not been reactivated.

Teen Leadership Development. The purpose of this program was to give low-income teenagers opportunities to develop skills in working with and leading other people. About 20 teenagers were recruited each year to work as counselors in the Summer Camp and Adventure Club programs.

Ginny Boncy's evaluation in February 1977 indicated that "the program featured training and orientation sessions, the giving of responsibility and building of self-confidence. This is a very successful program, though largely dependent on the camping program for its existence."

However, there was never any formal effort to measure whether teenagers participating in these programs progressed in their leadership skills, so it is impossible to determine exactly how effective the program was in achieving its goals. And the teen leaders experienced some role conflict (between being leaders and friends of the younger children), resulting in occasional violations of camp and Adventure Club rules.

Overall, the program probably was somewhat effective. It was phased out when the Adventure Club program disbanded, Ginny Boncy left LUM's staff, and LUM conducted the Summer Camp program in conjunction with the Southside Center.

Finally, two of LUM's programs to increase resources within low-income groups have been largely unsuccessful.

Adult Basic Education. In 1970, the Neighborhood Development Project considered a proposal "to hire an intern interested in urban ministry and give him a valuable insight into the problem of the inner city, and to use this intern as a referral agent to link up persons lacking a high school diploma with one of the two existing adult education programs in Lafayette." By fall 1970, the program changed "to meet those needing adult education on their level: giving them transportation, going to their home if needed, one-to-one tutoring situation, and more abstractly to deal with them as persons with a variety of educational and personal needs."

About 20 low-income people and 16 Purdue University students (tutors) became involved in the program between 1970 and 1972. The tutors met with their students twice a week for two hours each time. Minutes of the LUM board meeting in May 1972 indicate that "one of the students was able to take and pass the GED [General Education Diploma] test. Three 15-year-old girls, who would not be acceptable in other area programs, are currently being tutored."

However, the program had difficulties which outweighed its limited achievements. An internal evaluation indicated that the "toughest problem was reinforcing the student to make continued efforts for his GED after the illusion of getting an easy diploma had worn off. Students frequently sought the GED as an easy route to a diploma and often were frustrated with the reality of preparation. This presented the problem of keeping the student interested." LUM records also indicate that "most tutors began with a zest for tutoring. But as time passed, some failed to keep their commitment and missed a number of tutoring sessions. Students of these tutors expressed a feeling of guilt for the tutor's absence. The net result was a negative experience for the student." Finally, the program "failed to have a diagnostic test . . . to give an indication of the student's ability" and, as a result, often used "materials that weren't suited for our students."

The problems of diagnosis and suitable materials were corrected by 1972, but the problems of tutor and student motivation remained. By early 1972, LUM was hoping to incorporate the program into the Tippecanoe School Corporation's Adult Program. That merger occurred and LUM's direct involvement in adult basic education ended.

Community Infant Care Center. In October 1974, a single parent on welfare (call her Judy) approached LUM with a proposal for a Community Infant Care Center for children two years of age and under. LUM agreed to sponsor the center.

In the months which followed, LUM helped Judy obtain $2,300 in support from the Campaign for Human Development and recruit people to serve on the center's board of directors. When the time came for the board to hire a permanent staff for the center, Judy applied. However, the board told Judy she could not be hired because she did not have the credentials required by state law. The board told her it would have to hire someone with a degree in child development. Without Judy's energy and vision, the board lost its momentum and never developed the infant care center.

Emergency Relief

Over the years, LUM has not been actively involved in providing emergency relief, but the two programs it has operated have been very successful.

Centralized Emergency Fund (CEF). In May 1972, the community development division of the Greater Lafayette Community Centers proposed a task force "to assess the annual need among the various social service agencies in the town," "to establish a permanent emergency fund," and "to inform potential contributors." Out of the discussion came a proposal to form a "Community [later Centralized] Emergency Fund."

According to the original proposal, human service agencies working with low-income people could turn to the Community Emergency Fund as a "court of last resort" when they could not find the resources they needed to help anywhere else (e.g., when low-income people had unexpected medical expenses but did not meet the township trustee's residency requirements [at that time] of three years in Indiana and one year in Lafayette). The agencies would screen all cases and refer families and/or individuals to LUM, which would dispense the needed funds. LUM accepted this arrangement in August 1972.

Between 1973 and 1976, contributions to CEF ranged from $3,000 to $4,000. Disbursements grew steadily from $2,155.53 in 1973 to $4,096 in 1976. The number of recipients varied from 72 to 92 per year. The size of the average grant grew from $27.99 in 1973 to $48.76 in 1976.

Between 1976 and 1981, the fund grew in all respects. Contributions were $5,506.95 in 1977 but over five times that amount ($28,528.42) in 1981. Disbursements were $5,666 in 1977 but four times that amount ($24,760.81) in 1981. About 124 families or individuals were helped in 1977, but more than five times that number (594) were helped in 1981. During this five-year period, the amount distributed to each family or person remained quite stable ($40 to $45). Thus, LUM dispensed the same amount of money per applicant, but it reached more than five times as many people.

Advocates. When LUM adopted the Advocates program in 1978, the seven advocates were helping about 13 low-income families or individuals per month (i.e., about 160 per year). Between 1979 and 1981, LUM recruited and trained additional advocates (20 in 1981), mostly from member churches. These advocates helped 580 people in 1979; 1,091 in 1980; and 1,334 in 1981.

Increasing Local Churches' Own Involvement in Social Concerns

Prior to 1977-78, LUM did not sponsor programs with the expressed intent of affecting local churches and the priorities, attitudes, and beliefs of their members. However, by that time many people knew of LUM and many had been involved in its programs or served on its board. Thus, it is fair to ask whether LUM had had any effect on parishioners' outlooks before affecting their attitudes and behavior became a goal.

To examine these issues, I developed several indices: a four-item index of exposure to LUM;[8] a 12-item index of personal involvement in LUM;[9] a five-item index of the importance parishioners attached to social concerns;[10] a four-item index measuring the extent to which people explained poverty in terms of the poor's own attitudes and behavior;[11] a five-item index measuring the extent to which people explained poverty in terms of social policies and practices over which the poor have little or no control;[12] a three-item index of vertical belief;[13] and a three-item index of horizontal belief.[14]

People in the 1979 survey also asked to what extent to which LUM had influenced their lives. The response categories were: "overall, a negative effect," "no real effect," "some positive effect," "a very positive effect," and "one of the most important influences in my life."

Parishioners also were asked how they felt their churches should respond to several social and economic problems: poverty, relations between the rich and the poor, the township trustee system of poor relief, violations of housing codes, race relations, health care for the poor, and general conditions in the downtown area. Respondents were given four choices: "[their church] cannot or should not be involved at all"; "through the efforts of individual members, not church as a whole"; "through efforts of clergy and lay leaders on behalf of church"; and "whole church takes active, leadership role; sponsors efforts to solve the problem."[15]

Through 1979, 54 percent of all church members had had some exposure to LUM; seven percent had served on LUM's board; and six percent had been involved in its programs (see Table 3).[16] People in LUM's member churches had been more highly exposed to LUM, more involved on its board, and more highly involved in its programs, than people in non-member churches. People who had been most highly exposed to LUM also were more involved in its programs and had served on its board more than people who were less exposed to it. People who had been most involved in LUM's programs also were more exposed to its staff and programs and more often on its board than were people who had not been involved. Finally, people who served on its board were more exposed to LUM and more involved in its programs than were people who had never served on its board.

Table 3
EXPOSURE TO AND INVOLVEMENT IN LUM: 1979
(Percent)

	Exposure		Involved in Programs		Served on Board	
	Low	High	No	Yes	No	Yes
Totals	46	54	94	6	93	7
Member Church	33	67	93	7	92	8
Non-Member Church	81	19	98	2	99	1
Exposed	-	-	90	10	88	12
Not Highly Exposed	-	-	99	1	99	1
Personally Involved	12	88	-	-	67	33
Not Personally Involved	51	49	-	-	96	4
Board Member	7	93	68	32	-	-
Not Board Member	50	50	96	4	-	-

Overall, about 21 percent of church members said LUM had been a positive influence in their lives (see Table 4).[17] LUM had had the most positive impact on people in its member churches, people who had been exposed to it, people who had been involved in its programs, and people who had served on its board. And the more intimate parishioners' contact with LUM, the greater its influence. Over 60 percent of the people who had been involved in LUM's programs or on its board said LUM had been a positive influence in their lives.

Table 4
IMPACT OF LUM BY INVOLVEMENT IN LUM: 1979
(Percent)

	Influence			
	Negative	None	Somewhat Positive	Very Positive
Total	7.5	71.9	15.0	5.6
Member Churches	6.6	67.4	18.6	7.4
Not Member Churches	10.3	83.0	5.9	.8
Exposed	5.7	60.5	24.3	9.6
Not Highly Exposed	9.0	85.9	4.7	.5
Personally Involved	7.4	30.9	36.8	25.0
Not Involved	7.1	77.4	11.8	3.8
Board Member	4.3	33.0	29.8	33.0
Not Board Member	7.8	75.7	13.1	3.4

But, what kinds of effects had LUM had? I expected to find that people who had been involved in LUM's programs, had served on its board, and reported that it had had a positive influence on their lives would: attach high priority to social concerns; feel their churches and church leaders should be involved in social and community issues; tend to explain poverty in structural more than individual terms; and have a more integrated system of vertical and horizontal beliefs (see Tables 5, 6, and 7).

Table 5
IMPORTANCE OF CHURCH INVOLVEMENT IN SOCIAL CONCERNS BY INVOLVEMENT IN LUM
(Percent)

	Priority					Method			
	Unim-portant	Somewhat Imp't	Quite Imp't	Very Imp't	Should Not	Ind. Only	Leaders Only	Whole Church
Total	15.6	47.5	33.9	2.9	12.7	42.0	32.3	13.0
Member Churches	15.0	46.1	35.9	3.0	10.5	38.7	36.0	14.8
Not Member Churches	17.1	50.6	29.1	3.2	17.7	49.8	23.7	8.7
Highly Exposed	12.3	44.9	40.0	2.8	10.3	35.3	38.1	16.3
Not Highly Exposed	19.6	52.4	25.9	2.1	15.3	49.2	25.5	10.0
Personally Involved	10.1	37.7	43.5	8.7	3.9	33.3	43.1	19.6
Not Involved	16.7	50.0	31.6	1.7	13.8	43.2	30.6	12.4
Board Member	5.5	43.5	43.5	7.6	2.9	29.0	44.9	23.2
Not Board Member	16.6	48.8	32.3	2.3	13.7	43.2	30.6	12.6
LUM Positive Influence	7.3	40.0	47.3	5.5	5.5	24.6	44.7	25.1
LUM No/Negative Influence	18.8	51.5	28.2	1.6	14.9	46.3	29.2	9.6

Table 6
EXPLANATIONS OF POVERTY BY INVOLVEMENT IN LUM
(Percent)

	Individual				Structural			
	Not Imp't	Somewhat	Quite	Very	Not Imp't	Somewhat	Quite	Very
Total	14.7	42.2	37.2	5.9	44.6	40.2	13.1	2.0
Member Churches	14.7	43.2	36.9	5.1	42.5	41.9	13.4	2.3
Not Member Churches	14.1	39.5	38.2	8.1	49.2	35.6	13.6	1.6
Highly Exposed	14.6	42.3	37.8	5.2	42.0	41.7	13.8	2.5
Not Highly Exposed	15.5	44.2	35.5	4.9	47.3	39.7	12.3	.7
Personally Involved	15.9	42.9	38.1	3.2	40.6	29.7	28.1	1.6
Not Involved	15.0	42.8	37.1	5.1	45.8	40.6	11.8	1.9
Board Member	18.4	40.2	36.8	4.6	34.4	45.6	14.4	5.6
Not Board Member	14.6	42.4	37.5	5.5	46.1	39.9	12.4	1.6
LUM Positive Influence	18.5	43.8	32.7	5.0	33.1	44.5	17.9	4.6
LUM No/Negative Influence	14.5	42.8	37.7	5.0	48.5	38.9	11.6	1.1

Table 7
VERTICAL AND HORIZONTAL BELIEFS BY INVOLVEMENT IN LUM
(Percent)

	Vertical Beliefs				Horizontal Beliefs				Correlations
	Disagree	Uncertain	Agree	Strongly Agree	Disagree	Uncertain	Agree	Strongly Agree	
Total	1.6	3.6	18.4	76.4	7.5	23.8	45.0	23.8	-.01
Member Churches	2.2	4.4	21.2	72.2	4.6	20.5	49.0	25.9	+.07
Not Member Churches	.2	1.4	11.1	87.3	14.6	31.5	35.1	18.8	-.10
Highly Exposed	1.4	3.7	20.1	74.8	5.1	22.1	48.9	24.0	+.05
Not Highly Exposed	1.7	3.5	18.6	76.2	10.6	26.4	40.6	22.5	-.09
Personally Involved	1.4	5.7	21.4	71.4	8.5	12.9	50.0	28.6	+.07
Not Involved	1.8	3.7	18.9	75.6	7.7	25.7	44.0	22.6	-.03
Board Member	2.2	3.2	23.7	71.0	2.2	18.0	57.3	22.5	+.01
Not Board Member	1.6	3.6	18.3	76.5	8.1	24.4	44.5	23.0	-.03
LUM Positive Effect	1.5	4.3	19.4	74.8	3.7	18.2	50.9	27.1	+.04
LUM No/Negative Effect	1.8	3.5	19.3	75.4	8.6	26.0	43.5	22.0	-.03

Priorities. People who had been exposed to LUM attached somewhat higher priority to social concerns and were somewhat more likely to say their churches should be involved in community issues than people who had not been exposed to LUM. The biggest differences were between people who had been personally involved in LUM programs, served on its board, and/or said LUM had had a positive influence on their lives. These people were most likely to attach high priority to social concerns and feel that their churches and church leaders should participate in social and community issues.

Attitudes About Poverty. People who had been involved in LUM's programs, on its board, and said that LUM had had a positive influence on their lives were somewhat more likely than others were to believe that poverty results from the policies and practices of social institutions such as education, business, and politics. However, they were no different from people who had not been involved in their tendency to feel that poverty results from the attitudes and behavior of the poor (e.g., lack of effort or inability to manage money).

Religious Beliefs. There is little indication that involvement in LUM had helped foster a closer relationship between vertical and horizontal beliefs. People who had been exposed to LUM, involved in its programs, on its board, and said it had positively influenced their lives were somewhat more inclined than others were to agree with the three items comprising our index of horizontal belief. And, the correlations between vertical and horizontal belief were positive for those who had been exposed to LUM, involved in its programs or on its board, and said that LUM had had a positive influence on their lives (while the correlations were negative for others). However, the overall pattern indicated that the vertical and horizontal beliefs of people who had been most involved in LUM and said it had had a positive influence on their lives were not appreciably different from those of people who had not been involved. Though the correlations between their vertical and horizontal beliefs were positive, they were very small (e.g., the largest correlation of $+.07$ indicates less than one percent overlap between the two spheres of belief).

Thus, through mid 1979, LUM had had some effect on the priorities of people who had been involved in its programs or served on the board, less effect on their social attitudes, and almost no effect on their religious beliefs. Its effects mainly had been to nurture the importance some church members attached to social concerns and their awareness of the structural factors affecting poverty.

Now, LUM wanted to do more. It wanted to increase local congregations' own involvement in social concerns, make social concerns a high priority for more church members, foster more compassionate attitudes about poverty and the poor, and integrate the vertical and horizontal spheres of belief. Through 1981, LUM had sponsored eight programs in relation to these goals.

Table 8 indicates that LUM has had some success in fostering more social concern within local congregations (mean score = 3.24). The mean score for program development is 3.2 (somewhat effective) and the mean score for priorities, attitudes, and beliefs is 3.3.

Increase Congregational Programs

The Jubilee Christmas Shop and the Grow-a-Row project have been very effective means for stimulating more social concerns programs within local congregations.

Jubilee Christmas. Jubilee Christmas has stimulated considerable activity within local congregations. Each year, 20 to 30 local congregations contribute $4,000 to $8,000 in money and gifts. Moreover, five congregations have run their own Jubilee Christmas Shops. In 1981, two-thirds of LUM's member churches were involved in Jubilee Christmas in one way or another.

Grow-a-Row. The Grow-a-Row project was only in its second year in 1981, but half of LUM's member churches had embraced the program. They engaged youth and/or adult groups in the process of growing produce which they brought to LUM's downtown storage center for distribution in low-income neighborhoods. Some of the churches also have integrated the concept of sharing food with the poor into worship services.

Thirty-nine percent of LUM's member churches have participated in both the Jubilee Christmas *and* the Grow-a-Row program. Another 50 percent have participated in one or the other but not both. Only 11 percent have not participated in either.

The Christmas Project and Repairs on Wheels have been somewhat effective.

Table 8
EFFECTIVENESS OF LUM'S PROGRAMS TO INCREASE CONGREGATIONS' INVOLVEMENT IN SOCIAL CONCERNS

Programs to:	Counter Productive (X1)	Little or No Effect (X2)	Some Effect (X3)	Very Effective (X4)	Mean Score
Increase Church Sponsorship of Social Concerns Programs					
% = 100	-	20	40	40	
N = 5	-	1	2	2	3.2
Raise Priorities, Change Social Attitudes, Integrate Vertical and Horizontal Beliefs					
% = 100	-	-	67	33	
N = 3	-	-	2	1	3.3

Christmas Project. The Christmas Project has been conducted each year since 1972. Between 1972 and 1978, LUM conducted the program on behalf of local churches (i.e., identifying people to be visited, arranging the visits, and purchasing the gifts). During this time, volunteers from 10 to 15 local churches visited as many as 100 to 150 elderly and low-income people each year.

Since 1978, LUM has encouraged local congregations to conduct the program on their own (i.e., finding volunteers within the church, visiting the low-income and elderly people to see what they would like for Christmas, purchasing the gifts, and delivering them. Twenty-one percent of LUM's churches participated in the program in 1981.

Repairs on Wheels. LUM has had some success cultivating volunteer groups within nine percent of its member churches to help fix the homes of low-income people. All have been campus ministry programs at Purdue University. Two other campus groups which do not belong to LUM also have adopted the program. Thus, LUM has not succeeded in getting Repairs on Wheels groups started in community churches, but it has had some success fostering the program within religious programs on campus.

Thirty-two percent of LUM's member churches have adopted either the Christmas Project or the Repairs on Wheels program. Sixty-eight percent of LUM's churches have not become involved in either program.

Finally, one program has been largely unsuccessful: *Integrated Hands.* In 1972-74 (before LUM really defined program development within churches as one of its goals), Rev. Elly talked with members of several member churches on the near Northside to see if their churches might participate in efforts to bridge the racial gap in Lafayette. As reported earlier, Rev. Elly's efforts did not succeed in fostering more church involvement in this area.

Priorities, Attitudes, and Beliefs

Seeds of Vision. The most effective of the three programs designed to affect churchgoers' priorities, attitudes, and beliefs has been LUM's Seeds of Vision conference.

The conference in 1979 consisted of a keynote address by Rev. Donald Bakely of Cross-Lines Cooperative Council in Kansas City; lunch at which participants had to fill out poor relief eligibility forms to eat; eight workshops, and an ecumenical worship service. The workshops were on the following topics: How to get [your church] started [in social concerns]; How to know your community; Social concerns in the rural church; Impact—the importance of legislation; Poverty as a web; Programs in [social concerns] ministry; Housing—Lafayette's problem; and Prison—our response. The conference was held at the Southside Community Center.

The conference in 1980 consisted of a keynote address by George M. Webber (from the East Harlem Protestant Parish); lunch (with a special appeal by Baldemar Velasquez of the Farm Labor Organizing Committee); 14 workshops; and an ecumenical worship service. The workshops pertained to issues such as: the farmworker's struggle in Indiana and Ohio; food and health; federal funds and poverty; racism and racial reconciliation; poor relief; refugees; and how to develop a social concern program within a local congregation. The conference was held at First Christian Church.

About 170 people from 44 congregations attended the first conference, and 250 people from 63 congregations attended the second. These are large attendance figures for church gatherings in Lafayette and especially for gatherings having to do with social concerns.[18]

The conferences demonstrated that there was a large number of people in local churches who felt their churches ought to be involved in social concerns. There was a feeling among those in attendance that social concerns is a normal, church-like activity, not deviant and unchurch-like. In Rev. Dolphin's words:

> One thing the conference did was show that there are lots of other people out there that kind of share some concerns that we have and, "gosh, there's even a few churches that have something going." I notice that now there tends to be an embarrassment [among board members whose churches do not have social concerns committees]. It's sort of like now we know what needs to happen, whereas before I think it was the rare exception . . . [the conference] set up a

pattern that it was important for churches to be involved. And I think that thought is clearly more among us now than it's ever been.

The feedback LUM has obtained from the participants supports Rev. Dolphin's contention. One member of a local church indicated how the attendance at the 1980 conference gave her strength:

> I was struck by the sheer numbers present and the sense of a caring community throughout the day. Sometimes, particularly in the Reagan era, we have a sense of being alone in the struggle for social justice. It was with a feeling of solidarity that we shared with others on this day. The spirit of fellowship was very present as we communed at noon time. To bring us together in such a creative way made me feel 'in touch' with all mankind.

Another person added that the conference encouraged Christians to act:

> People of faith spend too little time acting upon what they say they believe on Sunday morning. Your conferences have allowed us/forced us to face up to and take actions with respect to our religious commitments . . . [they have] helped us to see some of the 'little people' who are doing this kind of work which encourages us to do the same."

And several others told of actions they had taken as a result of the conference. One woman said she and her husband "altered the way we celebrated Christmas this year [1980] as a direct result of suggestions from the 'Living more biblically for less' workshop." Another woman, who chaired the social concerns committee at a local church, heard a workshop leader describe how the leader's church got started in social concerns and reported that "we are now in the process of setting up a system similar to theirs." Another person said that as a result of Baldemar Valasquez' talk on migrants, she "went to the next Public Affairs Committee meeting at the YWCA and encouraged them to look into the farm workers' issue and make recommendations to the YWCA board."

The conference also fostered more social concerns within several local churches. Rev. Thomas Clifton, pastor at First Baptist Church told LUM:

> The "Seeds of Vision" Conference was one of the most motivating and inspirational events of my life. About a dozen persons from our Missions Committee attended the conference, and the "difference" is already being felt. We know we have to respond to the needs. And we are hoping to involve as many others as we can, to reach out in support of existing ministries and in the development of new responses.

At least two other congregations formed social concerns committees largely as a result of the Seeds of Vision conferences. These committees are now actively fostering more social concerns programs (e.g., Grow-a-Row, Jubilee Christmas) within their congregations.

But, the conferences have not affected everyone so positively. One person told LUM:

> . . . all I heard was that the poor were victims and I was the cause of their impoverishment by virtue of being a white, middle-class Protestant consumer. Sorry, but I won't buy that guilt trip.

Not much was heard about impoverishment of the spirit; indeed, the general impression was that the plight of the poor could somehow simply be solved by giving them money and unearned privileges through government resources.

And, the 1980 conference had some negative consequences within the host church. The conference was scheduled for a Saturday when the janitor at the church was to be on vacation. The church property chairman (who would have to supervise the clean-up in the janitor's place) became so upset that, despite reassurances from Rev. Dolphin and the pastor of the church, he resigned. The new church property chairman then became very upset that closed-circuit television sets would be used in the sanctuary as part of one multi-media workshop. Third, though LUM's clean-up crew put all the chairs back, it put too many chairs in some rooms and not enough in others. Fourth, the "church circle ladies" who are responsible for the kitchen and usually prepare meals for church gatherings were upset that LUM wanted to prepare its own low-cost lunch, wanted to serve it in a special way as part of a lunch program, and did not use the women's system for cleaning up the kitchen. Finally, a cup of coffee was spilled on a rug in the church parlor; the new church property chairman had the entire carpet cleaned so there would not be any spot on the rug when a women's class met in the parlor the next morning.

Thus, the conference itself was a great success insofar as the program and most participants were concerned, but caused some friction within a member church—a situation which probably reinforced some church members' views that churches ought not be involved in social concerns. When a seminary intern at the church asked the Social Ministries Committee in spring 1981 whether it would be willing to offer the church facilities to LUM again if it needed a place for another Seeds of Vision conference, he said "the overwhelming reaction was a vehement 'no' and it came from ladies who were involved in the Church Women Fellowship and were down in the kitchen."

The Seed. LUM's newsletter, *The Seed*, "contains several kinds of material: information about LUM, news about programs in member churches, up-dates on community developments affecting churches and low-income people, and appeals for action of one kind or another in response to these community developments."

The Seed was first published in 1979. It is sent to all LUM board members, people in leadership positions within LUM's member churches, and other individuals who express an interest in LUM's work in social concerns. By summer 1981, it was being sent to 1,507 people each month.

The main effects of a newsletter like *The Seed* are the transmission of information, reinforcement of existing attitudes, and stimulation of some action on the part of people who were predisposed to act. And there is some evidence that *The Seed* has had these effects. Pastors of member churches willingly provide LUM with the names and addresses of their leaders so LUM can send copies of *The Seed.* And nobody who has been put on the list by someone else has ever asked to be removed from it. Pastors and other church leaders also have reprinted articles from *The Seed* in their church newsletter (thus multiplying its potential impact). According to Rev. Dolphin, "that happens in some churches fairly regularly. I want it to happen in all churches." Third, people who receive *The Seed* also receive two solicitations from LUM each year: one for Summer Camp and the other for the Centralized Emergency Fund. Rev. Dolphin feels the increased contributions for camp and CEF are indications that *The Seed* is being read and favorably received: it is stimulating behavior which is grounded in attitudes favorable to social concerns and/or will foster such attitudes (research shows that people tend to form attitudes which are consistent with their behaviors [Davidson, 1985a]). Finally, in the 1980 evaluation of all LUM programs, the Program and Planning Committee felt "*The Seed* is most helpful as a means of raising social concerns as a parish priority, influencing church members' attitudes about social issues, and integrating their vertical and horizontal beliefs."

There also are two other indications that *The Seed* has been an effective means for fostering attention to social concerns. A member of the presbytery's Mission and Support Committee in up-state New York was so impressed with what he learned about LUM through the newsletter, he invited Rev. Dolphin to come to New York and explain how LUM has succeeded in fostering social concerns within local congregations. Rev. Dolphin spoke in three different communities, explaining the biblical basis for social concerns and showing how LUM's programs related to local congregations. Rev. Dolphin also feels *The Seed* is partly responsible for the Episcopal diocese of Indianapolis' increased support of LUM. Support has increased since Dennis Sorge, the representative from St. John's Episcopal Church, put the names of diocesan leaders on the mailing list for *The Seed*.

Survey/Consultation. The overall results of the 1979 survey were summarized in a report sent to each church. Each church also received a detailed breakdown of its own responses to each question. Thus, churches could compare their own responses with the overall pattern.

These documents became the basis for a consultation with representatives from the 30 churches which participated in the survey. Each church was invited to send three to five people (preferably the pastor and members of the church's social concerns committee). At the consultation, participants considered two issues: the extent to which their congregations were (not) involved in ecumenical and social outreach programs, and ways in which they might become more involved. Four local church leaders shared their thoughts on each of these subjects, after which representatives from the various churches discussed each issue for about 45 minutes. At the end of the morning, one representative from each church "reported in," describing the situation at his/her own church and some of the things that church could do in the area of social concerns. The participants also were told that LUM was eager to work closely with any congregation which wanted additional help in planning or executing a particular program.

The survey and consultation had some positive effects. Clergy in several local churches built sermons around the results of the survey or included references to it in sermons addressing the role of the church in the world. Fifteen of the 24 member churches invited to the consultation (62 percent) sent representatives (in most cases, two or three representatives). Three of the six non-member churches which participated in the survey also sent representatives. Like the Seeds of Vision conferences, the consultation reinforced the participants' interest in social concerns. The agreement among the four featured speakers (a white Presbyterian, a white Baptist, a black Baptist, and a white Roman Catholic) was a very compelling indication that social concerns can be a basis of interfaith and interracial cooperation. Finally, according to Rev. Dolphin:

> [The message] was that social justice and social concerns historically have been part of the church, but that in present circumstances we don't have the structures set up to make that a part of the church. By our structures, we tend to exclude it. What the consultation pointed out was that we need to find ways to include it. It sets up the agenda in the church to try to get a social concerns committee started.

At Immanuel [United Church of Christ, where the consultation was held], they've never had a mission council. They're on the verge of creating a mission council that's an official—not an ad hoc—structure within their church to deal with outreach and mission and social concern. That's significant.

However, several limitations prevented the survey and consultation from being more highly effective. Only five copies of the results were sent to each church. Second, participation in the consultation was voluntary and nine churches (38 percent) did not attend. Third, none of the participating congregations called LUM to follow up on ideas expressed at the consultation. Finally, conversations between one white and one black church concerning the possibility of meeting again to follow up on the consultation did not result in any concrete plans.

Effectiveness Over the Years

The data in Table 9 point to several conclusions concerning LUM's effectiveness over the years. First, LUM's overall effectiveness has increased, from a mean score of 2.8 in

Table 9
LUM'S EFFECTIVENESS, 1972-81[a]

	1972-77[b]	1978-81[c]
Total Effectiveness	2.8	3.3
On Behalf of Local Churches	2.9	3.3
(a) Alter policies and practices	(2.5)	(2.5)
(b) Cultivate relationships with/among the poor	(2.7)	(3.1)
(c) Increase resources	(3.5)	(3.8)
(d) Provide relief	(3.0)	(4.0)
Within Local Churches	2.5	3.3
(a) Increase programs	(2.5)[d]	(3.3)
(b) Alter priorities, attitudes, beliefs	(DNA)[e]	(3.3)

[a] All scores range from 1 (counterproductive) to 4 (very effective).
[b] Includes all programs started and ended between 1972 and 1977 *and* the mean score for all programs begun between 1972 and 1977 but which continued to operate after 1978.
[c] Includes all programs started since 1978 *and* the mean score for all programs between 1972 and 1977 but which continued to operate after 1978.
[d] Increasing church programs was not an official goal between 1972 and 1977, but it was an operative goal, so it was considered in the calculation of the subtotals and the total effectiveness scores at the top of the table.
[e] Altering priorities, attitudes, and beliefs was neither an official nor operative goal between 1972 and 1977, so it was not considered in the calculation of the total effectiveness scores at the bottom of the table (DNA = does not apply).

the 1972-77 period to a mean score of 3.3 for the 1978-81 period. Second, LUM's increased effectiveness has been most dramatic in its efforts to increase local congregations' own involvement in social concerns, where the mean score jumped from 2.5 to 3.3. Finally, LUM also has become more effective in its efforts to address the causes and consequences of poverty on behalf of local congregations, where the mean score rose from 2.9 to 3.3. Within this area, LUM has become especially effective in providing emergency relief; somewhat more effective at increasing resources in low-income groups and cultivating relationships with and among the poor; but no more effective in addressing institutional policies and practices which perpetuate poverty.

Conclusion

LUM has tried to increase local churches' own involvement in social concerns and to address the causes and consequences of poverty on behalf of local churches. Overall, LUM has been somewhat effective in achieving these goals and its effectiveness has increased over the years. It has been most effective on behalf of local congregations, especially providing emergency relief and increasing resources within low-income groups; it has been less effective in altering institutional policies and practices which perpetuate poverty (though it also has had some success in that area). Although LUM has been somewhat less effective in increasing local churches' own involvement in social concerns, its effectiveness in that area has increased sharply in recent years. It has increased local congregations' sponsorship of social concerns programs, and it has affected the priorities, attitudes, and beliefs of church members who have come in contact with its programs. Appendix B updates LUM's effectiveness through 1984.

Chapter 9 will try to account for LUM's increased effectiveness.

CHAPTER 9
ANALYSIS OF LUM'S EFFECTIVENESS
PUTTING THE RESOURCES TO GOOD USE

LUM's effectiveness has increased over the years. Between 1972 and 1981, it became more and more successful in its efforts on behalf of local churches and in fostering social concerns within local congregations. This chapter uses my theoretical framework to explain this increased effectiveness.

Societal ("Period") Factors

Structural Conditions: Secular Realm

Social Conditions. The nation's interest in social change waned during the 1970s and its interest in reaffirming traditional ways increased (see Chapter 7). I expected this trend would limit LUM's effectiveness. However, it did not. The programs LUM dropped between 1972 and 1981 (e.g., Adventure Clubs) were not controversial or oriented toward institutional change. They were dropped because they were no longer needed or no longer worked. And some of the programs LUM developed during the late 1970s and early 1980s (e.g., Advocates, Public Policy) *were* oriented toward institutional change. For example, LUM became more involved in issues related to the policies and practices of the township trustee system of poor relief.

Structural Conditions: Religious Sphere

Religious Policies and Practices. Chapter 7 showed that the main trend in religion during the 1970s and early 1980s was away from the social action emphasis of the 1960s and toward a more personal-spiritual emphasis. I expected this shift would reduce LUM's effectiveness, but it did not.

The growing religious conservatism was clearly incompatible with LUM's goals of altering policies and practices related to poverty and cultivating more relationships with low-income groups. However, LUM was just as effective in its efforts to change social policies and practices in the 1978-81 period as it had been earlier. And it was even more effective in cultivating relationships with and among the poor.

The national trend toward religious conservatism also was incompatible with LUM's goal of increasing social concerns within local congregations. The growing religious conservatism called for more emphasis on programs to enhance spiritual well-being, not social concerns related to poverty. It also included harsher (not more compassionate) attitudes about the poor. And it sought to reestablish the primacy of personal faith *over* social concerns (not the integration of the two). However, LUM conducted more programs and became more effective in its efforts to foster social concerns within local congregations than it ever had before.

The national trend toward religious conservatism was compatible with LUM's goals of increasing resources within low-income groups and providing emergency relief to low-income families and individuals. It probably contributed to churches' and churchgoers' willingness to support programs which accepted the legitimacy of prevailing institutions and called for charitable efforts to help the poor—efforts which religious liberals and conservatives would say are supposed to flow from personal faith and salvation.

Thus, LUM tended to become more effective in spite—not because—of the national trend toward a more personal-spiritual emphasis.

Ecumenism. According to the evidence presented in Chapter 7, there was a marked decline in interest in ecumenism at the national level. And support for relatively liberal ecumenical groups such as the World Council of Churches and the National Council of Churches waned.

I expected this trend would be incompatible with LUM's effectiveness. Church leaders would be more likely to stress the importance of denominational matters and question the efficacy of ecumenical organizations and activities. However, there is little or no evidence that it had much bearing on LUM's effectiveness. While interest in ecumenism declined, LUM's effectiveness increased.

Resources: Secular Realm

Economic Conditions. Economic conditions deteriorated during the 1970s and early 1980s. People with jobs found it increasingly difficult to make a dollar go as far as it did in the 1960s. And more and more people had no jobs at all.

I expected such a situation would limit LUM's effectiveness. However, indications are that they probably *contributed* to its effectiveness in several unanticipated ways. The deteriorating economy increased the number of people suffering from economic hardship and needing help with utilities, food, medical care, housing, and other essentials. Thus, LUM expanded the Centralized Emergency Fund and the Advocates program. It also put more emphasis on growing food (Grow-a-Row) and helping low-income people purchase food at reduced rates (Food Buying Club). And, these have been effective programs, bringing emergency relief and additional resources to large numbers of low-income people.

Resources: Religious Sphere

Religious Resources. Chapter 7 showed that human and economic resources within the religious sphere declined during the early and mid 1970s before increasing somewhat during the late 1970s. The decline was especially large in liberal Protestant denominations which were the backbone of ecumenical groups like LUM. And as VanderWerf (1976) and Johnson (1980) have indicated, the decline in church resources led to many cutbacks in the support of ecumenical groups and reductions in their effectiveness.

During the early to mid 1970s, LUM leaders felt denominational offices and local churches probably would put more of their resources into denominational and congregational programs and that the support of ecumenical, social action groups like LUM would not keep up with organizational and programmatic expenses. And as the evidence in Chapter 6 indicated, there was some basis for this assumption. Denominational support grew in terms of absolute (current) dollars, but did not always keep up with inflation. United Methodist leaders openly indicated that denominational priorities were more important than ecumenical ones and that, if need be, support of LUM might have to be reduced to meet more pressing, denominational expenses (though this reallocation of support never occurred). And local church support did not grow even in terms of current dollars during the mid 1970s.

Thus, national conditions probably had some chilling effect on LUM's effectiveness during the early to mid 1970s. That effect could be seen in the increased amount of time LUM's board and staff spent dealing with financial—rather than program—issues. It also was evident in LUM's inability to pay for the people and materials the staff felt it needed to conduct existing programs. And it was evident in LUM's inability to afford new programs.

The up-swing in national resources during the late 1970s and early 1980s led to some stabilizing of denominational support for ecumenical and social action groups like LUM. This development provided a context within which groups like LUM could pursue their goals with more confidence that the resources they needed might be available. After LUM's process of administrative succession was completed, the board and staff assumed that LUM could obtain the denominational and congregational support it needed to be effective. And the experiences of late 1979—when churches provided over $10,000 within two months to support the first Seeds of Vision conference, the Centralized Emergency Fund, and the first Jubilee Christmas Shop—seemed to confirm this assumption. The resources *were* there and contributed to the success of these programs.

Justification. Chapter 7 showed that Christianity's prophetic tradition justifying efforts to foster justice and equality persisted during the 1970s and early 1980s, though its spokespeople often were overwhelmed by voices stressing the need for more emphasis on personal faith and salvation. LUM's board and staff spent more time at meetings studying the scriptural bases for social involvement and church teachings related to justice and equality, which provided a sense of *ministry* that had not been expressed as often in LUM's earlier years. The biblical basis for LUM's efforts also began to appear in its explanation of old programs and its justification of new programs such as Jubilee Christmas. It also appeared in the content of *The Seed* and programs such as Seeds of Vision and the survey/consultation, where the purpose was to affirm Christianity's prophetic heritage and its implications for local churches.

The persistence of the prophetic tradition and LUM's greater reliance on it contributed to LUM's effectiveness in the late 1970s and early 1980s, especially its effectiveness in fostering social concerns within local churches. The more LUM drew upon biblical images and stories as bases for its programs, the more church members thought of it as a specifically-religious ministry (not "just another human service agency"). LUM could claim that, regardless of one's socio-political views, the Bible teaches that Christians have an obligation to struggle for justice and equality and to serve the poor. This approach stressed the unifying potential of social concerns. It also reassured churches and church members that LUM's goal was to strengthen the faith and its role in the world—not to introduce liberal, secular humanism into conservative religious groups. As a result, local churches were open to the ideas of adopting one of LUM's programs and/or participating in one addressing the parishioners' priorities, attitudes, and beliefs.

Personnel. Chapter 7 showed that there was an over-supply of clergy during the 1970s and this availability of personnel contributed to LUM's institutionalization, especially its success in finding a new director. It also contributed to the availability of two other ordained staff people and, thus, also affected the leadership dimension of LUM's institutionalization. However, there is no evidence that it had any direct impact on LUM's effectiveness.

Local ("Place") Factors

Structural Conditions: Secular Realm

Political Climate. According to my theoretical framework, the conservatism of the Lafayette area should have stifled LUM's efforts to reform structural conditions affecting poverty, organize the poor, and increase churches' involvement in social issues related to poverty. However, as the political climate became more conservative, LUM became more effective. Thus, contrary to my expectations, the area's political climate did *not* limit LUM's effectiveness.

Structural Conditions: Religious Sphere

Persistence of the Problem. Chapter 7 showed that poverty persisted in Lafayette during the 1970s, as did the lack of church involvement in issues related to its causes and consequences. LUM responded through the Advocates program's efforts to monitor the performance of township trustees, and the Public Policy Network which successfully challenged the county medical association to submit a proposal for a WIC program in Tippecanoe County. The large number of low-income people needing help also led to several programs designed to cultivate relationships with and among the poor (e.g., Advocates, the Food Buying Club), increase resources within low-income groups (the Food Buying Club, Grow-a-Row, and Repairs on Wheels), and to provide emergency relief (Advocates and the expansion of CEF). These new programs have been more effective than LUM's earlier programs were.

The 1976 evaluation pointed to the need for local congregations to do more on their own as well as through LUM. Their lack of involvement has meant that, when LUM has proposed programs such as Grow-a-Row and Jubilee Christmas Shops, local churches have not been able to refuse programs on the grounds of already being heavily involved in social concerns. Through 1981, a majority of LUM's member churches had adopted at least one-third of the programs LUM devised for them.

Cooperation. Chapter 7 indicated that ecumenism was a low-priority item for most church members in the Lafayette area. Interest in church unity and interfaith understanding was especially limited. However, there was an openness to "down to earth" interfaith activities.

This ecumenical situation had some impact of LUM's effectiveness. Local churches' willingness to respond *together* to LUM's programs was an important aspect of its increased effectiveness in the late 1970s and early 1980s. Roman Catholic and liberal Protestant congregations were not only willing to integrate some of LUM's programs (e.g., Grow-a-Row) into their own congregations; they also were willing to work together on several (e.g., Jubilee Christmas Shops). Catholics and Protestants have been willing to attend the Seeds of Vision conferences, listen to speakers from different denominational and theological backgrounds, share ideas in workshops, and join together in ecumenical worship services related to the themes of social concerns—things which might not have been possible two or three decades ago.

Competition. Finally, Chapter 7 showed that LUM has had little competition with similar groups. This lack of competition has meant that LUM could develop programs out in the open, without fear of having its ideas stolen by competitors. LUM also could develop programs for local churches with full knowledge of how many other programs the churches were sponsoring and how LUM's programs might affect them. LUM has not had to deal with the uncertainties which competitive organizations would introduce. And local churches have been able to associate LUM with social concerns related to poverty; they have not had to think in terms of several organizations. All of these circumstances have contributed to LUM's success in recent years.

Resources: Secular Realm

Community Size. Chapter 7 showed that the Lafayette area had a large and growing population. Lafayette's urban character meant there were large numbers of people in the immediate area who could work with LUM and/or utilize its services. Lafayette also performed the central place function which was conducive to LUM's effectiveness. Many people in the rural areas around Lafayette were attracted to the city for a wide variety of services, including these offered by LUM. These conditions have contributed to its effectiveness.

Resources: Religious Sphere

Potential Support Groups. The Lafayette area contains a large pool of Roman Catholic and liberal Protestant churches. The existence of these potential support groups has had some indirect impact on LUM's effectiveness, through it's impact on LUM's institutionalization (particularly its size, economic resources, and leadership). But, it also has had some direct effects. LUM's success in fostering more social concerns programs within local congregations has been due, at least partly, to the fact that the congregations it has worked with most closely have been Roman Catholic and liberal Protestant congregations—not more conservative or fundamentalist Protestant groups. Moreover, a majority of the non-member churches which have attended the Seeds of Vision conferences also have been Roman Catholic and liberal Protestant groups. These groups have been able to justify programs attempting to integrate social concerns into the life of the parish and to cultivate responsibility for the social and economic needs of low-income people. For example, all of the Roman Catholic and liberal Prostestant congregations agreed to participate in the 1979 survey. But several conservative Protestant congregations said "no." If most of the churches in the Lafayette area had been conservative Protestant congregations, LUM almost certainly would not have been as effective promoting social concerns within local churches.

Resources in Potential Support Groups. The substantial resources within LUM's member churches certainly have contributed to the effectiveness of programs it has conducted on their behalf. Churches have given large amounts of money to Summer Camp and the Centralized Emergency Fund, toys and other goods to the Jubilee Christmas Shops, and volunteers to programs such as Volunteer Transportation and Advocates. The quantity and quality of these resources have been keys to the success of these programs.

However, resources have not been highly related to LUM's effectiveness within local congregations (see Table 1).[1] The congregations which have been most willing to adopt programs LUM has created have been the large, *less* affluent churches (100 percent) and the *small*, more affluent churches (80 percent). The least responsive churches have been the small, less affluent churches (56 percent) and the large, more affluent churches (50 percent).

Table 1
CONGREGATIONS' PARTICIPATION IN LUM'S PROGRAMS BY SIZE AND AFFLUENCE[a]

	Less than 1/3		More than 1/3	
	N	%	N	%
Large, Less Affluent	0	0	4	100
Small, More Affluent	1	20	4	80
Small, Less Affluent	4	44	5	56
Large, More Affluent	3	50	3	50

[a]Four member churches were not included in this analysis because they did not belong to LUM when I did the 1979 survey (hence I did not have data on the family incomes of their members) and/or they did not belong in 1980 when some of the programs were sponsored.

Overall, then, church resources have helped LUM achieve some of its goals, but has had little or no bearing on others.

Organizational Factors

My theoretical framework suggested that LUM's institutionalization (especially dimensions having to do with resources) would have positive implications for its effectiveness, but that LUM's effectiveness in pursuing some of its goals would not have important implications for its effectiveness in pursuing others.

Institutionalization

Table 2 indicates how much and what kind of an impact each dimension of institutionalization has had on LUM's effectiveness. Seven dimensions positively affected both goals; one dimension negatively affected one goal; and seven dimensions had no observable impact on either goal.

Table 2
IMPACT OF INSTITUTIONALIZATION ON EFFECTIVENESS

	Effectiveness		
	On Behalf of Churches	Within Churches	Total
Purpose	+	+	2
Economic Resources	+	+	2
Bureaucratization	+	+	2
Leadership	+	+	2
Flexibility	+	+	2
Intra-organizational relations	+	+	2
Inter-organizational relations	+	+	2
Administrative Succession	-	0	1
Membership	0	0	0
Size	0	0	0
Formalization	0	0	0
Complexity	0	0	0
Distribution of Authority	0	0	0
Productivity	0	0	0
Stability	0	0	0

\+ = positive effect
0 = no effect
\- = negative effect

Purpose. Between 1972 and 1977, LUM assumed local congregations were not interested in social concerns and that it would have to "do social concerns" on their behalf. With this orientation, LUM was somewhat effective in addressing the causes and consequences of poverty on behalf of churches.

LUM's decision in 1977 to foster more social concerns within local congregations has had a substantial impact on its effectiveness. Three of the programs LUM created between 1977 and 1981 for this purpose have been highly successful (Grow-a-Row, Jubilee Christmas, and Seeds of Vision), and three have been partially successful (Repairs on Wheels, *The Seed*, and the survey/consultation). Thus, the shift in LUM's purpose has contributed to LUM's effectiveness.

Economic Resources. The resignations of Rev. Elly (September 1977), Ginny Boncy (October 1977), Veronica Blann (July 1978), and Sharon Shrottenbach McCabe (September 1978) resulted in salary savings which allowed LUM to accumulate reserves it had never had. The grant from Lilly Endowment in 1979 provided additional capital. With these resources, LUM was able to develop several relatively expensive programs in 1979: its monthly newsletter, *The Seed*; its first Seeds of Vision conference; the survey of 30 local churches; and the first Jubilee Christmas Shop. LUM's resources also contributed directly to the effectiveness of these programs. For example, LUM could afford to invite excellent keynote speakers for the Seeds of Vision conferences. And written feedback indicates the excellence of the speakers contributed greatly to the conferences' positive impact on those who attended. The grant from Lilly allowed LUM to conduct the survey without cost to the churches.

The effectiveness of these new programs resulted in substantial increases in local church support of LUM (from $15,210.04 in 1979 to $21,340.74 in 1980 and $26,567.60 in 1981). These new resources, in turn, allowed LUM to hire new staff people in 1980 and 1981 to conduct its food programs (Grow-a-Row, which has been very effective and the Food Buying Club, which has been somewhat effective), and to increase the amount of staff time devoted to the highly successful Advocates program (from three-quarters to full-time).

Increased income from "other" sources also has had a direct impact on the effectiveness of specific programs. LUM has sent a letter each fall to people receiving the newsletter, soliciting contributions to the Centralized Emergency Fund. As the circulation and effectiveness of the newsletter have increased, so have contributions to CEF. And as these contributions have increased, CEF has been able to serve more and more people. LUM also has sent a letter each spring, asking people who receive the newsletter to donate "camperships" so low-income kids can attend LUM's Summer Camp. Contributions for camp have increased since the mid 1970s, allowing LUM to invest more into the quality of the camp program.

Bureaucratization. In the early 1970s, there were few job descriptions or personnel policies. Thus, staff members had a great deal of freedom to operate in almost anyway they pleased.

This freedom produced behavior which limited the organization's effectiveness. One staff member was allowed to work at home so she could have time with her young family. Her absence from the office led to a lack of information about her programs and an inability among other staff members to contribute to her work. And, until it became an issue in 1977, another person was allowed to work at home to minimize the risk of a miscarriage. Her absence from the office contributed to breakdowns in communication with office volunteers and frictions with other staff members who had to deal with problems in her absence.

As LUM's board and new director developed greater emphasis on the needs of the organization and staff members' accountability to those needs, effectiveness increased. Staff members were held accountable to job descriptions or personnel policies which had not existed before. Except when their work required being out of the office, they were expected to work in the office. And when organizational needs demanded it, they were expected to help one another. These more bureaucratic conditions contributed to the effectiveness of LUM's programs between 1979 and 1981.

Leadership. Rev. Elly and Rev. Dolphin were alike in many respects (e.g., both viewed their work with LUM as ministries and they both stressed the importance of "initiating structures"), but their differences have had important implications for LUM's effectiveness. Rev. Elly's focused style and involvement in many different programs were largely responsible for LUM's effectiveness during the early and mid 1970s. However, they also contributed to his frustration, sense of loneliness, and ultimately the "burn out" he experienced. Moreover, staff members' tendencies to view their work as a "job" limited LUM's effectiveness.

Rev. Dolphin's style has allowed him to devote more attention to administrative matters and a few programs while challenging board and staff members to view their work as ministry and to initiate new ideas and programs. The result has been a greater utilization of available talent and increased effectiveness.

Flexibility. LUM always has had some degree of flexibility in its programming, dropping the Adult Basic Education program in 1972, the Integrated Hands project in 1974, the Spanish-Speaking Persons Task Force in 1975, and the Community Infant Care Center in 1975.

But, LUM's flexibility was most apparent in 1978 and 1979. During those two years, LUM dropped four older and partially successful programs (Adventure Clubs, Good Friends, Teen Leadership Development, the Human Development Coalition) and one highly successful one (the Pastoral Counseling Center). In their places, LUM added five highly successful programs (Advocates, Jubilee Christmas, Seeds of Vision, Shamrock Park, and Grow-a-Row), four which were partially successful (*The Seed*, Public Policy, the survey/consultation, and Repairs on Wheels), and one (the Mother's Group) which failed. Since 1979, LUM has dropped the unsuccessful Mother's Group and developed the more successful Food Buying Club. The net effect of this flexibility has been to increase LUM's effectiveness on behalf of local churches and within local churches.

Intra-Organizational Relations. Relations among board and staff members have correlated with LUM's effectiveness. When intra-organizational relations were moderately positive between 1972 and 1974, LUM initiated and/or adopted fourteen new programs, twelve of which were at least somewhat effective (five of which were very effective). As intra-organizational relations deteriorated between 1975 and 1977, only two new programs were started, one of which was very effective and one of which failed. As intra-organizational relations improved between 1977 and 1981, eleven new programs were started, ten of which have been at least somewhat effective (five of which have been very effective). While other factors (e.g., leadership) probably had greater causal influence on LUM's effectiveness, there is little doubt that relations among board and staff members have had some impact of their own on how well programs have been conducted.

Inter-Organizational Relations. LUM's relations with churches and low-income groups also have had some impact on its effectiveness.

Between 1972 and 1977, LUM assumed churches were not willing to participate in social concerns and that its role was to "do social concerns" on their behalf. This emphasis fostered a gap between LUM and local churches. Local churches were not sure what LUM was doing with their resources. And LUM's staff and board felt alienated from local churches which they felt did not care about biblical issues of justice and equality.

When LUM expanded its purpose to work more closely *with* local churches, relations with member churches improved, and their willingness to participate in programs increased. The churches with which LUM has been most successful establishing positive relations are the ones which also have participated most in its programs.

LUM has always sought to establish positive relations with low-income groups, mainly through programs intended to serve their interests. LUM's reputation spread gradually among low-income people who received rides in LUM's mini-bus or from a volunteer driver, attended Summer Camp, or were part of the Spanish-Speaking Persons Task Force. However, each of these programs was directed at relatively small and somewhat isolated groups: the aged, school-aged children, and Spanish-speaking people. Thus, when Rev. Dolphin arrived in early 1978, he felt LUM's relations with the poor in general needed improvement.

The CEF program was expanded to serve 400-500 people per year. The Advocates program was created and by 1981 was helping over 1,000 people per year. These programs have increased low-income people's perception of LUM as a group which treats them kindly as it seeks to help them. They have expressed this perception to LUM board and staff members, frequently contrasting their positive feelings about LUM with their negative feelings about township trustees. They also have expressed it by telling their friends to go to LUM. My conversations with low-income people waiting to see an advocate revealed that nearly half learned of LUM from others who had been helped by an advocate. This perception also became the dominant theme in a *Journal-Courier* article entitled "Poor Find a Friend at Urban Ministry" (February 24, 1982). Thus, LUM's effectiveness in serving low-income people has improved its relations with low-income groups which, in turn, has contributed to the effectiveness of its programs.

Administrative Succession. Since LUM did not try to foster social concerns within local churches between 1972 and 1977, the process of administrative succession did not limit LUM's effectiveness in that area. However, it did limit LUM's effectiveness in addressing the causes and consequences of poverty on behalf of local churches.

Rev. Elly was personally responsible for three of the five most effective programs LUM started between 1972 and 1974, and he contributed significantly to a fourth. As he shifted his attention to pastoral counseling and organizational matters within LUM, LUM's effectiveness declined (at least in the short run). Programs headed by other staff members also floundered. Once Rev. Elly's successor was found, LUM turned its attention back to programs, and organizational effectiveness increased.

None of the other dimensions of institutionalization had any observable, causal influences on LUM's effectiveness.

Effectiveness

My theoretical framework suggested that LUM's effectiveness in any one area of endeavor would be relatively independent of its success in any other area. To test this hypothesis, I needed to examine the relationships among LUM's goals: (1) whether LUM's four goals on behalf of local churches have influenced each other; (2) whether its four goals within congregations have affected each other; (3) whether LUM's four goals on behalf of local congregations have influenced its efforts within local congregations; and (4) whether LUM's effectiveness within local congregations has influenced its effectiveness on their behalf. The results are presented in Table 3.

On Behalf of Local Congregations. Three of LUM's five programs to affect social policies relating to poverty have had no observable impact on LUM's efforts to cultivate relations with and among the poor, to increase resources in low-income groups, and/or to provide emergency relief to low-income families and individuals. However, the Revenue Sharing Task Force succeeded in obtaining funds for human service agencies and, thus, increased the flow of resources into low-income families served by these agencies. And monitoring the policies and practices of township trustees has increased emergency relief for low-income people.

Some efforts to cultivate relations with and among the poor have had positive effects on LUM's efforts to increase resources within low-income groups. Organizing the poor into a Food Buying Club has increased the amount of food getting to low-income people. And the Spanish-Speaking Persons Task Force had some positive effect on medical services and police protection available to Hispanics. However, these programs have been only partial successes. And none of LUM's other efforts to cultivate relationships with and among the poor have had observable effects on its effectiveness in other areas.

LUM's success increasing resources within low-income groups has had little or no

Table 3
RELATIONSHIPS AMONG DIMENSIONS OF LUM'S EFFECTIVENESS

	On Behalf of Churches				Within Churches			
	Alter Structures	Organize the Poor	Increase Resources	Provide Relief	Sponsor Programs	Raise Priorities	Change Attitudes	Integrate Beliefs
On Behalf of Churches								
Alter Structures	-	0	+	+	0	0	0	0
Organize the Poor	0	-	+	0	+	0	0	0
Increase Resources	0	0	-	0	0	0	0	0
Provide Relief	+	+	++	-	0	0	0	0
Within Churches								
Sponsor Programs	0	+	+	0	-	+	0	0
Raise Priorities	0	0	0	0	0	-	N.E.	N.E.
Change Attitudes	0	0	0	0	0	N.E.	-	N.E.
Integrate Beliefs	0	0	0	0	0	N.E.	N.E.	-

0   No effect
+   Some modest effect
++ Considerable effect
N.E. Not examined; priorities, attitudes, and beliefs were treated together

effect on other programs it has conducted on behalf of local churches. The exception is the Food Buying Club. Obtaining food at reduced rates has contributed to the willingness of low-income to participate as leaders in the club.

LUM's two emergency relief programs have had important implications for effectiveness in other areas. The advocates' experiences trying to help low-income people obtain poor relief from the township trustees led to LUM's partially successful efforts to challenge the policies and practices of the trustees' offices. Efforts to help people with utility bills led to efforts to challenge the policies of state-operated Project Safe. The Advocates and CEF programs also led to LUM's efforts to foster closer relationships among the poor. For example, families LUM has helped through the Advocates program have been invited to the Jubilee Christmas Shop. Finally, the relief LUM has provided through the Advocates and CEF has enhanced its efforts to increase resources within low-income groups. Children in families LUM has helped through the Advocates program have been invited to the Summer Camp program. And LUM's recognition that a substantial number of CEF requests were for food led to LUM's creation of the Grow-a-Row program and the Food Buying Club—both of which have been relatively successful in increasing the amount of food in low-income neighborhoods.

Social Concerns Within Local Congregations. Feedback from board members whose churches have participated in Grow-a-Row and Jubilee Christmas is that social concerns can bring church members together without a great deal of organizational effort. The experience of working together on a social concerns project has challenged the myth that involvement in social concerns is necessarily divisive and costly, and has increased parishioners' willingness to consider other social concerns programs. For example, Christ United Methodist Church and Immanuel United Church of Christ had such positive experiences working separately on the Grow-a-Row project in the summer of 1981, they decided to co-sponsor a Jubilee Christmas Shop of their own in December 1981. Thus, program sponsorship can influence the priority parishioners attach to social concerns.

However, program sponsorship does not necessarily have this effect. First Christian Church allowed LUM to use its facilities for the 1980 Seeds of Vision conference—an experience which fostered more negative than positive feelings about social concerns. There also is no indication that churches' sponsorship of the Christmas Project or the Repairs on Wheels program has affected the priority parishioners attach to social concerns.

There also is no indication that these programs have had any appreciable effect on either parishioners' social attitudes or their religious beliefs. However, the relative newness of LUM's efforts to work within local churches may contribute to this pattern. Over time, these programs might have more effect.

Some of LUM's efforts to alter parishioners' priorities, attitudes, and beliefs have fostered more church sponsorship of social concerns programs, but others have not. Board members who have grown to appreciate the importance of social concerns and developed a greater understanding of how social institutions impact on low-income people have been instrumental in stimulating social concerns within their congregations.But, LUM's programs to affect parishioners' priorities, attitudes, and beliefs have not resulted in many new church programs. The highly successful Seeds of Vision conference has predisposed churches and churchgoers to social concerns but has not stimulated new programs. The survey and consultation demonstrated the need for more parish outreach, and provoked some sermons on the subject, but did not stimulate new programs. And LUM's newsletter, *The Seed*, has been instrumental in making people aware of programs such as Grow-a-Row, Jubilee Christmas, the Christmas Project, and Repairs on Wheels, but it has been the effort of individual board members—not the newsletter—which has fostered the adoption of these programs within local churches.

On Behalf of and Within Local Congregations. LUM's efforts to alter social policies and practices perpetuating poverty and cultivate relationships with and among the poor caused two churches to withdraw from LUM, thus, limiting LUM's ability to foster social concerns within those parishes. Neither LUM's sponsorship of the Advocates program, nor any of its other programs to challenge the structure of poverty and organize the poor, has not limited its effectiveness in working with any other churches.

In two noteworthy cases, LUM's efforts to cultivate relationships with and among the poor have fostered church sponsorship of social concerns programs. During the early to mid 1970s, LUM tried to increase local churches' contact with the elderly and poor through the Christmas Project. These efforts led to some congregations' willingness to conduct the program on their own. And the first Jubilee Christmas Shop in 1979 was so successful that First Christian Church decided to sponsor one of its own, and Dayton United Methodist Church and Memorial Presbyterian Church of Dayton co-sponsored one in 1980. Immanuel United Church of Christ and Christ United Methodist Church co-sponsored one in 1981.

LUM's effectiveness in increasing resources within low-income groups and providing emergency relief to low-income families and individuals has had little or no effect on its work with local churches. These have been essentially separate spheres of work for LUM.

Social Concerns Within Local Churches and on Their Behalf. Churches' willingness to sponsor Jubilee Christmas Shops and the Christmas Project has fostered some closer relationships with and among low-income people. Their willingness to form Repairs on Wheels groups and to participate in the Grow-a-Row project have increased the flow of resources into low-income areas. However, only six churches are involved in the Christmas Project, only five have (co-)sponsored their own Jubilee Christmas Shop, and only three have developed Repairs on Wheels groups, so the contacts between the churches and the poor remain limited. Moreover, the development of programs within local churches has not produced efforts to alter policies and practices perpetuating poverty or to provide emergency relief to low-income families and individuals.

LUM's effectiveness in changing parishioners' priorities, attitudes, and beliefs has had little impact on its efforts to address the causes and consequences of poverty on behalf of local churches. The Seeds of Vision conference in 1979 did produce the idea of a Jubilee Christmas and, thus, fostered greater contact between churches and low-income people. However, there is no evidence that any of LUM's other efforts to affect priorities, attitudes, and beliefs have had any such impact.

Conclusion

The purpose of this chapter has been to explain why LUM's effectiveness has increased over the years. None of the three structural factors at the societal level (social change, religious policies and practices, and ecumenism) had any major impact. The one secular resource factor at the societal level (economic conditions) had effects which were contrary to my expectations: the worse the economy got, the *more* effective LUM became. Two resource factors within the religious sphere (religious resources and justification) had the effects I expected them to have. As religious resources became more plentiful in the late 1970s and early 1980s, LUM benefited and its programs became more effective. And, as LUM's grounding in Christianity's prophetic heritage increased, so did its effectiveness. The availability of religious personnel had no appreciable impact.

Local conditions had far more to do with LUM's effectiveness. Six of the seven local factors (community size, the persistence of the problem, the existence of potential support groups, the abundance of resources with these churches, favorable attitudes toward interfaith cooperation, and a lack of competition with other groups had the positive effects I expected them to have. One structural factor (political climate) did not have the expected effects.

Finally, organizational factors had important implications for LUM's effectiveness. Eight of the fifteen dimensions of institutionalization had some observable impact. Purpose, economic resources, bureaucratization, leadership, flexibility, intra-organizational relations, and inter-organizational relations contributed to LUM's effectiveness in pursuing both of its major goals. The process of administrative succession temporarily limited LUM's effectiveness in addressing the causes and consequences of poverty on behalf of local churches (though the successful completion of that process allowed LUM to become more effective in the long run).

Table 4
SUMMARY OF ENVIRONMENTAL FACTORS INFLUENCING
LUM'S EFFECTIVENESS

	Period		Place		
	Structural Conditions	Resources	Structural Conditions	Resources	
Secular	0 of 1	1 of 1	0 of 1	1 of 1	(2 of 4)
Religious	0 of 2	2 of 3	3 of 3	2 of 2	(7 of 10)
	(0 of 3)	(3 of 4)	(3 of 4)	(3 of 3)	

By and large, LUM's effectiveness in pursuing any one of its eight specific goals had little or no impact on its effectiveness in pursuing its other goals. However, LUM's success in providing emergency relief increased its effectiveness in achieving all of its other goals on behalf of local churches. And its effectiveness in fostering social concerns programs within local churches contributed to its impact on the priority parishioners attach to social concerns, its effectiveness in cultivating relationships with and among the poor, and its success in increasing resources within low-income groups. Two other goals also had some effects worth noting. LUM's partial success in altering social policies and practices contributed to its effectiveness in increasing resources within low-income groups and providing emergency relief. And its effectiveness in cultivating relationships with and among the poor increased its effectiveness in increasing resources within low-income groups and fostering social concerns programs within local churches.

CHAPTER 10
SUMMARY AND IMPLICATIONS

The mobilization of social movement organizations has been at the heart of this volume. Here I summarize my treatment of this problem using an open system approach (including emphases on structural conduciveness and resource mobilization), and the results bearing on each of the research hypotheses I derived from that approach. Finally, I consider this study's implications for future theory and research on social movement organizations, and for religious leaders interested in ecumenical urban ministries.

Summary

It is more difficult to start social movement organizations (which call on value incentives to change society) than it is to start organizations which use economic incentives to provide services society wants. Among other things, it is hard to find competent people who are willing to donate the time and energy needed to form organizations which are designed to promote change and, thus, are likely to provoke at least some resistance.

It also is more difficult to institutionalize organizations intent on changing society than it is to institutionalize ones which deliver services. People are more likely to question the legitimacy of groups promoting change; they also are more likely to try to "destabilize" such groups.

Finally, it is more difficult to build effective change-oriented organizations than it is to build effective service-oriented organizations. It is easier to "sell" services than it is to "sell" change.

But, social movement organizations have been formed, many have been institutionalized, and some have been relatively successful. For example, several hundred ecumenical urban ministries were formed in the 1960s. Some folded within two or three years, but many persist. Some have been largely unsuccessful, but others have been able to achieve significant changes in society and/or local churches.

These variations among ecumenical urban ministries provoke three questions. First, how and why did these urban ministry organizations get started? What conditions in society and in local communities gave rise to such groups? What kind of people participated in the formation of such groups?

Second, under what conditions could ecumenical urban ministries establish themselves as enduring and viable organizations? What societal, local, and organizational factors contributed most to the institutionalization of ecumenical urban ministries?

Finally, to what extent, and under what conditions, could ecumenical urban ministries achieve their goals? What circumstances affected their ability to stimulate social concerns within local congregations and/or to address the causes and consequences of poverty on behalf of local churches?

I explored these issues while evaluating the Lafayette Urban Ministry between 1975 and 1981. I cannot generalize from LUM's experience to all ecumenical urban ministries, but what I have learned has implications for future analyses of similar groups and for religious leaders who are interested in the church's role in issues related to poverty.

Formation, Institutionalization and Effectiveness

I assumed that the process of organizational formation encompasses all the people and activities involved in the creation of a group which, heretofore, has not existed. The evidence reinforced the view that formation is a complicated process which can take a long period of time to complete. LUM began as the Neighborhood Development Project in 1962, but it was not until the late 1960s that Rev. Elly pressed for the formation of a community-wide, ecumenical urban ministry. It took approximately four more years before the necessary lay and clergy support were secured and sufficient economic resources were obtained. The formal recognition of LUM's formation occurred in December 1971.

I assumed that the process of institutionalizing a social movement organization encompasses eight structural dimensions and seven process dimensions. A highly institutionalized social movement organization has a clear sense of purpose; formulates membership criteria related to its sense of purpose; grows in size; obtains the economic resources it needs to function and build a reserve; keeps written records; develops departments and programs oriented toward achieving its goals; formulates personnel policies stressing organizational needs but also reflecting a concern for the well-being of individual staff people; and develops a decentralized pattern of decision making. It also: succeeds in replacing key administrative personnel; recruits strong leaders; builds a stable membership; is flexible when it needs to be; is productive; cultivates positive relations among its members; and is on good terms with its constituencies.

The evidence tends to support these expectations. The closer LUM got to this model, the more viable it became.

Finally, I assumed that organizational goals are relatively independent of one another. Thus, a group can achieve some of its goals without necessarily achieving others. By and large, the results support this view, though they also indicate that some goals are more closely related than others.

Open System Approach

I used an open system approach in a search for factors to help explain LUM's formation, institutionalization, and effectiveness. Within that context, I drew upon the traditional social movement literature calling attention to structural conditions in society, and the growing literature on resource mobilization. Together, these perspectives suggested seven societal ("period") factors, seven local ("place") factors, and twenty-one organizational factors.

The results support the use of an open system approach. With an open system approach, I looked for conditions outside of LUM which might have important effects on its formation and survival. If I had not taken these factors into account, I could not have explained LUM's experiences as fully as I have been able to.

The open system approach also called attention to the dynamics within social movement organizations. If I had focused on relatively permanent, structural conditions within LUM, I would not have been able to understand how the organization adapted to changing conditions.

With the open system approach, I also considered the role other groups play in determining the effectiveness of organizations like LUM. If I had assumed that effectiveness is a function of conditions inside the group, I would have missed many of the environmental forces that had even more to do with LUM's achievements.

Table 1 indicates how much environmental factors influenced LUM's experiences. Period *and* place factors contributed to all three processes (formation, institutionalization, and effectiveness). Their influences were similar with regard to LUM's formation, though local factors had more to do with LUM's institutionalization and effectiveness than societal factors did.

Table 1
SUMMARY OF ENVIRONMENTAL INFLUENCES
(Number of Factors Having Important Effects)

Factors	Formation	Institutionalization	Effectiveness
Period	7 of 7	3 of 7	3 of 7
Place	6 of 7	6 of 7	6 of 7
Secular	3 of 4	1 of 4	2 of 4
Religious	10 of 10	8 of 10	7 of 10
Structural	6 of 7	3 of 7	3 of 7
Resources	7 of 7	6 of 7	6 of 7

Secular *and* religious factors were important, though factors within the religious sphere had somewhat more impact.

Structural Conduciveness

The results also affirm my assumption that structural conditions in society and in local communities affect the mobilization of social movement organizations (see Table 1). The structural conditions I examined were most consistently related to LUM's formation, but several also had important effects on LUM's institutionalization and effectiveness.

Table 2 summarizes the effects specific structural conditions had.

Structural Conditions in Society: Secular Realm. I expected a *societal tendency to question the legitimacy of its social institutions* would be positively related to formation, institutionalization, and effectiveness; a tendency to reaffirm traditional social arrangements would inhibit the three processes. These expectations were partially supported. The change-orientation of the 1960s contributed to LUM's formation in 1971, but LUM became more highly institutionalized and more effective in spite of the growing conservatism of the 1970s and early 1980s.

Structural Conditions in Society: Religious Sphere. My expectation that *challenges to traditional religious policies and practices* would contribute to the mobilization of groups like LUM was only partially supported. The religious ferment in the 1960s stimulated LUM's formation, but the religious conservatism of the 1970s and early 1980s did not

Table 2
SUMMARY OF FINDINGS ON FACTORS AFFECTING THE FORMATION, INSTITUTIONALIZATION, AND EFFECTIVENESS OF LUM

	Formation		Institutionalization		Effectiveness	
	Expected	Result	Expected	Result	Expected	Result
Period Factors						
A. Structural Conditions: Secular Realm						
Social Conditions (change)	+	+				0
B. Structural Conditions: Religious Sphere						
Policies and Practices (changing)	+	+	+	0	+	0
Cooperation (possible)	+	+	+	0	+	0
C. Resources: Secular Realm						
Economic Conditions (prosperity)	+	+	+	0	+	0
D. Resources: Religious Sphere						
Economic Resources (abundant)	+	+	+	+	+	–
Justification (possible)	+	+	++	++	++	++
Personnel (available)	+	+	++	+	++	0
Place Factors						
A. Structural Conditions: Secular Realm						
Political Climate (liberal)	+	0	+	0	+	0
B. Structural Conditions: Religious Sphere						
Problem (exists/persists)	+	+	++	++	++	++
Cooperation (possible)	++	++	++	+	++	+
Competition (little)	+	+				
C. Resources: Secular Realm						
Community Size (large)	+	+	+	+	+	+
D. Resources: Religious Sphere						
Support Groups (exist)	+	+	+	+	+	+
Resources in Support Groups (abundant)	+	+	+	++	++	++

Organizational Factors

A. Formation Factors

Leadership (secured)	+	+	NA	NA	NA
Lay Support (secured)	+	+	NA	NA	NA
Clergy Support (secured)	+	+	NA	NA	NA
Economic Resources (secured)	+	+	NA	NA	NA

B. Institutionalization Factors

Purpose	NA	NA	+	+*	+
Membership	NA	NA	NA	+	0
Size	NA	NA	NA	+	0
Economic Resources	NA	NA	+	+*	+
Complexity	NA	NA	NA	0	0
Formalization	NA	NA	+	+	+
Bureaucratization	NA	NA	NA	+	0
Distribution of Authority	NA	NA	+	+*	+
Administrative Succession	NA	NA	+	+*	-
Leadership	NA	NA	NA	+	+
Stability	NA	NA	NA	0	0
Flexibility	NA	NA	+	+	+
Productivity	NA	NA	NA	+	0
Intra-organizational relations	NA	NA	+	+	+
Inter-organizational relations	NA	NA	+	+	+

C. Effectiveness Factors

On Behalf of Churches	NA	NA	+	+	0
Within Churches	NA	NA	+	+	0

+ = Positive relationship expected and/or found
0 = No relationship expected and/or found
- = Negative relationship expected and/or found
NA = No hypothesis advanced (not applicable)
* = Especially important factors

have much bearing on either its institutionalization or its effectiveness.

Ecumenism did not play the role I expected it to play. Interest in ecumenism during the 1960s probably contributed to the formation of ecumenical groups like LUM. However, while interest in ecumenism declined during the 1970s and early 1980s, LUM became more highly institutionalized and increasingly effective.

Structural Conditions at Local Level: Secular Realm: The evidence did not support my expectation that a *liberal political climate* would be more conducive to mobilization than a conservative climate would be. LUM was formed and became institutionalized and increasingly effective in an area with a very conservative political climate. The ecumenical urban ministry in Memphis also was formed and has functioned in a conservative climate (Takayama and Darnell, 1979).

Structural Conditions at Local Level: Religious Sphere. The problem which triggered LUM's formation was local churches' habit of not dealing with the causes and consequences of poverty. The *persistence of this problem* also was one of the reasons LUM was able to become a more viable and effective organization over time. Takayama and Darnell (1979) also found that churches' non-involvement in poverty and racial issues contributed to the formation of the ecumenical urban ministry in Memphis.

As I expected, the considerable *interfaith cooperation* in the Lafayette area prior to LUM contributed to LUM's formation. And, though interest in ecumenism may have declined during the 1970s, many of the local congregations which had been most ecumenical over the years continued to work together, a condition which contributed to LUM's institutionalization and effectiveness.

I assumed that the *lack of competition* with other groups with similar goals would contribute to LUM's mobilization. The evidence supports this hypothesis.

Overall, local structural factors were more important than societal structural factors. Nine of my 12 hypotheses concerning local structural factors were supported, compared to only three of nine hypotheses concerning societal conditions. Also, structural conditions within the religious sphere were more important (11 of 15 hypotheses) than structural conditions in the secular sphere (one of six hypotheses).

Resource Mobilization

The resource mobilization perspective suggests that two conditions are necessary for social movement organizations to be formed, institutionalized, and effective: resources must be available, and they must be mobilized. Groups must secure the resources they need, maintain them over time, and put them to good use. The evidence also is consistent with this approach.

Table 1 indicated that the availability of resources affected all of LUM's experiences. Table 2 specifies some of these effects.

Societal Resources: Secular Realm. I expected *economic prosperity* would be positively related to formation, institutionalization, and effectiveness; a poor economy would tend to stifle these processes. These expectations were only partially supported. The economic prosperity of the 1960s contributed to LUM's formation. However, the economic downturn in the 1970s had little or no impact on LUM's institutionalization and *contributed* to LUM's increased effectiveness.

Societal Resources: Religious Sphere. I expected *an abundance of human and economic resources within the religious sphere* would contribute to the mobilization of groups like LUM. The abundance of religious resources in the 1960s did foster LUM's formation in 1971. The decline in religious resources during the early to mid 1970s probably limited LUM's institutionalization and effectiveness during that period, and the increase in resources was conducive to LUM's institutionalization and increased effectiveness during the late 1970s and early 1980s.

My expectation that *an ideological basis justifying social reform* would favor formation, institutionalization, and effectiveness was supported. Christianity's prophetic tradition was used to justify LUM's formation in the late 1960s and early 1970s. And as LUM increasingly called upon that heritage to explain its goals and programs during the late 1970s and early 1980s, the organization became more highly institutionalized and increasingly effective.

Resources at Local Level: Secular Realm. As I expected, *Lafayette's urban characteristics* contributed to LUM's mobilization. This finding compares favorably with the urban character of Memphis, where another ecumenical urban ministry was studied (Takayama and Darnell, 1979).

Resources at Local Level: Religious Sphere. Roman Catholic and liberal Protestant congregations accounted for over half of the churches and churchgoers in Tippecanoe county. In accordance with my expectations, they played a disproportionate role in LUM's formation, institutionalization, and effectiveness. The same has been true for the ecumenical urban ministry in Memphis (Takayama and Darnell, 1979).

The data also were consistent with my expectation that *support groups would have to have substantial resources* for groups like LUM to be mobilized. The abundance of resources in LUM's member churches contributed to its formation, institutionalization, and its effectiveness on behalf of churches (though not its effectiveness within them).

Thus, resource factors at the societal and local levels were about equal in impact. Nine of the 12 hypotheses concerning societal resources factors were supported and, in a tenth case (the impact of economic conditions on effectiveness), the factor was important but its influence was opposite to my expectations. All nine of my hypotheses concerning local resources factors were supported. Moreover, resources in both the secular realm and the religious sphere were important. Five of six secular resource factors had some impact, as did 14 of 15 religious resource factors.

The resource mobilization perspective also stresses the need for organizations to mobilize these resources (see Table 2).

Organizational Factors Affecting Formation. Leadership, lay and clergy support, and *economic resources* were important factors in LUM's formation. Rev. Elly's commitment and competence were key ingredients. Lay support came from highly educated, relatively liberal, professionals and spouses who felt they and their churches ought to be involved in social concerns. Clergy support came from a small number of relatively young, Presbyterian colleagues who (compared to other clergy in Lafayette) were somewhat more community-oriented in their conceptions of their ministries, somewhat more liberal politically, and somewhat more likely to feel that support of NDP and LUM was in their professional self interest. Theologically, they were neither more liberal nor more conservative than other mainline Protestant and Roman Catholic clergy. Finally, LUM obtained the resources it needed from denominational bodies, local congregations, and community organizations.

Organizational Factors Affecting Institutionalization. I expected that six dimensions of institutionalization would play particularly important roles in LUM's overall institutionalization. The results indicated that the four most important dimensions were *leadership, purpose, administrative succession,* and *economic resources.* Staff and board leadership combined to affect all other dimensions of LUM's institutionalization. Rev. Elly's more focused style of leadership was effective during LUM's formative years, but Rev.

Dolphin's more distributed style was more compatible with LUM's needs in the late 1970s and early 1980s. Board leadership—especially the leadership of highly educated, liberal, professionals—also was crucial. The clarification of LUM's goals (especially its increased emphasis on promoting social concerns within local churches) also contributed to its viability. LUM's success in recruiting Rev. Dolphin also was a key to its institutionalization—a key which many other ecumenical urban ministries did not have. Finally, LUM was able to obtain the economic resources it needed to pay its staff, conduct its programs, and develop a cash reserve.

Other factors which contributed to LUM's institutionalization were membership, size, complexity, bureaucratization, distribution of authority, stability, productivity, intraorganizational relations, and inter-organizational relations.

LUM's effectiveness in achieving its goals also contributed to its institutionalization. As expected, its effectiveness within local congregations contributed more than its effectiveness on behalf of local congregations, though both were important.

Organizational Factors Contributing to Effectiveness. Eight dimensions of institutionalization contributed to LUM's effectiveness: its increasingly clear sense of *purpose, economic resources, bureaucratization, success in replacing Rev. Elly, staff and board leadership, flexibility, positive relations within the group*, and *positive relations with constituent groups.*

The evidence also confirmed my expectation that LUM's *effectiveness* in achieving any one of its goals would be largely independent of its success in achieving its other goals. However, success in increasing congregations' own involvement in social concerns and providing emergency relief on their behalf had some impact on LUM's overall effectiveness.

In short, the theoretical framework I used to examine LUM was quite useful, though the results indicate several areas where modifications could be made.

Implications

These findings have important implications for future theory and research on social movement organizations (especially ecumenical urban ministries).

Theory

Though a closed system approach may be appropriate for some types of organizational analysis, it is not an appropriate mode for analyzing the formation, institutionalization, and effectiveness of social movement organizations. A closed system approach would not allow one to examine the societal and local conditions which affect the likelihood of social movement organizations being formed. It also would not permit analysis of the contextual factors which affect their viability. Finally, it would overlook the impact other people and groups have on organizational effectiveness.

Sociologists interested in the mobilization of social movement organizations are much better off using an open system approach. As this study has shown, that approach expands the researcher's vision to include societal factors which increase and decrease the likelihood that social movement organizations will be formed at a given period in time and in particular localities. It ensures that the analyst gives proper credit to environmental influences which transcend organizations and their individual members. It also reduces the risk (evident in some of the literature on charismatic leaders) that analysts might give too much credit to individuals involved in the process of starting social movement organizations (or too much blame, should the organizations not be formed).

The open system approach also alerts sociologists to the role societal and local factors play in social movement organizations' efforts to survive and become viable parts of the social fabric. As the evidence from this study suggests, environmental factors have important implications for the institutionalization of social movement organizations. Structural conditions and the expansion and contraction of resources can mean the difference between organizational vulnerability and vitality.

Finally, the open system approach fosters an awareness of how much organizational effectiveness depends on the responses of people outside the organization. Researchers need to understand how other groups' positive and negative reactions can affect the achievement of organizational goals.

Thus, if I were to do another study of social movement organizations, I once again would use an open system approach.

Within this context, I also would stress the value of combining two theoretical traditions: structural conduciveness and resource mobilization. My results have reaffirmed the importance of structural conditions in society and, especially, in local communities. To overlook these factors would be a major mistake. They help explain why resources are mobilized in some contexts but not others. But, the results also reaffirm the importance of resource mobilization. One needs to consider resources if one is to explain why some seemingly conducive contexts give rise to social movement organizations while others do not.

Thus, one implication of this analysis is to caution against a tendency to pit one of these theoretical approaches off against the other. Rather than choosing one or the other, we ought to seek some integration of the two.

Structural Conduciveness. On the basis of what I've learned in this project, I would assume that some structural conditions have more overall impact than others. For one thing, I would assume that, when it comes to explaining groups like LUM, local factors are more important than societal factors. The most important local structural conditions appear to be the existence/persistence of a problem needing resolution, the willingness of potential support groups to cooperate, and the absence of competition with other organizations with similar goals. Societal factors are important insofar as organizational formation is concerned, but have less impact on the institutionalization and effectiveness of groups like LUM.

I also would assume that structural conditions within the religious sphere are more important than factors in the secular realm. Religious conditions which seem especially important are churches' failure to deal with the causes and consequences of poverty, cooperation among potential support groups, and a lack of competition with similar groups. Religious conditions at the societal level may have important implications for the formation of ecumenical urban ministries, but do not have much impact on their institutionalization or effectiveness. Secular factors at the societal level (social change) may only affect formation, and secular conditions at the local level (political climate) may have little or no impact.

Resource Mobilization. Though structural conduciveness is an important consideration, it is not sufficient. Organizations also must be able to secure, organize, use, and maintain the resources they need to function. If they do not mobilize these resources, they have little or no chance of becoming viable and successful organizations.

If I were to do another study of ecumenical urban ministries, I would assume that the availability of resources is even more important than structural conditions. Resources at all levels (societal and local) and of all types (secular and religious) have important implications.

The resources which seem to affect all three processes (formation, institutionalization, and effectiveness) are human and economic resources within the religious sphere, religious justification for social reform, an urban population, the availability of potential support groups, and substantial resources within these groups. Those which affect one or two of the processes are the nation's economy and the availability of leaders.

But, all these resources must be mobilized. Ecumenical urban ministries must attract capable leaders, gain the support of volunteers who share their objectives, and secure sufficient economic resources if they are to be formed. This study and others (e.g., Oberschall, 1973; Snow, Zurcher, and Ekland-Olson, 1980) indicate that social networks are important mechanisms in the mobilization of these resources.

Revising my initial expectations about institutionalization, I now would assume that four dimensions are most important: leadership, purpose, administrative succession, and economic resources (in that order). They seem to have the greatest impact, though several other dimensions also cannot be overlooked. I would continue to assume that organizational effectiveness also impacts on institutionalization. The more successful a social movement organization is in achieving its goals, the more likely it is to become a viable organization in the future.

Finally, several organizational factors need to be considered if one wants to explain the effectiveness of social movement organizations. One needs to examine the extent to which a group has been institutionalized, paying special attention to the group's sense of purpose, economic resources, the extent to which bureaucratization has occurred, leadership, flexibility, intra-organizational relations, and inter-organizational relations. Other factors also have affected LUM's success over the years, but these seemed to be especially important.

One should *not* assume that an organization's success in achieving some goals will necessarily affect success in achieving others. A better assumption is that effectiveness in any one area is relatively independent of effectiveness in any other area. If success in one area spills over to another, it is likely to be the result of circumstances that need to be studied (and not the result of some "natural" process of organizational integration). The two goals which might have the most effect on others are fostering social concerns programs within local churches and providing emergency relief on behalf of churches.

Research

This analysis suggests several lines of research, all of which would permit the testing and further refinement of the theoretical reformulations stated above.

One possible direction for future research is to examine the formation, institutionalization, and effectiveness of other ecumenical urban ministries. Just as Takayama and Darnell's (1979) analysis of MIFA helped sharpen the focus of my study of LUM, the theoretical reformulations growing out of this study could provide a framework for examining similar organizations in other communities. The testing and retesting of an open system approach stressing structural conduciveness and resource mobilization could contribute to the development of an even more precise understanding of ecumenical urban ministries.

These studies could take several forms. Some researchers might wish to conduct case studies, as Takayama and Darnell and I have done. There are many such organizations around the country, but sociologists know relatively little about them. Case studies would produce a great deal of additional information about the cities where they are located, the ways in which they have been organized, and the goals they are attempting to pursue. They also would give us some feeling for the extent to which the theoretical approach outlined above is meaningful to all ecumenical urban ministries or only certain ones.

A second type of research would provide even more direct evidence on the variations among urban ministries. As Takayama (1977, 1983) has suggested, sociologists also could conduct longitudinal analyses of several ecumenical urban ministries. These studies might lack the qualitative depth of case studies, but they would yield important information about organizational types, how the types operate, and the extent to which they are affected by the same forces we have examined. They also would lend themselves to statistical analyses of the relative importance of various factors (something I have not been able to do with the precision I would like).

Yet another line of research would involve analyses of social movement organizations in other institutional spheres. One could study movement organizations in the spheres of family, education, work, politics, and leisure. Once again, these studies could be case analyses and/or surveys. Whatever form they might take, they could indicate the extent to which the theoretical framework outlined above is applicable to other substantive areas. To the extent it is, it could become an element in the development of a more general theory concerning the mobilization of social movement organizations within spheres.

Finally, researchers could look into social movement organizations which cut across spheres. Groups in this category deal with issues such as civil rights, peace, aging, the environment, welfare rights, and labor (Perrow, 1979). It is not clear how these groups compare descriptively with other types of social movement organizations. Nor is it clear whether they face similar, or very different, problems related to formation, institutionalization, and effectiveness. Finally, it is not clear whether the theoretical approaches used to study religious (or other institutional) groups can be generalized to these groups. We must answer these questions before we fully understand the mobilization of social movement organizations.

Policy

Several policy implications for religious leaders emerge from the study of ecumenical urban ministries as social movement organizations. The assumption that urban ministries are different from established religious organizations suggests they have special problems which many other religious groups do not have. They have the special problem of finding leaders who have the commitment and competence needed to lead organizations that want to change the world around them. They also have the special problem of trying to become viable while also trying to change some of the very groups they hope will support them (i.e., "biting the hand that feeds them"). Finally, they have the special problem of trying to achieve goals calling for reform of policies and practices which other aspects of society tend to reaffirm.

Thus, whenever denominational, congregational, and ecumenical leaders evaluate urban ministries, they must be careful to use criteria which are appropriate to social movement organizations, and not to simply superimpose criteria used to evaluate all other religious organizations.

Formation. The results offer some guidance to people considering the formation of ecumenical urban ministry groups in other communities. It is not surprising that urban ministry groups like LUM sprang up in many communities during the mid to late 1960s. Most all the period conditions were ripe for it. And, many localities had the characteristics and individuals needed to create such groups. Thus, groups similar to LUM also were formed in communities such as Memphis (Takayama and Darnell, 1979). If all the societal and local factors converge again at some future point, the time once again would be ripe to form such groups. These groups might not take exactly the same form, but groups with similar purposes probably could be formed.

If none of these factors exist at any particular time or place, it is very unlikely that groups like LUM could be formed. If the national context were not conducive to it; if the area were rural; if religious conditions were not conducive to it; and if the right kinds of individuals did not live in the area, it would be very difficult to start an ecumenical urban ministry such as LUM.

Finally, between these two extremes are situations where *some* favorable conditions exist but others do not. If the period conditions existed, but the local conditions did not, groups such as LUM probably could not be formed. The national context would be favorable, but the local resources needed to form such a group simply would not exist.

If the national conditions were not favorable (e.g., as I write in 1984), but local conditions were, it still might be possible to form groups such as LUM. The absence of a favorable national context would increase the difficulty of starting such groups in local communities. But, if the local conditions are favorable, it still might be possible to create an urban ministry. The right conditions would be the following:

1. a large, urban population
2. the existence of the problem (lack of church involvement in issues related to poverty)
3. the existence of several Roman Catholic and liberal Protestant congregations
4. abundant resources in these congregations
5. a willingness among these congregations to work together and share their resources
6. a lack of competition with other ecumenical groups trying to increase churches' involvement in social concerns

Four other factors pertaining to the incipient group also would be important. One is having committed and competent leadership. It is significant that both Rev. Elly and Rev. Dolphin had urban ministry experiences during their seminary training. These experiences heightened their commitment and increased their competence. If seminaries cultivate such experiences for their students, they can contribute to the formation of ecumenical urban ministries like LUM. If they do not offer such programs, they choke off one of the essential factors needed to form such groups.

Highly educated, relatively liberal professionals and spouses who believe they and their churches ought to be involved in social concerns also can play an important role in the formation of groups like LUM. These people are a relatively small percentage of all churchgoers and are only a subset of affluent members, but they can be a potent force when their talents and attitudes are channeled into activities related to social concerns. They may not get as excited about some other aspects of parish life, but they may be a critical source of ideas and energy in the area of social concerns. Religious leaders should cultivate and call upon their abilities. It would be a major loss to the church if they failed to do so.

The findings also indicate that leaders of ecumenical urban ministries cannot engage in such challenging work alone. They are likely to turn to colleagues in their denomination—especially others who have worked in other aspects of church life and have a community-oriented concept of ministry—for support. This support system may be a key factor in the leader's ability to carry on "when the goin' gets tough." The lack of such a network might contribute to the "burn out" among leaders of such groups and the premature demise of the organizations they are trying to form.

Finally, leaders of ecumenical urban ministries must secure the economic resources their organizations need to function. It is best that they look to denominational agencies, local congregations, and individuals for support. These sources are most closely related to the ministries' goals, are likely to have resources, and form a natural social network for the people who are most likely to participate in ecumenical urban ministries.

Each of these local and organizational factors seem to contribute to the formation of groups like LUM. If they were present, they might be able to overcome the negative impact of an unfavorable national context.

Institutionalization. The results also offer some guidance to people who have an interest in institutionalizing urban ministry organizations. First, religious leaders could use my multi-dimensional approach to institutionalization to evaluate urban ministries. They could monitor changes in components such as organizations' sense of purpose, membership criteria, size, resources, and productivity quite easily. They also could assess more qualitative matters such as styles of leadership, intra-organizational relations, and inter-organizational relations.

With this scheme, they could detect patterns that might be problematic. I argued that institutionalization would be difficult, if not impossible, if ecumenical urban ministries: have an unclear sense of purpose; have membership criteria that are not related to their sense of purpose; fail to attract new members; do not secure the resources they need to meet expenses and build some reserves; are too informal in their record keeping; do not cultivate new committees and programs; are too bureaucratic or not bureaucratic enough; are too highly (de)centralized; fail to replace their key administrative staff; lack strong staff and board leadership; experience rapid turnover or losses among their members; are not flexible; are unproductive; are dominated by lack of respect, avoidance, and conflict among their members; and experience strained relations with constituent groups.

On the other hand, ecumenical urban ministries with the following characteristics are likely to survive and be viable organizations: a clear sense of purpose; membership criteria based on a clear sense of purpose; a growing number of members; resources which exceed expenses; formal records; a variety of committees and programs; a balanced approach to organizational needs and the needs of individual members; some centralization of authority but a significant sharing of authority among members; success replacing key administrators; strong staff and board leadership; stability among members; flexibility; productivity; positive relations among members; and positive relations with constituent groups.

A variety of national, local, and organizational factors probably contributed to the demise of many ecumenical urban ministries during the 1960s and 1970s. But groups such as LUM can be institutionalized even in the context of a poor economy and a national mood of social and economic conservatism. Second, national religious conditions (especially the availability of resources, personnel, and an ideological justification for reform) also need to be considered. If these conditions exist, the chances of institutionalizing a group such as LUM are improved; if they do not exist, the chances of institutionalization occurring are seriously limited. But, local conditions are even more important, especially the six listed above in our discussion of organizational formation.

Finally, ecumenical urban ministries can have some control over their own institutionalization. Staff leadership may have its greatest impact on an organization's size, economic resources, administrative succession, complexity, stability, productivity, intra-organizational relations, and inter-organizational relations. Board leadership may affect virtually all structural dimensions (except perhaps complexity) and three of seven process dimensions (administrative succession, intra-organizational relations and inter-organizational relations). A clear understanding of the organization's official goals is crucial, along with a close correspondence between its official and operative goals. The organization also must succeed in replacing key administrative personnel with people whose leadership styles are compatible with organizational needs. It must seek and obtain economic resources it needs from groups which are directly related to its purpose, and see that its expenses are less than its income, so it can cultivate some reserves for use in emergency situations. Finally, it must be able to demonstrate success in achieving its goals.

The more of these conditions which exist, the greater the chances are of institutionalizing groups like LUM. Other factors are not totally unimportant, but these conditions may provide the keys to the development of viable ecumenical urban ministries.

Effectiveness. Societal factors have some impact on effectiveness. A bad economy can have multiple effects on a group like LUM, but—contrary to our expectations—the net effect may be to *increase* effectiveness. Though religious leaders might bemoan such trends for other reasons, they might find they have desirable implications for their efforts to increase local churches' involvement in social concerns related to poverty. An abundance of religious resources and the existence of an ideological justification for social reform also may contribute to the effectiveness of groups like LUM.

However, the results suggest that the effectiveness of urban ministries like LUM is more a result of factors which "are closer to home." The chances of success are greatest in communities with large, urban populations, where churches are not involved in social concerns, where there are several Roman Catholic and liberal Protestant churches which are willing to share their resources, and where there is a lack of competition with other ecumenical groups trying to increase churches' involvement in social concerns.

Several factors within urban ministry groups also are important. The clarity of an organization's official and operative goals has important implications for its effectiveness, as does the adequacy of the economic resources it obtains from its support groups. The more the group can balance its organizational needs and the needs of its individual members (bureaucratization), the more successful it is likely to be. The replacement of administrative staff is crucial, as is staff and board leadership. The group ought to be flexible in its programming so it can respond to changing conditions within the community, local churches, and low-income groups. Relationships within the group and with other constituent groups also ought to involve respect, trust, and cooperation (though some conflict with other groups may be desirable, even required, in relation to the achievement of particular goals).

Finally, while there are no necessary connections among urban ministry goals, some goals may have more impact on a group's overall effectiveness than others. The most important goals seem to be fostering social concerns programs within local congregations, and providing emergency relief on their behalf. Two other goals which might have some spill-over effect would be altering social policies and practices which perpetuate poverty, and cultivating relations with and among the poor. The inter-relation of these, and other dimensions of organizational effectiveness, would be increased to the extent that religious leaders deliberately build in ways in which one program might lead to others (as LUM has done with the Advocates program). Any such connections between programs are desirable because they enhance specific programs and contribute to the overall effectiveness of the group. Isolated programs (e.g., service-oriented programs such as Volunteer Transportation) may require enormous resources but may not do a great deal to enhance a group's overall effectiveness.

This analysis also suggests some programmatic guidelines for leaders of urban ministries with goals similar to LUM's. By their very nature, ecumenical urban ministries tend to be reform oriented. They seek changes in local communities, low-income groups, and local congregations. However, LUM's experience suggests it also is wise to complement this change orientation with service-oriented programs. Low-income people need assistance as well as advocacy. Local churches need to be reinforced as well as reformed in the area of social concerns. Some combination of service and change also might promote institutionalization and effectiveness. As Takayama (1979) has noted, purely change-oriented urban ministry which focuses exclusively on *issues* would be vulnerable, given its dependence on local congregations which focus more on *solidarity.*

Most of LUM's efforts to change policies and practices in the community have focused on agencies related most closely to the consequences and victims of poverty (e.g., human service agencies, poor relief). Moreover, LUM's approach in this area has been to express its intent to assist or strengthen these groups without threatening them. Other urban ministry groups also should be able to conduct programs such as the Revenue Sharing Task Force and the Public Policy Network with considerable assurance that such efforts would be well received by the community as a whole, including members of local churches.

LUM has focused less attention on reforming policies and practices in the economic and political spheres. However, in spring 1981, LUM's board discussed the pros and cons of moving more in this direction (especially in regard to changing the way the township trustee system of poor relief is run). Board members generally were willing to support more programs in the economic and political spheres, but they also seemed conscious of two potential problems. First, some church members believe the poor are responsible for their own problems and, thus, might not appreciate LUM's involvement in the economic and political spheres. Second, some church members and others in the community might perceive any efforts to change economic and political policies as efforts to tear down the system rather than build it up. As Appendix B shows, both of these reactions have occurred. But, as LUM's experience also shows, ecumenical urban ministries can deal with these reactions if they explain that economic and political reform are necessary parts of a well-rounded program, use Christianity's prophetic heritage to explain their actions, and demonstrate how the poor are victims of injustice.

With regard to cultivating closer relationships with and among the poor, LUM has been most successful with projects, such as Jubilee Christmas Shops, which LUM conducts on its own, which LUM's staff takes the lead in creating, when LUM's staff is most excited about the concept of program, and when the project is relatively short-term. Ecumenical urban ministries could develop similar projects in the future with some confidence that they would be quite effective.

LUM has been less successful with projects such as Good Friends and the Christmas Project which its staff is less excited about and gives low priority, with projects such as the Spanish-Speaking Persons Task Force and Integrated Hands where LUM's staff shares responsibility with other groups or depends on other groups for leadership, and with projects which involve the establishment of long-term relationships over racial, ethnic, and economic divisions in the community. If ecumenical urban ministries are to succeed in building enduring relationships which transcend long-standing social divisions, their staffs must attach high priority to the programs and work vigorously to support the participants as they struggle to engage in behavior they are not accustomed to.

LUM has been most successful providing services which are familiar to middle class churchgoers, do not require professional skills, and do not involve extended relationships with low-income people. Programs such as Summer Camp, providing rides, and fixing homes and park shelters are rather traditional patterns of church action. They can be done by almost anyone. They also do not impose any demands or expectations on low-income people. If ecumenical urban ministries designed similar programs in the future, they could do so with some confidence that they would be relatively successful.

LUM has been less successful with programs which involve relations with low-income people for the purpose of changing their behavior. Adult education and working with low-income youngsters require special skills that many untrained people do not have; and they involve expectations that low-income people will change their behavior. Ultimately the success of such programs depends on the abilities of the project leaders and the willingness of low-income people to change. If either one or both of these conditions are lacking, the projects are likely to fail.

LUM has demonstrated that an ecumenical urban ministry also can stimulate social concern within local congregations. Sixty percent of LUM's member churches have participated in and/or responded to at least 40 percent of its programs. Another 25 percent of the churches have been involved in one-third of LUM's programs. This is a major accomplishment for a social movement organization that seeks to reform its parent organizations.

Local churches have responded more enthusiastically to some programs than others. The most effective programs have been those which provide imaginative ways of extending people's behavior along familiar lines of activity. For example, churches have embraced the Seeds of Vision conferences and the Jubilee Christmas Shop with considerable excitement. The least successful programs have fallen into three categories: (1) those—such as the Christmas Project—which offer a conventional format and require that people engage in behavior which may not have any meaningful impact in the long run; (2) those—such as Integrated Hands—which require behaviors which are not extensions of ordinary patterns of activity; and (3) those—such as the survey/consultation—which stress information and require no change in behavior. Programs which lack imagination and consequence or which stress education and information are not likely to foster changes in attitude or behavior.

Conclusion

I have sought some understanding of how social movement (ecumenical urban ministry) organizations can be formed, institutionalized, and effective. The results suggest that an open system approach stressing structural conduciveness and resource mobilization is a useful framework for examining these issues. Because they are social movement organizations, ecumenical urban ministries face some difficulties that other religious organizations do not face. But, the evidence from this study also indicates that they can be viable and effective instruments for building a more just and equal world.

FOOTNOTES

Chapter 1

¹Bureaucracies emphasize service more than social movement organizations do, but they also can engage in some forms of social change. Social movement organizations can provide some services, but they place greater emphasis on change than bureaucracies. Bureaucracies stress financial compensation, but also call on value incentives to make work meaningful. Social movement organizations also provide financial support for their members, but they stress value incentives more than most bureaucracies.
²See Starr (1979) and Lofland and Jamison (1984) for a similar distinction between "adversary" and "exemplary" groups.

Chapter 2

¹More radical social movement organizations which do not try to work with parent organizations (e.g., "poor people's movements") can develop when the economy is either quite strong or quite weak (Piven and Cloward, 1977).
²When there is no problem to solve, people do not form groups. If a group were formed to deal with a problem which did not really exist, it would have a difficult time sustaining the motivation of its members. Moreover, group members would be hard pressed to persuade others that the problem is serious enough to warrant their support.
³Levels three and four do not preclude the formation, institutionalization, and effectiveness of new groups (indeed, Emery and Trist suggest level three might even foster greater program effectiveness), but they make these processes more difficult. The new group is likely to spend a great deal of time competing with other groups for "domain," and using its resources to control its environment. Moreover, parent organizations such as dioceses, presbyteries, and other judicatory-level agencies have only limited resources so, if confronted with applications from several similar groups in the same community, they are likely either to fund one or two and deny the others, or fund several at reduced levels that will make it difficult for the groups to survive and be effective.
⁴In its popular usage, charisma usually means some intangible, spiritual, or personal quality which makes the leader attractive to others and contributes to his/her ability to persuade others of the rightness of his/her message. But, in the sense that Weber (1964) first used the concept, charisma did not refer to an inner quality of an individual. It referred to a special *relationship* between a leader and his/her following in which the followers granted the leader privileges because *they felt* he/she possessed transcendental qualities. It also entailed "a radical reorientation on the part of the followers" (Wilson, 1978:110). Thus, charisma was attributed to a leader by others who were willing to accept the obligations of a relationship with the leader.
⁵Professionals can support the growth of such groups in several ways. University professors can "set up a special course as a conduit through which university students could be channeled into community organizations for course credit" (Rothschild-Whitt, 1976:80). Professors also can analyze and write about the groups activities. Social workers and staff persons in human service agencies can share information about the needs in the community, especially the needs of low-income and other "hurting" people. And lawyers, teachers, and psychologists can provide needed advice to the group and its constituents.
⁶The other nine dimensions of institutionalization are not unimportant. Indeed, each dimension is important in its own right and probably affects at least one other dimension to some extent. For example, productivity probably has some impact on the group's resources: the more productive the group is, the more likely it is to obtain the resources it needs to conduct its programs. However, I assume that these nine dimensions are more likely to be independent, or functions, of the six dimensions I consider most important.

Chapter 3

¹I was due for a sabbatical and wanted to explore ways of developing a more organizational approach in my professional work and integrating my professional interests in the sociology of religion, social stratification, and racial and ethnic minorities with my personal interest in church programs relating to the causes and consequences of poverty.
²I considered ways in which I might combine a reading program with some practical, "hands on," experience. I told Rev. Elly of my interests, and he told me more about LUM and some problems it was experiencing at the time. We agreed that LUM would be a meaningful setting for me to explore some of my own ideas and that, simultaneously, I could contribute to LUM.

I developed a proposal for Lilly Endowment's Faculty Open Fellowship program. The proposal indicated that I would (a) spend fall 1975 on sabbatical expanding my understanding of "complex organizations" generally and religious organizations in particular, and (b) spend spring and summer 1976 evaluating LUM and recommending ways it might become an even stronger group.
³Takayama and Darnell (1979) also report that an evaluation was instrumental in the institutionalization of the urban ministry organization in Memphis. Thus, one of the lessons from these studies is that organizations which are willing to sponsor evaluations and take the evaluators' recommendations seriously can be strengthened.
⁴Instead of a one-year relationship with LUM, I was involved for about seven years (1975-81). During this time, my relationship with LUM went through three relative distinct stages: non-participant observer (1975-76), very active

participant-observer (1977-79), and somewhat active participant-observer (1980-81).

Non-participant observer (1975-76). During this stage, my role was mainly that of an observer. I deliberately kept a low profile and tried to learn as much as I could about the organization. This was clearly the most detached stage of my relationship with LUM.

Very active participant-observer (1977-79). During this stage, I assumed the more active role of participant observer, serving as chair of the Program and Planning Committee and attending numerous meetings related to various aspects of LUM's survival. This involvement increased my opportunities to observe LUM from various angles and to learn how others outside of LUM perceived it. This more active role reduced the detachment I had during the 1975-76 stage, though I did all I could to maintain my ability to critique the organization's behavior.

Somewhat active participant-observer (1980-81). The third stage of my relationship with LUM began in 1979 as I was trying to find funds to conduct the second evaluation of LUM. I was able to secure some funds for that evaluation from Lilly Endowment through the Indiana Council of Churches' program to evaluate ecumenical organizations around the state. Once the evaluation project began in fall 1979, I relinquished my role with the Program and Planning Committee and assumed a less active role (though I could not return to exactly the same low-profile role I had played in 1975-76).

[5]Copies of the questionnaire can be obtained by writing to me at the Department of Sociology and Anthropology, Stone Hall, Purdue University, West Lafayette, IN 47907.

Chapter 4

[1]How could this collision have occurred? In its dealings with Rev. Elly, presbytery emphasized the possibility for a community ministry at Hope Chapel. This possibility was reiterated in a letter Rev. Elly received from Rev. Kenneth Edelman (moderator at Hope Chapel while that church searched for a new pastor). These utterances, in combination with Rev. Elly's predisposition toward community ministry, led him to believe that the people of Hope Chapel wanted a pastor who would conduct an experimental-community ministry as well as a traditional-pastor ministry. Rev. Sala reiterated this emphasis in his "Charge to the Congregation" at Rev. Elly's installation in June 1967.

[2]Rev. Elly expressed his frustration to the people of Hope Chapel in the 1968 annual report:

> The lack of commitment and atmosphere is discouraging to the pastor. The congregation seems to have turned inward, measuring success by numbers and interested in maintaining the building because it is a reminder of past days which were more pleasant and easier to live in. As such, Hope Chapel has lost a sense of mission and hope. Pessimism and discouragement threaten to douse the fire of God's Spirit. Joseph Kraft commented once in an editorial:
>
> ". . . Man is not at his best when exclusively preoccupied with his own affairs. Self-absorption generates pettiness. Life thus lived is what Hobbes said it was: solitary, poor, nasty, brutish, and short."

[3]For example, the February 1969 board minutes include the following entry:

> Mr. Elly brought an idea to the members of the Board for their consideration. He suggested that the NDP now start to relate itself to other Presbyterian churches in and around Lafayette. If any of these churches express a willingness to participate in the Project, they can have representation on the Advisory Board. The churches in question are: Bethany, Dayton, Faith, Elston and Central. Some of these churches have already been exposed to a presentation of activities at the Neighborhood Development Project.

Chapter 5

[1]Mainline denominations experienced especially large increases in membership during the 1950s and early 1960s. These increases were due mainly to the post-World War II baby boom. As that boom ended in the mid-1960s, membership in these groups began to decline. This led to downturns in church building, baptisms, and Sunday school enrollments. However, the positive effects of abundance outweighed the negative effects of the downturns through the late 1960s. It was not until the early 1970s that mainline groups became alarmed. Moreover, per capita contributions in mainline churches rose during the 1960s.

[2]There also were other indications of the conservative political climate in the Lafayette area. Billboards and signs urging the United States to withdraw from the United Nations and demanding that we impeach former Supreme Court Justice Earl Warren were common along roadsides in Tippecanoe and surrounding counties. Tippecanoe County was among the last two of 17 eligible counties to apply for food stamps. And when the county received notification that it would get food stamps, the Lafayette *Journal-Courier* (November 9, 1971:A-14) editorialized that the program was "good for those 2,300 families who have been lining up for such commodities as are being handed out as township relief. It is also good for the taxpayers who, besides being reassured that the poor are being well-served, will find savings of some $20,000 a year in local tax monies."

[3]Rev. Elly indicates few people asked him about the statistical evidence concerning the extent of poverty. Most people *assumed* there was *some* poverty in the county and particularly in certain parts of the community "which everyone knows are poor." The Southside of Lafayette where Hope Chapel is located is one such area. When Rev. Elly spoke to people about poverty in Lafayette, they assumed the validity of his claims largely on the grounds that he lived in the area and, thus, must know what he is talking about.

[4]Lafayette and West Lafayette were quite different types of communities. West Lafayette residents were highly educated, professionally-employed people with high incomes and expensive homes. The largest single employer

was Purdue University. Lafayette's residents, as a rule, were much more diverse. The majority were high school and college graduates, but many were not. They had a wide range of incomes and homes. Many were professionally-employed, while many others worked for large manufacturing firms such as Alcoa, National Homes, and Eli Lilly Co. (to name just a few).

[5]The Federation of Churches' records indicate there were 124 Christian congregations in the county. Seven of these (6 percent) were Roman Catholic. About 40 percent of all Protestant congregations were affiliated with liberal denominations. Johnson, Picard, and Quinn's (1974) listing of churches and church memberships indicates there were six Roman Catholic congregations (8 percent) with a total membership of 18,138 (36.2 percent of all church members in the county). Approximately 57 percent (N = 43) of all 70 Protestant congregations and 44 percent of all Protestant churchgoers were liberal.

The percentage of liberal Protestant groups depends on how one categorizes the congregations. I assumed all congregations within a liberal denomination also were liberal and/or whatever errors were made on this basis were more or less canceled out by comparable errors made in assuming all congregations in the conservative denominations also were conservative.

[6]To obtain data on these issues, I culled LUM records for the names of lay people who participated in any NDP activities before NDP became LUM at the end of 1971. Rev. Elly and I went through that list of names to confirm their involvement and to see if he could think of any other people who had been involved but were not on the list. These processes produced a total of 66 names.

Rev. Elly then rated each of these people from 1 (limited support) to 10 (active support). He rated 30 people ≤ 5, indicating they had not been very active in or supportive of NDP. He rated 36 other people ≥ 6, indicating they were NDP's most active supporters. I then called all of the most active supporters I could reach (i.e., those who were still alive and living in the Lafayette area). I was able to contact 18 (50 percent) of the 36 most active people.

[7]Most of the clergy who were in the Lafayette area in the late 1960s, including many of those who support LUM, had left the community for other positions. Thus, it was impossible to obtain precise data on all the variables I felt would contribute to support of LUM's formation. Nor was it possible to compare directly the clergy who supported LUM with other clergy in the area. However, I was able to obtain some data on the variables from Rev. Elly, who remains in the community as a pastoral counselor.

[8]Assuming there were at least 150 clergy in the area at the time (over 100 churches, with at least one—and as many as three or four—clergy staff), the eleven who supported LUM's formation represented less than 10—perhaps as little as 5—percent of all the local clergy. Many of the others were not approached and, thus, should not necessarily be thought of as having opposed LUM's formation, though some may have.

[9]I attempted to judge the relative importance of these factors as sources of clergy support for NDP. The most significant factors seem to have been their affiliation with Presbyterian church; their activity in hierarchical church work in addition to their pastorates and, in one case, involvement in a campus ministry; their tendency to define colleagues as an important part of one's professional identity, and a tendency to define colleagues as an important part of one's professional identity, and a tendency to view support of NDP as being in one's professional self-interest. Being young and theologically moderate to liberal also were important factors, but to a lesser extent. Viewing the community as part of one's ministerial role also contributed to support for NDP, but to an even lesser extent. Finally, political orientation seemed to be relatively inconsequential.

Chapter 6

[1]The argument for the first motion was that participation of the poor serves the interests of both LUM and low-income people: it would increase poor people's input into LUM and it would empower the poor (giving them greater access to resources and a right to vote on how these resources were utilized in relation to the poor). The argument for the second motion was that two representatives from each group would "guarantee meaningful participation." Counterargument revolved around four issues: (1) it might be better for low-income people to participate in LUM's program committees—rather than on the board of other committees which they might not have much interest in; (2) having two representatives from each group—a total of 10—might make the board too big; (3) such a large percentage of low-income seats "might make the churches which pay the bill a little nervous"; and (4) because LUM did not have well-developed, on-going relationships with people in these low-income groups, it might have difficulty finding representatives from each who would serve on the board.

[2]From 1972 to 1976, federal funds comprised a substantial proportion of all "other" funds. Since 1976, LUM has used almost no federal money. Individual gifts have comprised the largest share of "other" funds.

[3]Since 1981, LUM has developed a task force which is addressing the problem of poor relief on a state-wide basis (see Appendix B).

[4]In 1977, the board accepted the following description of its members' responsibilities:
1. Members of the Board of Directors are *directors* (not managers or supervisors).
   A. They are primarily concerned with the financial situation of LUM, in order to assure that LUM is in a sound and secure financial position.
   B. The Board employs a Pastor-Director (a manager and supervisor) to run the day-to-day operations of LUM. The Board supervises the Pastor-Director in a broad and general sense. The Pastor-Director is accountable to the Board for the efficiency and effectiveness of the LUM operation.
2. Members of the Board of Directors assure that the objectives and mission of LUM are achieved.
   A. They establish general and broad policies and plans for LUM.
   B. The Board makes major decisions which will affect the general direction and control of LUM.

3. Each member of the Board of Directors is accountable to the member church which he/she represents. The Board member communicates and coordinates with their pastor, social concerns committee, and church members regarding LUM matters.

The prevailing expectation is that any issues presented to the board will have been discussed within the appropriate committee(s) and/or the Executive Committee.

[5] See job description in Appendix A.

[6] The committee tended to view its support of LUM as payment of Rev. Elly's salary (i.e., support of a particular Presbyterian minister, not necessarily LUM as an organization). Thus, if Rev. Elly left and was not replaced by another Presbyterian, the committee was inclined to reduce its support. The committee also was not sure LUM would survive Rev. Elly's resignation and had considered alternative uses of its money in 1978 if LUM folded. A third consideration was that with Rev. Elly's resignation, LUM's salaries would be reduced for several months. Thus, the committee felt LUM would need less money. Assuming it would continue to provide some support, the committee felt it could reduce the amount of money it contributed to LUM.

[7] LUM's representatives argued that presbytery's money was more than Rev. Elly's salary; without it, LUM could not survive. They said presbytery's support of LUM during the transition period would be especially important because local churches might be even more inclined to cut their support and withdrawal of presbytery's support might cause even more local congregations to withdraw their support. They also said that, while other groups like LUM had not survived, LUM *would* survive because LUM's officers and the people who were engaged in the process of finding a replacement for Rev. Elly were highly qualified people with experience in searching for people to fill religious and academic positions. Finally, they argued that, while LUM's salaries would decline somewhat in future months, the organization would experience transition costs which were not in the budget and that presbytery's full support was needed because it would be two to three years before the new director's efforts to cultivate new sources of support would pay off.

[8] By this time, there were growing indications that the northern conference of the United Methodist church and some local United Methodist congregations might reduce their support of LUM. Conversations with United Methodist leaders over a period of several weeks indicated that several factors might be involved: (1) a United Methodist retirement home was in financial trouble and the conference might need to reallocate money to save it; (2) United Methodists perceived themselves as being more denominationally-oriented (i.e., less ecumenically-oriented) than Presbyterians and denominational concerns were increasing; (3) some United Methodist leaders did not feel they were getting their money's worth out of their church's investment in LUM; (4) some United Methodist leaders did not like LUM's recent emphasis on stimulating more programs within local congregations; (5) some leaders felt United Methodist interests had not been adequately represented in the search for LUM's new director; and (6) the committee did not nominate a United Methodist to be director.

[9] The focused approach remained Rev. Elly's style when he left LUM to form the Lafayette Pastoral Counseling Center. He became its first staff person and people tended to associate it with him.

[10] Thus, he was going in many different directions at once. In a memo to the Personnel Policies and Salary Review Committee in November 1974, he acknowledged: "I am dynamic, multi-faceted, and my interests in people, issues and events range widely. Consequently, I over-extend myself in terms of time not ability. I am aware of this and working on narrowing my focus slightly . . . the struggle to balance LUM commitments, counseling request, continuing education and family responsibilities still continues."

[11] The present size and turnover rate combine to foster less intimacy among board members. Members are not as likely to know one another's names as they used to.

[12] While relations with member churches have improved, several difficulties remain. When Rev. Dolphin first arrived, he was very favorably impressed by the pastors of Lafayette churches. In March 1978, Rev. Dolphin observed that Lafayette's clergy were "strong, competent, and supportive; they are a great resource for the growth of LUM." By the 1980s, Rev. Dolphin was more sanguine in his assessment of local pastors. He indicated that "one of the major disappointments" in his first two years with LUM was "the fact that pastors really don't care about social concerns; they are not opposed; they just don't care."

LUM's relationship with its member churches also is hampered by the fact that some representatives are not well integrated into their congregations and/or are not on good terms with their pastors. In a show of hands at a LUM board meeting in December 1980, about one-third of the representatives indicated they did not belong to their congregations' social concerns committees or were not accountable to any group in their church for their work with LUM.

[13] The most serious conflict LUM has ever had with a human service agency occurred during late 1980 and early 1981. In 1978, LUM struck an agreement with the Southside Community Center regarding the Summer Camp program. The agreement said that "the Greater Lafayette Community Center (Southside) takes primary responsibility for the staffing, planning, and execution of the camp program" and that "The Lafayette Urban Ministry takes primary responsibility for the raising of funds to support youngsters' participation in the camp program." In 1978, Rev. Dolphin felt the Southside Center did not exercise much leadership in planning the camp, complaining that there was no schedule of activities until one week before the camp. In 1979, he said Southside's planning was poor and there was too much use of foul language by Southside's staff members. In 1980, Southside Center assigned a person to direct the camp who had been put on probation by the Southside board. Rev. Dolphin said he was "not willing to leave the running of camp in the hands of someone [Southside Center] had put on notice," especially with the director of the center going on vacation "when last minute plans were being made." Camp generally went well, but Rev. Dolphin was very disturbed by the Southside Center's staff members' attitudes toward the campers and a food fight which he said was instigated by Southside staff members.

After camp, Rev. Dolphin told the board he was upset with Southside Center's handling of camp over the last three years and that he was not sure he wanted to continue the arrangement whereby LUM raised money to support a camp which Southside Center planned. In December 1980, the Executive Committees of the two groups met. In two hours, it became clear that the two groups no longer had a sense of mutual respect and confidence in one another. For example, LUM's representatives asked to tape record the meeting. Southside Center's representatives said they wanted to maintain the relationship with LUM, but it was revealed later that they had scheduled a week for camp in 1981 under Southside Center's name only. It also was clear that the two groups had different assumptions about low-income youngsters and the nature and staffing of camp. In January 1981, LUM's board voted to sever the relationship with the Southside Center and fund its own camp.

But, the friction between the groups persisted. In spring 1981, LUM sent out a solicitation letter for its 1981 camp. It included a xerox copy of a newspaper article about the 1980 camp. The Southside Center's staff objected to LUM's use of the article on two grounds: it indicated that LUM co-sponsored the camp with Southside Center (which it did in 1980) and left people with the impression that it would do so again in 1981 (which it would not). The Southside Center threatened legal action if LUM did not send out a letter of explanation to all the people who received the first solicitation. LUM felt justified in using the article and thought it had done both groups a favor by not broadcasting the fact that they had experienced conflict. LUM also felt Southside Center probably wanted LUM to send the follow-up letter simply as a way of telling people on LUM's list about Southside's camp. But LUM sent out a letter which appeased Southside Center and increased donations to LUM's camp by $1,000.

Chapter 7

[1]In January 1981, United Way sent a document called "Statement on United Way Priorities" to all United Way agency presidents. In that document, the United Way board expressed the following scenario: (1) during the 1950s, human service agencies "were still, of necessity, focusing service efforts on our most destitute and needy citizens"; (2) the "War on Poverty of the 1960s and the Economic Opportunity of the 1970s brought massive investments of Federal dollars to bear on the problems faced by our lowest income citizens"; (3) that "it appears likely that such programs will persist into the 1980s"; (4) "1980 has been increasing pressure on and erosion of those citizens formerly labeled 'middle class' "; (5) "it is doubtful that the Federal government can or will address the needs of this group, given the incredibly large investments already institutionalized for the lowest income citizens"; and (6) therefore, "more emphasis, can and should be placed on allocations to those services needed, even more so now, by middle and lower income families struggling to maintain their families in the fact of rising inflation." It was recommended that "United Way be alert to and cognizant of the growing need to provide family recreation, education, and social services to the average working citizen and family."

In December 1981, local United Way agencies met to discuss how the reduction in federal funds for social programs would reduce their budgets, staffs, and services, and how they could cope with the situation. The agencies unanimously opposed the cutbacks and searched for ways to increase their resources so they could maintain their budgets, staffs, and services. But, instead of siding with the agencies in their time of crisis, the United Way representative told the agencies that United Way, nationally and locally, supported the federal cutbacks and the concept of "maximum local determination of services to be provided." Once again, when United Way had a choice of siding with middle- and upper-income people (by favoring the cutbacks and more local control) or siding with local agencies and the lower-income people they served (by opposing the cutbacks in federal programs), United Way chose to side with middle- and upper-income people.

[2]I also have collected information concerning the amount of money local churches spend on programs and activities relating to poverty. Indications are they spend only about one or two percent of their income on such matters (and part of that is their pledge to LUM).

[3]Davidson and Knudsen's (1977) study of Protestant students from six denominations coming into Purdue University as freshmen in 1975 revealed a similar pattern. The top four items on the list of programs they "definitely" wanted to participate in were: traditional worship services (52 percent), study groups on the Bible (26 percent), retreats (22 percent), and marriage preparation and life planning programs (20 percent). At the bottom of the list were action programs on racial justice (10 percent), action programs on hunger (9 percent), working in community centers (9 percent), and study groups on ethics (8 percent).

[4]Respondents also were asked to rate 12 community problems from "not a real problem" to "serious problem." Two problems stood out: drugs and alcoholism (63 percent) and the decline in religious and moral values (53 percent). The items at the bottom of the list were: agencies serving the poor not adequately funded (22 percent); housing codes not enforced (19 percent); the township trustee system of poor relief (17 percent); conditions in the downtown area (16 percent); relationships among various races (12 percent); and relationships between the rich and the poor (10 percent).

I also asked church members whether their churches should be involved in solving these community problems, and if so, how? Answers to each topic were divided into four categories: (1) churches should not/cannot be involved; (2) churches should only be involved through the action of their individual members; (3) clergy and religious leaders should act on behalf of the churches; and (4) the whole church should take an active leadership role by sponsoring efforts to solve the problem.

The respondents were most convinced that their church as a whole should sponsor efforts to deal with the problems of declining religious and moral values (74 percent), isolation and loneliness (57 percent), drugs and alcohol (57 percent), and quality of family life (57 percent).

They were more divided on how to handle the problems of poverty, health care for the poor, race relations, and the funding of social service agencies. Overall half of church members felt either that church leaders should work in these areas on behalf of churches, or that churches as a whole should take a leadership role in solving these problems. However, 40-50 percent of the members felt churches should not be involved in these areas, or should be only at the individual level.

Finally, the prevailing view was that churches should not be organizationally involved in the problem of relations between the rich and poor, the township trustee system, conditions in the downtown area, and the enforcement of housing codes. Over half of churchgoers felt either that churches should not be involved at all, or that they should be involved only through individuals.

5During its withdrawal from the area of social concerns, the Federation of Churches spun off one of its programs: the Food Pantry. It became the only other ecumenical group in town with an interest in social concerns. The Food Pantry solicits foods and some small amounts of money from local churches. The money is used to buy food, which is distributed to low-income individuals and families on an emergency basis by volunteers from local churches. Compared to LUM, the Food Pantry asks the churches for different types of support, has no paid staff, a much smaller budget, and a much more specific purpose.

Two other ecumenical groups have solicited funds from local churches: the Pastoral Counseling Center which Rev. Elly started and Rev. William Vamos' Center for Christian Growth. However, these groups have not dealt with social concerns, have not asked for representatives as LUM has, and have asked for relatively small amounts of money. Thus, LUM had not had to compete with them to institutionalize itself.

6Census figures for 1980 show that the population in Lafayette dropped to 43,011 (a 4.4 percent loss) between 1970 and 1980, but there are two good reasons for believing this decline was not real. First, the data collection procedures for the census in Lafayette were so confused that census officials had to be brought in from Chicago to straighten out the mess. It is quite widely believed that many Lafayette residents were not counted. Second, the number of dwelling units in Lafayette increased by 14.5 percent.

7That model specified three of the four goals LUM now considers to be part of its efforts to increase local churches' own involvement in social concerns: (1) to increase churches' sponsorship of social programs; (2) to increase the priority church members attach to social concerns; and (3) to integrate the vertical and horizontal dimensions of faith.

With regard to low-income people, the model also stated three of the four functions LUM now seeks to perform in its efforts to address the causes and consequences of poverty: (1) to alter social policies and practices that perpetuate poverty, (2) to increase resources within low-income groups, and (3) to provide emergency relief to low-income families and individuals.

8A fourth function was specified with regard to LUM's goal of increasing local churches' own involvement in social concerns: to foster more compassionate attitudes about poverty and the poor among church members. A fourth function also was specified in relation to LUM's goal of addressing the causes and consequences of poverty: to cultivate closer relationships with and among low-income people. (Both of these goals had been implicit in LUM's activities over the years but were made explicit in 1980.)

9The possibility of recruiting more mainline Protestant denominations was addressed rather matter-of-factly. There seemed to be an assumption that this was a good and manageable task that would not involve any particular problems.

The discussion of recruiting more conservative or fundamentalist Protestant groups was more troublesome. On the one hand, the board recognized that such churches attracted many low-income people and therefore should be involved in LUM to a greater extent. On the other hand, there was an awareness that such churches probably would have different views on LUM's role in the community.

LUM had a long-standing desire to recruit Catholics to the board but also a lack of progress on this front—due to Protestant uncertainties over how to approach Catholics (e.g., whether to go to the bishop or to the local pastors). I indicated my interest in seeing the six local Catholic congregations join. Rev. Elly and I promised to pursue this possibility.

Finally, the discussion of Jewish involvement in LUM raised some questions about the nature of LUM's ministry. LUM had grown out of a Protestant heritage and defined itself as a Christian ministry. For example, many of its goal statements and objects indicate that various activities are to be done "in the name of Jesus Christ." How could this continue to be if Jews were to be involved? No clear answer emerged.

10Essentially, having low-income people on LUM's board would serve the interests of both groups. If LUM were to recruit low-income people to its board, it would increase their access to organizations that make a difference in the community (e.g., LUM itself, LUM's member churches, human service agencies with which LUM interacts). It also would increase their say in decisions, many of which affect the low-income community in particular. Thus, it would step in the direction of leadership development and empowerment of the low-income community. It also would give low-income people an opportunity to learn how at least some portions of "the system" operate. Finally, by tackling the objective circumstances of exclusion, LUM would contribute to some reduction in the low-income community's sense of alienation and its debilitating consequences in many aspects of their lives.

The recruitment of low-income people would increase LUM's awareness of the community as a whole: the priorities of the middle and upper classes would come mainly through representatives of member churches (though not exclusively) and the priorities of lower and working class people would come through low-income representatives (though, again, not exclusively). LUM also might find how similar the views of higher and lower income people are, as well as where they differ.

11I summarized the sociological evidence concerning the relationships between several factors and low-income people's participation in groups like LUM (Smith, Eddy, and Baldwin, 1972; Smith, 1973). Low income youth, adults of various racial and ethnic backgrounds, and older people are not likely to be as active as the middle-class and middle-aged people who make up the LUM board at present. Therefore, if only one representative were chosen from each group, LUM could expect their participation to be inconsistent; considerable effort might be required on the part of LUM staff and board to maintain and enhance their participation.

Also, if only one person were chosen, making a total of five low-income representatives, that small group probably would feel overwhelmed by a group of 25 to 30 middle class church people (especially given voting procedures that stress majority-rules). They might feel isolated, fearful, reluctant to share ideas, or intimidated.

Therefore, I argued, at least two representatives from each low-income group should be recruited to the LUM board (i.e., at least 10 low-income representatives).

[12]After the process of administrative succession was completed, the role of at-large members declined and the role of member church representatives increased. However, the important role that at-large members played during this period is one reason why the board in 1980 voted to keep a certain number of at-large positions available for church members and/or low-income people who have a special interest in LUM's work.

[13]LUM no longer saw itself as a human service agency and wanted the autonomy to conduct justice-oriented (not just service-oriented) programs—something which it felt the local United Way would not approve of. In light of the federal cutbacks, United Way's support of federal cutbacks, and other United Way policies (which I reviewed earlier), LUM's decision not to depend on the government and United Way for support appears to have been a very wise one.

[14]Some United Methodist congregations were concerned at first that LUM might try to turn everything over to local churches, but that concern has diminished.

[15]My description and account of LUM's effectiveness follow in Chapters 8 and 9. Each program was rated on a four-point scale ranging from counterproductive (score 1) to very successful (score 4).

Chapter 8

[1]Over 100 people (mostly middle-class people from local agencies or with an interest in improving services to the poor) attended the workshop. The participants established the following list of problems needing attention: (1) comprehensive, low-cost health care accessible to low-income people; (2) coordination, evaluation, and planning of human services; (3) legal services for low-income people; (4) more funding and coordination of funding for human service agencies; (5) more public education about human needs among government officials, school officials, providers of service, and the community at large; (6) problems related to housing especially for the poor; (7) the lack of supermarkets in the downtown area; and (9) better transportation for the community as a whole and especially for low-income people. Task forces were created to deal with each of these problems.

[2]The pros, essentially, were (1) that the program would provide LUM with more direct contact with low-income people; (2) that some church members already associated Advocates with LUM, but LUM had no control over the program; (3) if LUM adopted Advocates, it could play a larger role in educating church members and others about the need for Advocates, and (4) Advocates seemed scripturally sound and compatible with the gospel message of seeking justice. The cons were (1) the increased burden it would put on LUM's staff to nurture and conduct the program and (2) the possibility that some member churches might object to LUM's sponsoring a program that might involve conflict with established institutions.

[3]WIC "provides specified nutritious food supplements and nutrition education to women who are pregnant, postpartum or breastfeeding and to children who are less than five years of age. Program participants must be at 'nutritional risk' due to inadequate nutrition and income." The program "is sponsored by the United States Department of Agriculture, administered state-wide by the Indiana state board of health, and operated locally by various community health or human service agencies."

[4]These problems were: training in writing resumes, emphasizing skills over formal training and degrees; adopting a family, giving the support needed; creating new jobs; solving problems of underemployment; temporary housing, finding ways to give visibility to Lafayette's minority groups; helping people learn English; compiling a list of skilled and semi-skilled persons and contacting businesses in an effort to connect the two.

[5]A supporter of the mayor responded in a Letter-to-the-Editor in April 1979 which described what the administration had done on behalf of Spanish-speaking people but indicated that "the Mayor's job is not to spoon-feed these people or give them preferential treatment.... What more could the city of Lafayette give these people than an opportunity? What else do they want?" Members of the SSPTF responded with several Letters-to-the-Editor criticizing the writer's patronizing view of Spanish-speaking people and asserting the legitimacy of Hispanics' efforts to make the political process work on behalf of their interests.

[6]After the 1981 camp in June, one of the counselors sent LUM a letter in which he summarized his very favorable experiences and those of the youngsters he worked with most closely:

SUMMER CAMP IS . . .

Just a note to commend you on the success of Urban Ministry's camp. I'm a different person because of my experience.   I had the pleasure of watching eleven boys blossom and flourish. It made me realize that they really do hold the secret of entering heaven. Unless we can become like them . . . we learned so much together. We learned to share and care for others. We learned that it's okay to be afraid, to cry, to feel lonely because with friends it's not nearly so painful. So many lives were positively changed by a few days at camp. I'll never forget what a good time the group had. So much laughing and loving went on; discovering new things. It was wonderful.

At night, before lights out, I'd talk to each of the guys about the day and each one of them gained some very high-level insights. So here it is from

Joe: who is still "slightly allergic" to the dark, but not so afraid anymore.
Billy: who can hug a grown man so tight that tears fall from his eyes.
Scott: who can preach a more convincing sermon on "the wages of sin is hell and damnation."
Charles: who learned the joys of sharing.

James: who learned if you put out your hand and trust, someone will take it.
Mickey: who is a confident swimmer—now.
Victor: who flew like superman (from his top bunk).
Travis: who discovered a new breed of animal never seen before—the chipmunk.
Ricky: who made a lot of new friends before he has to move away.
Mike: who learned that even though he's only 8-years-old, he is created by God and therefore good.
And Clarence: who learned to say "I love you" in a multitude of ways.

Clarence Semmes
Volunteer Counselor

[7] LUM's rationale for rejecting the vans was as follows: (1) LUM's transportation service had demonstrated agencies' need for a more comprehensive system, but it was not more appropriate for them to develop their own transportation service than for them to depend on LUM; (2) expanding LUM's transportation service would not be consistent with its emerging focus on local churches and low-income groups and its diminishing focus on agencies; (3) the size of the transportation program might threaten LUM's ability to move into new areas; (4) "it would not be good long-range investment of staff time or resources"; and (5) "costs and administrative uncertainties are too great."

[8] This index indicated the frequency with which people had "heard a sermon in . . . church given by an Urban Ministry staff member," "heard your pastor say a good word about the Lafayette Urban Ministry," "received the Urban Ministry's newsletter *The Seed*," and "heard an Urban Ministry staff member in a discussion group or church class." Alpha = .71.

[9] This index consisted of 12 items measuring the number of times church members had "personally donated money or goods to the Lafayette Urban Ministry as a general donation," to its Summer Camp or to the Centralized Emergency Fund; participated in the Advocates program, the Volunteer Transportation Service, Summer Camp (as a counselor), Adventure Clubs, the Christmas Project, the Spanish-Speaking Persons Task Force, Good Friends, and the rehabilitation of Shamrock Park; and "asked the Urban Ministry for help of any kind." Alpha = .74.

[10] This index included five items: "encouraging individual members to carry out acts of charity to needy persons," "supporting and organizing local church programs for aiding needy persons," "studying social issues in the light of Biblical teachings," "encouraging individual members to support social reform," and "providing church support for the poor and oppressed in organizing for their rights." Respondents rated these items on a six-point scale ranging from "very unimportant; lowest priority" to "very important; highest priority." Alpha = .82.

[11] Church members were asked how important the following things were in explaining poverty in Tippecanoe County: "lack of thrift and proper money management by the poor," "lack of effort by the poor themselves," "loose morals and drunkenness," "lack of ability and talent among poor people." Alpha = .73.

[12] This index consisted of five items: "failure of society to provide good schools for many Americans," "prejudice and discrimination against Blacks and other minorities," "low wages in some businesses and industries," "failure of private industry to provide enough jobs," and "being taken advantage of by rich people." Alpha = .78.

[13] Respondents were asked to indicate the extent to which they agreed or disagreed with three statements: "Jesus is the Divine Son of God and I have no doubts about it"; "I know there is a personal God and I have no doubts about it"; and "I am sure there is a life after death." Alpha = .75.

[14] This index consists of three items: "helping one's fellow man in need is more important than any personal religious belief or practice"; "to love God means caring for others in need; faith without good works is dead"; and "the way I treat my fellow man will determine my fate in the hereafter." These items were not as highly correlated as I would have liked (Alpha = .46). The relatively low correlation among them probably reflects the churches' failure to develop an integrated view of parishioners' relationships with other people and the role these relationships play in one's personal salvation.

[15] Respondents could check more than one category and some did. I recoded the multiple-checks to reduce the number of response categories, while retaining the respondents' message. For example, if someone checked "individuals," "leaders," and "the whole church," I recorded that as "whole church" to indicate that the person wanted the whole church (not just individuals) to be involved.

[16] In light of the several programs LUM has conducted since 1979 (e.g., the two Seeds of Vision conferences, the Grow-a-Row project), the number and percentage of churchgoers who have been exposed to LUM and/or participated in its programs certainly has grown even larger.

[17] Respondents were asked how much effect several groups had had on their lives. I ranked the groups in terms of the percentage of people who said they had had at least "some positive influence." Pastors ranked first (82.6 percent) followed by church committees people had been a part of (79.3 percent), "evangelists, worship services or sermons on TV or radio" (54.2 percent), "revivals or religious retreat you have attended (53.7 percent); Church Women United (which had positively affected 29.7 percent of all female respondents); LUM (20.6 percent) and the Tippecanoe County Federation of Churches; (10.7 percent). Thus several other groups had had more influence on respondents' lives, but LUM had had more impact than the county Federation of Churches which had been in existence three times as long.

[18] The author and Rev. Dolphin, separately and together, have attended other church conferences on social concerns. Attendance at these conferences has ranged from 25 to 50 people.

Chapter 9

[1] Since the average member church had 714 members, those with less than 714 members were considered small

and those with 714 or more members were considered large. Since 35 percent of the people in the average member church had family incomes of $25,000 or more, churches where the average was 35 percent or more were considered more affluent. Churches were divided into two groups according to their participation in LUM's programs: those which had participated in more than one-third of LUM's programs and those which had participated in one-third or less.

APPENDIX A

MAJOR DUTIES AND RESPONSIBILITIES OF THE ADMINISTRATIVE OFFICER

A. In the area of *Administration* the Administrative Officer:
   1. will work closely with the Board of Directors and supporting groups and institutions to provide support and guidance in the mission of Lafayette Urban Ministry and in seeking to secure the necessary funds (private or public) for the operation of the Lafayette Urban Ministry.
   2. administer the policies of Board of Directors.
   3. will direct and supervise all professional salaried and secretarial staff and work study students.
   4. will work with appropriate Board committees to prepare and propose to the Board an annual financial and human resource budget for Lafayette Urban Ministry.
   5. will identify annual objectives for the approval, revision or rejection by the Board of Directors of the Lafayette Urban Ministry.
   6. will present in an annual report to the Board of Directors an evaluation of the objectives, activities, and programs of the Lafayette Urban Ministry with emphasis on financial and budget information.
   7. will develop and maintain communication with the sponsors of Lafayette Urban Ministry, the churches of the Community, the people which Lafayette Urban Ministry seeks to serve and the community at large.
   8. will be responsible in consultation with the Board and its appropriate committees for hiring, promoting and terminating all salaried employees of Lafayette Urban Ministry.
B. In the area of *Program* the Administrative Officer:
   1. will be responsible for planning, implementing and evaluating the present programs of Lafayette Urban Ministry (such as Volunteer Transportation Service, Good Friends visitation, youth programs, summer camping program, community development, etc.) in consultation with the Board of Directors and such future programs as may be approved by the Board.
   2. will be responsible for defining needs and developing new programs (or gaps in present programs) to meet the issues of concern to the poor and powerless of the Lafayette Urban community consistent with the purpose of the Lafayette Urban Ministry.
   3. will direct and encourage all volunteer staff connected with the Lafayette Urban Ministry programs.

Qualifications, Skills and Knowledge
   1. Training and/or experience in administration, business, or civic organizations (community, religious, voluntary) or programs relating to low-income or minority groups.
   An academic degree would be helpful but is not necessary.
   2. Experience working with religious groups or knowledge of how ecumenical groups and various denominations function.
   3. Skill in preparing concise and persuasive reports and proposals involving large amounts of factual information.
   4. Ability to delegate authority.

5. Ability listen to various points of view and to deal tactfully with controversial issues in churches and the community as a whole.
6. Skills in raising funds from a variety of agencies (state, federal, private and religious) and writing financial grant proposals.

Miscellaneous

Both lay persons and clergy are encouraged to apply for this position.

Compensation and expenses, depending upon qualifications (including cash salary, housing allowance, car allowance, study leave, vacation, pension, etc.): $13,000 - $15,000.

The Lafayette Urban Ministry is an Equal Opportunity Employer.

Position available approximately November, 1977.

APPENDIX B

UPDATING LUM'S INSTITUTIONALIZATION AND EFFECTIVENESS: 1981-84

This volume has focused on LUM's experiences through 1981. But, some important developments have taken place since then. This update describes what has happened with regard to LUM's institutionalization and effectiveness through the end of 1984.

Institutionalization

LUM has become an even more viable social movement organization since 1981. Let me summarize what has happened on all 15 dimensions of institutionalization.

Purpose. LUM's two major goals remain the same: to promote social concerns within local churches, and to address the causes and consequences of poverty on their behalf. However, its work on behalf of local congregations has changed in two ways. LUM has increased its efforts to change social structures affecting the poor (especially the township trustee system of poor relief). It also has intensified its efforts to build closer relationships with and among the poor (especially in the area of neighborhood development).

Membership. Criteria for membership in LUM have not changed since 1981. However, some additional emphasis has been placed on increasing low-income people's involvement in LUM's activities. Four low-income people have been invited to board meetings; two have attended. Three others have participated on the task force studying the problems of poor relief.

Size. In 1981, LUM's board consisted of 29 local churches and three at-large members (total = 32). By 1984, LUM had 34 member churches and two at-large members (total = 36).

The new member churches included one United Methodist congregation (Congress Street), one Lutheran congregation (Prince of Peace), one Southern Baptist church (Calvary Baptist), one Christian Church-Church of God (Christian Campus House), and one non-denominational group (Abundant Life Fellowship). The two at-large members were Gary Henriott (formerly the representative from Immanuel United Church of Christ and now the chair of the Indiana Task Force on Poor Relief) and Kathy Rosaria (who works with the North Central Labor Council).

The staffing pattern also has changed. The number of full-time people has grown from two to three, while the number of part-time people has declined from four to one (a net reduction of one half).

Thus, the ratio of staff members to board members has grown from one staff member to every eight board members in 1981 to one staff member to every 10.3 board members.

Economic Resources. LUM's income more than doubled, going from $93,215 in 1981 to $202,796 in 1984. Cash reserves, which were $23,439 in 1981, increased to $38,185.

Denominational pledges grew from $35,650 in 1981 to $46,000 in 1984, but levels of actual support declined slightly to $43,000 as denominational agencies experienced some difficulty raising mission money and reallocated some support. Presbytery gave LUM $26,000; the United Methodist conference gave $10,000; the United Church of Christ, $5,000; and the United Episcopal Charities, $2,000.

Congregational support increased considerably, going from $26,567 in 1981 to

$40,647 in 1984.

The biggest growth was from "other" sources (e.g., direct mailings to individuals for Summer Camp and the Centralized Emergency Fund). This portion of LUM's budget grew from $30,998 in 1981 to $121,218 in 1984.

Formalization. There has been no appreciable change in LUM's formal record keeping, except to improve some of the language in its personnel policies document.

Complexity. In 1981, all of LUM's programs were oriented toward the Greater Lafayette area. While the vast majority of its programs are still focused on Lafayette, there has been a marked increase in LUM's activities outside of Lafayette. This vertical differentiation has occurred mainly as LUM's Indiana Task Force on Poor Relief has established chapters in Columbus, South Bend, Goshen, Indianapolis, and Mt. Vernon, and has become more active monitoring the state legislature's activities in the area of poor relief. It also has occurred as word of LUM's effectiveness has spread and groups in other communities have called on LUM's staff for advice. For example, after consultation with LUM's staff, a church in South Bend has started a Jubilee Christmas Shop of its own.

LUM also has added five programs oriented toward Lafayette. These include a Host-Hostess program, which was introduced in 1982; an annual Clothing Give-a-way, which started in 1983; and Energy Fast Day, which was held in 1983; a Voter Registration program, which started in 1984; and petition drives, two of which were done in 1984. The Food Buying Club, Volunteer Transportation, and the Christmas Project were terminated in 1982.

There have been no changes in the number of committees.

Bureaucratization. There have been no important changes in personnel policies since 1981.

Distribution of Authority. The distribution of authority was estimated by dividing the total number of directors, officers, and committee chairs by the total number of board and staff members. LUM continues to have one director and four officers. The number of committees remains at five, but the chair of the Indiana Task Force on Poor Relief now is included in the Executive Committee and reports to the board three to four times a year. The total size of the board and staff has grown to 39.5 (36 board members and 3.5 staff people).

The director, four officers, five committee chairs, and the chair of the task force comprise a core of 11 decision makers, who represent 28 percent of all the people on the board and staff (the same as it was in 1981).

Administrative Succession. Rev. Dolphin continues as LUM's director, so LUM has not had to deal with the problem of administrative succession.

Leadership. Rev. Dolphin's leadership style has not changed much since 1981. He continues to rely heavily on other staff and board members. Indeed, he says with the increased size of the board and a slightly smaller staff, he must rely even more on others: "There's no way I can be on top of everything all the time."

He also continues to concentrate on LUM, local churches, and low-income people, but pressures have increased to work with urban ministry groups elsewhere in the state (e.g., Patchwork Central in Evansville) and local groups (e.g., United Way, human service agencies). Rev. Dolphin has given higher priority to religious groups dealing with social concerns than to human service agencies.

Board leadership remains strong. All officers and committee chairs are now representatives of member churches. And the board has handled major issues decisively.

Flexibility. LUM's total program remains relatively fixed, but there still is considerable flexibility. The Food Buying Club, Volunteer Transportation, and the Christmas Project were dropped in 1982. Six new programs were added: the Host-Hostess program, the Indiana Task Force on Poor Relief, the Clothing Give-a-way, the Energy Fast Day, Voter Registration, and the petition drives.

Stability. Through 1984, 38 local churches have joined LUM. Four of these have dropped their memberships; one of these rejoined in 1981. Thus, LUM has retained 92 percent of the congregations which have ever joined.

However, it continues to struggle with rapid turnover among member church representatives. Rev. Dolphin has come to accept this turnover as "the nature of the beast," but also laments its impact on board leadership. It takes new board members several months to learn how the organization runs and a year or so to feel comfortable enough to chair a committee. At that point, they might be ready to assume even more responsibility, but with board members turning over about every two years, many leave before their leadership has been fully expressed.

There has been increased stability among the staff. As the full-time staff has increased from two to three and the part-time staff has shrunk from four to one, continuity has increased.

Productivity. In 1981, LUM's four staff people (two full-time and four part-time) conducted 12 programs (i.e., three programs per staff person). In 1984, LUM's 3.5 staff members conducted 12 programs (i.e., 3.4 programs per staff person). Thus, LUM's productivity has continued to be quite high. According to Rev. Dolphin, LUM's staff is now about as productive as it can be.

Intra-organizational Relations. Growth in the size of the board and the turnover among board members have imposed some limits on board members' ability to develop close personal relationships. Rev. Dolphin has tried to promote close bonds by having board members introduce themselves at meetings and, occasionally, by breaking the board into small discussion groups.

Within this context, there appears to be considerable trust and confidence. There are no observable factions or signs of conflict. Board members feel comfortable voicing both approval and dissent.

Staff-board relations also remain positive.

Inter-organizational Relations. Relations with member churches have remained positive.

Relations with denominational bodies have varied. Relations with the United Church of Christ and Episcopal diocese are growing, as evidenced by their continued financial support and the frequency with which these groups call attention to LUM's programs in their publications. Presbytery's moral support remains intact, though its financial support has shifted slightly as its funding of two new ecumenical groups (a retreat center and a branch of Habitat for Humanity) has increased. The moral and financial support of the northern conference of the United Methodist church were in doubt during the last several months of 1984, when denominational officials indicated they might reduce their support of LUM because of its increased pressure on the township trustees (many of whom are United Methodists). However, after several months of uncertainty, LUM learned that conference support had been reaffirmed.

Relations with the poor have continued to grow as more and more low-income people turn to LUM for help (see later section on effectiveness). LUM's efforts to reform poor relief also have solidified its credibility among low-income people. The one area where LUM has never had much success is in bringing low-income people onto its board.

Conflict with township trustees has intensified as LUM's task force on poor relief has grown. The task force has mobilized support for some legislation trustees have opposed, and opposed some legislation they have supported. Through its newsletter, *The Overseer*, it also has exposed deficiencies in the system (e.g., the failure of some trustees to comply with laws concerning accountability). It also has turned considerable media attention on problems with poor relief. Trustees have responded by urging its supporters to reduce their support. This conflict is likely to persist until there are changes in the way poor relief is handled.

Finally, LUM maintains good working relations with human service agencies. Agencies call LUM 10 to 12 times a week for information or assistance of one kind or another. However, LUM's staff often has declined invitations to participate in meetings called by agency leaders. LUM's staff recognizes that its reluctance to become more involved in agency concerns may faster some ill-will, but insists that its first priority is to churches and low-income people, not agencies.

In short, LUM has branched out into riskier areas of social change. Yet, it has grown in size and resources; leadership remains strong; stability persists (except for turnover among board representatives); and productivity remains high. Relations within the group remain positive, as are relations with most denominations, member churches, and the poor. Relations with human service agencies are business-like, while relations with township trustees involve considerable conflict.

Effectiveness

LUM has continued to pursue four goals on behalf of its member churches and four within them (see Table 1, Chapter 8). I have organized this update around these goals.

Changing Policies and Practices on Behalf of Churches. The advocates continue to monitor the policies and practices of groups such as the utility companies, and the Public Policy Committee continues to examine issues such as voter registration.

But, the major development in this area has been the formation of the Indiana Task Force on Poor Relief in 1982. The task force has studied the strengths and weaknesses of Indiana's poor relief system as administered by township trustees, concluding that the system needs to be changed (specifically, that it should be moved from the township level to the county level of state government).

It also monitors the actions of township trustees (e.g., their failures to comply with state regulations) and actions of the state legislature concerning bills relating to poor relief.

Finally, it publishes regular reports through its newsletter, *The Overseer*, which reached about 1,600 people around the state in 1984. These reports are intended to promote public awareness of Indiana's poor relief system and actions which might improve that system.

The task force has made substantial progress in the direction of systemic change. Task force chapters have been formed in five other communities. Public awareness has increased as the news media have picked up on task force reports. Progressive bills have passed in the state legislature and regressive ones have been defeated. A bill has been submitted to shift the poor relief system to the county level. Support for the bill has grown as newspaper and political leaders in several cities have endorsed the proposed changes.

Cultivating Relations with and among the Poor. LUM has discontinued two somewhat successful programs in this area: the Christmas Project and the Food Buying Club. The Christmas Project was over-shadowed by Jubilee Christmas. The Food Buying Club was dropped because families felt the amount of effort required to run the program did not result in sufficient savings. In their place, LUM has expanded the Grow-a-Row project to include neighborhood gardens. With help from LUM volunteers, residents of six to seven low-income neighborhoods work on summer gardens. This approach has been more successful in cultivating bonds with and among the poor and yielding significant savings. LUM also has instituted an Host-Hostess program which fosters ties between church members who volunteer their time to serve as hosts and hostesses for the low-income people who come to LUM's office for assistance.

Increasing Resources within Low-Income Groups. Grow-a-Row, Repairs on Wheels, and Summer Camp continue to function much as they did in 1981. Two to three tons of food are distributed each year. Twenty-five to 30 home repairs are made each month. And 100 to 125 low-income youngsters go to camp each summer.

The Volunteer Transportation program, which helped only 10 riders in 1981, was discontinued in March 1982.

Emergency Relief. LUM continues to train advocates. In 1981, 20 advocates helped 1,334 people. In 1984, 25 advocates helped 3,315 people.

The Centralized Emergency Fund has grown rapidly. In 1981, LUM distributed $24,760 to 594 families. In 1984, it distributed $50,825 to 1,264 families (about 70 percent of the low-income families in Tippecanoe County).

Increasing Church Sponsorship of Social Concerns Programs. The two programs which member churches have embraced most readily have been Jubilee Christmas and Grow-a-Row.

Jubilee Christmas has gained more widespread acceptance than any other program. Churches and individual donors quickly "buy into" the concept of giving gifts in a way which does not undercut low-income parents. Thus, it has become one of LUM's most successful programs.

In 1981, 109 low-income families were invited to the Jubilee Christmas Shop LUM conducted at Central Presbyterian Church and there were four satellite shops at member churches. In 1984, 308 families were invited to LUM's Jubilee at St. Thomas Aquinas Center and there were eight satellite shops.

Churches also have been inclined to adopt the Grow-a-Row project. In 1981, 14 member churches participated in Grow-a-Row. In 1984, 28 member churches were involved. Volunteers from 13 non-member churches also participated.

LUM also has made some progress promoting Repairs on Wheels groups within local churches, especially those with large student populations. In 1981, only three of LUM's member churches had such groups. In 1984, seven had them.

Changing Priorities, Attitudes, and Beliefs. LUM's two main vehicles for changing the priorities, attitudes, and beliefs of church members have been its monthly newsletter, *The Seed*, and its Seeds of Vision conferences.

In 1981, *The Seed* was being sent to about 1,500 people. By 1984, it was going to about 2,400 people (a 60 percent increase). Thus, word of LUM's activities was reaching more and more people.

LUM conducted a Seeds of Vision conference in spring 1982. The keynote speaker was James A. Forbes from Union Theological Seminary. Workshops were organized around three concepts: The Call (sessions on Biblical Prophets, the Parables of Jesus, and Prayer and Justice), The Challenge (sessions on poor relief, human rights, integrating social concerns into church school programs, and abolishing nuclear weapons), and The Church in Action (session on how churches can be involved in refugee resettlement, feeding the hungry, and health care). The day ended with an ecumenical worship service.

The 350 people in attendance responded with much the same enthusiasm as they did in the two previous conferences.

Compared to 1981, then, LUM is considerably more effective in changing social policies and practices on behalf of local churches and providing emergency relief to low-income people. Its effectiveness within local churches also has increased. Its efforts at cultivating relations with and among the poor and increasing resources with low-income groups are about as effective as they were in 1981.

REFERENCES

Aldrich, Howard E.
    1979   *Organizations and Environments*, Englewood Cliffs, N.J.: Prentice Hall
    1971   "The Sociable Organization: A Case Study of MENSA and Some Propositions," *Sociology and Social Research* 55 (July):429-441

Altizer, Thomas and William Hamilton
    1966   *Radical Theology and the Death of God*, Indianapolis: Bobbs-Merrill.

Amerson, Philip A. and Jackson W. Carroll
    1979   "The Suburban Church and Racism: Is Change Possible?" *Review of Religious Research* 20 (Summer):335-349.

Bahr, Howard M., Louis Franz Bartel, and Bruce A. Chadwick
    1971   "Orthodoxy, Activism, and the Salience of Religion, *Journal for the Scientific Study of Religion*, 10 (Summer):69-75.

Bendix, Reinhard
    1956   *Work and Authority in Industry*, New York: John Wiley and Sons.

Benestad, J. Bryan and Francis J. Butler
    1981   *Quest for Justice*, Washington, D.C.: U.S. Catholic Conference.

Berger, Peter L.
    1963   "A Market Model for the Analysis of Ecumenicity." *Social Research* 30 (1):77-90.
    1961   *The Noise of Solemn Assemblies*, Garden City, New York: Doubleday.

Bissaillon, Francis Philip
    1972   "Church Structure and Decision-Making: A Study of Three Denominations? Responses to the Black Manifesto." Master of Science Thesis, Department of Sociology and Anthropology, Purdue University.

Blizzard, Samuel W.
    1956a   "The Minister's Dilemma," *Christian Century* 73 (April 25):508-509.
    1956b   "Role Conflicts of the Urban Protestant Parish Ministers," *The City Church*, 7 (September):13-15.
    1958a   "The Protestant Parish Minister's Integrating Roles," *Religious Education* 53 (July/August):374-380.
    1958b   "The Parish Minister's Self-Image of His Master Role," *Pastoral Psychology*, 9 (December):25-32.

Blume, Norman
    1970   "Clergyman and Social Action," *Sociology and Social Research* 54 (January):237-248.

Boyd, Malcolm
    1969   *The Underground Church*. Baltimore: Penguin.

Brewer, Earl D.C. et al.
    1967   *Protestant Parish*, Atlanta: Communication Art Press.

Brown, Robert McAfee
    1969   *The Ecumenical Revolution*. New York: Doubleday.

Burkey, Richard M.
    1978   *Ethnic and Racial Groups*. Menlo Park, California: Cummings Publishing Company.

Campbell, Ernest Q. and Thomas F. Pettigrew
    1959   *Christians in Racial Crisis*, Washington, D.C.: Public Affairs Press.

Cambell, Thomas C. and Yoshio Fukymama
    1970   *The Fragmented Layman*, Philadelphia: Pilgrim Press.

Campolo, Anthony
    1971   *A Denomination Looks at Itself*, Valley Forge, Pennsylvania: Judson Press.

Carroll, Jackson W. and Robert Wilson
    1980   *Too Many Pastors? Understanding the Clergy Job Market*. New York: Pilgrim Press.

Cavert, Samuel McCrea
    1968   *The American Churches in the Ecumenical Movement, 1900-1969*. New York: Association Press.

Champion, Dean J.
    1975   *The Sociology of Organizations*, New York: McGraw-Hill.

Clark, Henry
    1965   *The Christian Case Against Poverty*. New York: Association Press.

Cox, Harvey G.
    1968   "The 'New Breed' in American Churches: Sources of Social Activism in American Religion," in William McLoughlin and Robert Bellah (eds.), *Religion in America*, Boston: Beacon Press.

D'Antonio, William V., James D. Davidson, and Joseph A. Schlangen
    1966   *Protestants and Catholics in Two Oklahoma Communities*, Department of Sociology, University of Notre Dame, mimeograph.

Davidson, James D.
1985a "Captive Congregations: Why Local Churches Don't Pursue Equality," in John Rouse, Stephen Johnson, and Joseph Tamney (eds.), *The Political Role of Religion in the United States*, Boulder, CO: Westview.
1985b "Theories and Measures of Poverty: Toward an Holistic Approach," *Sociological Focus*, August.
1980a "An Evaluation of the Tippecanoe County Federation of Churches." Department of Sociology and Anthropology, Purdue University.
1980b "Churches and Churchgoers in Lafayette, Indiana." Department of Sociology and Anthropology, Purdue University.
1977 "Socio-Economic Status and Ten Dimensions of Religious Commitment." *Sociology and Social Research* 61 (July):462-485.
1975 "Glock's Model of Religious Commitment: Assessing Some Different Approaches and Results," *Review of Religious Research* 16 (Winter):83-93.
1972 "Religious Belief as an Independent Variable," *Journal for the Scientific Study of Religion* 11 (March):65-75.
1970 "Protestant Churches as Voluntary Associations," Indiana Academy of Social Science, *Proceedings 1969*, 110-123.

Davidson, James D. (with Ronald Elly, Thomas Hull and Donald Nead)
1976 *The Lafayette Urban Ministry: A Model for Urban Ministries and an Evaluation of LUM*, Lafayette, IN: Lafayette Urban Ministry.

Davidson, James D. and Dean D. Knudsen
1977 "A New Approach to Religious Commitment," *Sociological Focus* 10 (April):251-273.

Davidson, James D. and Michael K. Roberts
1984 "Pursuing Equality," presented at annual meeting of the Society for the Scientific Study of Religion, Chicago, October.

Davidson, James D., Dean D. Knudsen, and Stephen R. Lerch
1983 "Involvement in Family, Religion, Education, Work and Politics," *Sociological Focus*, 16 (January):13-36.

Davidson, James D., Gerhard Hoffman, and William R. Brown
1978 "Measuring and Explaining High School Interracial Climates," *Social Problems* 26 (October):50-70.

Demerath, N. J., III
1968 "Trends and Anti-Trends in Religious Change," pp. 349-448 in Eleanor Sheldon and Wilbert Moore (eds.), Indicators of Social Change. New York: Russell Sage.
1965 *Social Class and American Protestantism*, Chicago: Rand McNally.

Demerath, N. J., III and Phillip E. Hammond
1969 *Religion in Social Context*. New York: Random House.

Dixon, Robert and Dean R. Hoge
1978 "Models and Priorities of the Catholic Church as Held by Suburban Laity," *Review of Religious Research* 20 (Spring):150-167.

Documents
1983 *County and City Data Book*, Washington, D.C.: Bureau of the Census.
1982 *Handbook of Basic Economic Statistics*, Washington, D.C.: Economic Statistics Bureau.
1981 *Labor Market Review and Planning Information*, Lafayette, IN: Indiana Employment Security Division.
annual *Roster of State and Local Officials of the State of Indiana*, Indianapolis, IN: State Board of Accounts.
annual *Statistical Abstracts*, Washington, D.C.: U.S. Department of Commerce.
1980 *Census Summary, 1980*, Lafayette, IN: Tippecanoe County Area Plan Commission.

Earle, John R., Dean D. Knudsen, and Donald W. Shriver, Jr.
1976 *Spindle and Spires*, Atlanta: John Knox Press.

Egan, John J., Peggy Roach, and Philip J. Murnion
1979 "Catholic Committee on Urban Ministry: Ministry to the Ministers," *Review of Religious Research* 20 (Summer):279-290.

Emery, F. E. and E. L. Trist
1967 "The Causal Texture of Organizational Environments," pp. 435-447 in Walter A. Hill and Douglas M. Egan (eds.) *Readings in Organizational Theory: A Behavioral Approach*. Boston: Allyn and Bacon.

Encyclopedia Americana
annual *The Americana Annual*, New York: Americana Corporation.

Esman, Milton J.
1972 "Some Issues in Institution Building Theory," pp. 65-90 in D. Woods Thomas, Harry R. Potter, William L. Miller, and Adrian F. Aveni, Institution Building: A Model for *Applied Social Change*, Cambridge, Mass.: Schenkman Publishing Co.

Etzioni, Amitai
1965 "Dual Leadership in Complex Organizations," *American Sociological Review* 30 (October):688-698.
1964 *Modern Organizations*, Englewood Cliffs, NJ: Prentice-Hall.

Evans, Bernard F.
1979 "Campaign for Human Development: Church Involvement in Social Change," *Review of Religious Research* 20 (Summer):264-278.

Feagin, Joe R.
1978 *Racial and Ethnic Relations*, Englewood Cliffs, N.J.: Prentice-Hall.
1975 *Subordinating the Poor*, Englewood Cliffs, N.J.: Prentice-Hall.
1965 "Prejudice, Orthodoxy, and the Social Situation," *Social Forces*, 44 (September):45-56.

Fichter, Joseph
1968 *America's Forgotten Priests: What They Are Saying*. New York: Harper and Row.

Fischer, Claude S.
1975 "Toward a Subcultural Theory of Urbanism." *American Journal of Sociology* 80 (May):1319-1341.

Flacks, Richard
1971 "Revolt of the Young Intelligentsia: Revolutionary Class and Post-Scarcity America," in Roderick Aya and Norman Miller (eds.), *The New American Revolution*, New York: Free Press.

Fuchs, Victor
1967 "Redefining Poverty and Redistributing Income," *The Public Interest* 8:88-95.

Gamson, William A.
1975 *The Strategy of Social Protest*, Homewood, IL: The Dorsey Press.

Garrett, William R.
1980 "Interplay and Rivalry Between Denominational and Ecumenical Organization," pp. 246-362 in Ross P. Scherer (ed.) *American Denominational Organization*, Pasadena, CA: William Carey Library.

Gaustad, Edwin
1968 "America's Institutions of Faith," in William McLoughlin and Robert Bellah (eds.), *Religion in America*. Boston: Beacon Press.

Gibbs, David R., Samuel A. Mueller, and James R. Wood
1973 "Doctrinal Orthodoxy, Salience, and the Consequential Dimension," *Journal for the Scientific Study of Religion*, 12 (March):35-52.

Glock, Charles Y. and Rodney Stark
1966 *Christian Beliefs and Anti-Semitism*, New York: Harper and Row.
1965 *Religion and Society in Tension*, Chicago: Rand McNally.

Gorsuch, Richard L. and Daniel Aleshire
1974 "Christian Faith and Ethnic Prejudice: A Review and Interpretation of Research," *Journal for the Scientific Study of Religion*, 13 (September):281-307.

Graham, James
1970 *The Enemies of the Poor*, New York: Vintage.

Greeley, Andrew M.
1976 *The American Catholic: A Social Portrait*. New York: Basic Books.

Greenwood, Elma L.
1967 *How Churches Fight Poverty*. New York: Friendship Press.

Hadden, Jeffrey K.
1969 *The Gathering Storm in the Churches*, New York: Doubleday.

Hadden, Jeffrey K. and Raymond C. Rymph
1966 "Social Structure and Civil Rights Involvement: A Case Study of Protestant Ministers." *Social Forces* 45 (September):51-61.

Hadden, Jeffrey K. and Charles F. Longino, Jr.
1974 *Gideon's Gang*, New York: Pilgrim Press.

Hall, Richard H.
1972 and
1982 *Organizations: Structure and Process*, Englewood Cliffs, NJ: Prentice-Hall (first and third editions).

Hamilton, Richard F.
1972 *Class and Politics in the United States*, New York: Wiley.

Hammond, Phillip E. and Robert Mitchell
1965 "Segmentation of Radicalism: The Case of the Protestant Campus Minister," *American Journal of Sociology* 71 (September):133-143.

Harrison, Paul M.
1959 *Authority and Power in the Free Church Tradition*, Princeton: Princeton University Press.

Hessel, Dieter T.
1979 "Solidarity Ethics: A Public Focus for the Church." *Review of Religious Research* 20 (Summer):251-263.

Hogan, Thaddeus
1982 "Christian Unity: Our Unfinished Task," *Catholic Update* (January):1-4.

Hoge, Dean R.
　　1976　　*Division in the Protestant House*, Philadelphia: Westminster Press.
Hoge, Dean R. and Jeffrey Faue
　　1973　　"Sources of Conflict Over Priorities of the Protestant Church," *Social Forces*, 52 (December):178-194.
Hoge, Dean R., Everett Perry, and Gerald L. Klever
　　1978　　"Theology as a Source of Disagreement about Protestant Church Goals and Priorities," *Review of Religious Research* 19 (Winter):116-138.
Hougham, Anne and James D. Davidson
　　1979　　"Toward a Relative Approach to Poverty," presented at annual meeting of North Central Sociological Association, Cincinnati.
Hunter, James Davison
　　1980　　"The New Class and the Young Evangelicals." *Review of Religious Research* 22 (December):115-169.
Jacquet, Constant H.
　　annual　*Yearbook of American and Canadian Churches*. Nashville: Abingdon Press.
Jenkins, J. Craig
　　1983　　"Resource Mobilization Theory and the Study of Social Movements," *Annual Review of Sociology* 9:527-553.
　　1977　　"Radical Transformation of Organizational Goals," *Administrative Science Quarterly* 22 (December):568-586.
Johnson, Benton
　　1967　　"Theology and the Position of Pastors on Public Issues," *American Sociological Review*, 32 (June):433-442.
Johnson, Douglas W.
　　1980　　"Program Dissensus Between Denominational Grass Roots and Leadership and Its Consequences," pp. 330-345 in Ross Scherer (ed.) *American Denominational Organization*. Pasadena, CA: William Carey Library.
　　1969　　"A Study of New Forms of Ministry," Department of Research, Office of Planning and Program, National Council of Churches.
Johnson, Douglas W., Paul R. Picard, and Bernard Quinn
　　1974　　*Churches and Church Membership in the United States*, Washington, D.C.: Glenmary Research Center.
Johnson, Douglas W. and George W. Cornell
　　1972　　*Punctured Perceptions*, New York: Friendship Press.
Johnstone, Ronald L.
　　1975　　*Religion and Society in Interaction*, Englewood Cliffs, N.J.: Prentice-Hall.
Keedy, T. C.
　　1958　　"Anomie and Religious Orthodoxy," *Sociology and Social Research*, 43 (September-October):34-37.
Kelly, James R.
　　1979　　"The Spirit of Ecumenism: How Wide How Deep, How Mindful of Truth." *Review of Religous Research* 20 (Spring):180-194.
Kim, Gertrud
　　1980　　"Roman Catholic Organization Since Vatican II," pp. 84-129 in Ross Scherer (ed.) *American Denominational Organization*, Pasadena, CA: William Carey Library.
Knapp, Forrest L.
　　1966　　*Church Cooperation*. New York: Doubleday.
Knoke, David and James R. Wood
　　1981　　*Organized for Action*, New Brunswick, N.J.: Rutgers University Press.
Lee, Robert
　　1960　　*The Social Sources of Church Unity*. New York: Abingdon Press.
Lenski, Gerhard
　　1961　　*The Religious Factor*, New York: Doubleday.
Litterer, Joseph A.
　　1963　　*Organizations: Structure and Behavior*, New York: Wiley.
Lofland, John and Michael Jamison
　　1984　　"Social Movement Locals: Modal Member Structures," *Sociological Analysis* 45 (Summer):115-129.
Maniha, John and Charles Perrow
　　1965　　"The Reluctant Organization and the Aggressive Environment," *Administrative Science Quarterly* 10 (September):238-257.
Marrett, Cora Bagley
　　1980　　"Influences on the Rise of New Organizations: The Formation of Women's Medical Societies," *Administrative Science Quarterly*, 25 (June):185-199.

Martin, William
    1972   *Christians in Conflict*, Chicago: Center for the Scientific Study of Religion
Marty, Martin
    1981   "The New Christian Right," pp. 605-606 in *1982 Book of the Year*, Chicago: Encyclopedia Britannica.
    1970   *Righteous Empire*, New York: Dial Press.
Marx, Gary T.
    1967   "Religion: Opiate or Inspiration of Civil Rights Militancy Among Negroes," *American Sociological Review*, 32 (February):64-22.
McCarthy, John D. and Mayer N. Zald
    1977   "Resource Mobilization and Social Movements: A Partial Theory," *American Journal of Sociology* 82 (May):1212-1241.
    1973   *The Trend of Social Movements in America: Professionalization and Resource Mobilization*, Morristown, N.J.: General Learning Corporation.
Modras, Ronald E.
    1968   *Paths to Unity*. New York: Sheed and Ward.
Money
    1982   "Which States Tax Most," February, page 62.
Myers, Phyllis Goudy and James D. Davidson
    1984   "Who Participates in Ecumenical Activity?" *Review of Religious Research* 25 (March):185-203.
Myers, Phyllis Goudy
    1984   The Formation of Organizations: A Case Study of the North American Soccer League, doctoral dissertation Department of Sociology and Anthropology, Purdue University.
Nelson, Hart M., Raytha Yokley, and Thomas Madron
    1973   "Ministerial Roles and Social Actionist Stance: Protestant Clergy and Protest in the Sixties," *American Sociological Review* 38 (June):375-386.
Oberschall, Anthony
    1973   *Social Conflict and Social Movements*, Englewood Cliffs, N.J.: Prentice-Hall.
Parella, Frederick J., Jr.
    1975   *Poverty in American Democracy.* Washington, D.C.: U.S. Catholic Conference.
Pennings, Johannes M.
    1980   "Environmental Influences on the Creation Process," in John R. Kimberly et al. (eds.), *The Organizational Life Cycle*, San Francisco: Jossey-Bass.
Perrow, Charles
    1979   "The Sixties Observed," pp. 192-211 in Zald and McCarthy (eds.), *The Dynamics of Social Movements*, Cambridge, Mass.: Winthrop Publishers.
    1961   "The Analysis of Goals in Complex Organizations," *American Sociological Review* 26 (December):688-699.
Photiadis, John D. and Jeanne Biggar
    1963   "Religiosity, Education, and Ethnic Distance," *American Journal for Sociology*, 67 (May):666-672.
Photiadis, John and Arthur L. Johnson
    1963   "Orthodoxy, Church Participation, and Authoritarianism," *American Journal of Sociology*, 69(November):244-248
Piven, Frances Fox and Richard A. Cloward
    1977   *Poor People's Movements: Why They Succeed, How They Fail*, New York: Pantheon Books.
Pope, Liston
    1942   *Millhands and Preachers*, New Haven: Yale University Press.
Potters, Bobby
    1975   "Poverty in Indiana: Magnitude and Intensity of the Problem." *Law and Poverty* 1 (December):17-28.
Pugh, D. S., D. J. Hickson, C. R. Hinings and C. Turner
    1968   "Dimensions of Organization Structure," *Administrative Science Quarterly*, 13 (June):65-91.
Quinley, Harold E.
    1974   *The Prophetic Clergy*, New York: John Wiley and Sons.
Quinn, Gary J. and James D. Davidson
    1976   "Theology: Sociology = Orthodoxy: Orthopraxis," *Theology Today*, 32 (January):345-352.
Rokeach, Milton
    1969   "Value Systems in Religion" and "Religious Values and Social Compassion," *Review of Religous Research*, 11 (Fall):3-39.
Roof, Wade Clark
    1980   "Socioeconomic Differentials Among White Socioreligious Groups in the United States." *Social Forces* 58 (September):280-289.
Ross, G. Alexander
    1980   "The Emergence of Organization Sets in Three Ecumenical Disaster Organizations: An Empirical and Theoretical Exploration," *Human Relations* 33 (Summer):23-39.

Rothschild-Whitt, Joyce
    1976   "Conditions Facilitating Participatory-Democratic Organizations," *Sociological Inquiry*, 46 (2):75-86.
Salisbury, W. Seward
    1962   "Religiosity, Regional Sub-Culture and Social Behavior," *Journal for the Scientific Study of Religion*, 2 (Fall):94-101.
Santa Ana, Julio, de
    1979   *Good News to the Poor*, Maryknoll, NY: Orbis Press.
Scherer, Ross P.
    1980   *American Denominational Organization*, Pasadena, California: William Carey Library.
Sider, Ronald J.
    1980   *Cry Justice*. New York: Paulist Press.
    1977   *Rich Christians in an Age of Hunger*, Downers Grove, IL: InterVarsity Press.
Siffin, William J.
    1972   "The Institution Building Perspective: Properties, Problems, and Promises," pp. 113-148 in D. Woods Thomas, Harry R. Potter, William L. Miller, and Adrian F. Aveni, *Institution Building: A Model for Applied Social Change*, Cambridge, Mass.: Schenkman Publishing Co.
Smelser, Neil J.
    1963   *Theory of Collective Behavior*, N.Y.: Free Press.
Smith, David Horton, Richard Eddy, and Burt R. Baldwin
    1973   *Voluntary Action Research: 1973*, Lexington, MA: D. C. Heath and Company.
    1972   *Voluntary Action Research: 1972*, Lexington, MA: D. C. Heath and Company.
Snow, David A. Louis A. Zucher, Jr., and Sheldon Ekland-Olson
    1980   "Social Networks and Social Movements: A Microstructural Approach to Differential Recruitment," *American Sociological Review*, 45 (October):787-801.
Stark, Rodney and Charles Y. Glock
    1969   "Prejudice and the Churches," in Charles Y. Glock and Ellen Siegelman (eds.), *Prejudice U.S.A.*, New York: Praeger Press.
    1968   *American Piety*, Berkely: University of California Press.
Stark, Rodney and Bruce D. Foster
    1979   "In Defense of Orthodoxy: Notes on the Validity of an Index," *Social Forces* 48 (March):383-393.
Starr, Paul
    1979   "The Phantom Community," pp. 245-273 in John Case and Rosemary Taylor (eds.) *Co-ops, Communes, and Collectives: Experiments in Social Change in the 1960s and 1970s*, N.Y.: Pantheon Books.
Stinchcombe, Arthur L.
    1965   "Social Structure and Organizations," pp. 142-193 in James G. March (ed.) *Handbook of Organizations*, Chicago: Rand McNally.
Stuhr, Walter
    1972   *The Public Style: A Study of Commitment Participation of Protestant Ministers*, Chicago: Center for the Scientific Study of Religion.
Swanson, Guy
    1968   "Modern Secularity: Its Meaning, Sources, and Interpretation," pp. 801-834 in Donald Cutler (ed.), *Religious Situation: 1968*. Boston: Beacon Press.
Takayama, K. Peter
    1983   "The Decline of the 1960s Religious 'Justice' Movement Organizations," presented at annual meeting of the Society for the Scientific Study of Religion, Knoxville, Tennessee.
    1980   "Strains, Conflicts, and Schisms in Protestant Denominations," pp. 298-329 in Ross P. Scherer (ed.), *American Denominational Organization*, Pasadena, CA: William Carey Library.
    1977   "The Rise and Decline of Interfaith Coordinating Organizations: Comparative Study," proposal submitted to Research Award Committee of the Society for the Scientific Study of Religion.
Takayama, K. Peter and Susanne B. Darnell
    1979   "The Aggressive Organization and the Reluctant Environment: the Vulnerability of an Inter-Faith Coordinating Agency," *Review of Religious Research*, 20 (Summer):315-334.
Thomas, Woods, Harry R. Potter, William L. Miller, and Adrian F. Aveni
    1972   *Institution Building: A Model for Applied Social Change*. Cambridge, Mass.: Schenkman.
Tilly, Charles
    1974   "The Chaos of the Living City," pp. 86-108 in Charles Tilly (ed.) *An Urban World*, Boston: Little, Brown, and Company.
    1973   "Do Communities Act?" *Sociological Inquiry* 43 (3,4):209-240.
Ullman, Edward
    1941   "A Theory of Location of Cities," *American Journal of Sociology* 46 (May):835-864.

Vander Werf, Nathan H.
   1976   "The State of the Local Regional Ecumenical Movement in the USA," in Living Ecumenism Series, No. 4, New York: The Commission on Regional/Local Ecumenism, National Council of Churches.

Vanfossen, Beth E.
   1979   *The Structure of Social Inequality*, Boston: Little Brown and Co.

Warren, Roland L.
   1967   "The Interorganizational Field as a Focus for Investigation," *Administrative Science Quarterly*, 12 (December):396-419.

Weber, Max
   1964   *The Theory of Social and Economic Organization*, Talcott Parsons (ed.), Glencoe, Ill.: Free Press.

Wilson, John
   1978   *Religion in American Society*, Englewood Cliffs, N.J.: Prentice-Hall.

Winter, J. Alan
   1977   *Continuities in the Sociology of Religion*, New York: Harper and Row.

Wood, James L. and Maurice Jackson
   1982   *Social Movements*, Belmont, CA: Wadsworth.

Wood, James R.
   1981   *Leadership in Voluntary Organizations*, New Brunswick, N.J.: Rutgers University Press.
   1972   "Unanticipated Consequences of Organizational Coalitions: Ecumenical Cooperation and Civil Rights Policy," *Social Forces* 50 (June):512-521.
   1970   "Authority and Controversial Policy: The Churches and Civil Rights," *American Sociological Review* 35 (December):1057-1069.

Wuthnow, Robert
   1976   "Recent Patterns of Secularization: A Problem of Generations?" *American Sociological Review* 41 (October):850-867.
   1973   "Religious Commitment and Conservatism: In Search of an Elusive Relationship," in Charles Y. Glock (ed.), *Religion in Sociological Perspective*, Belmont, California: Wadsworth.

Zald, Mayer N.
   1982   "Theological Crucibles: Social Movements in and of Religion," *Review of Religious Research* 23 (June):317-336.
   1970   *Organizational Change: The Political Economy of the YMCA*, Chicago: University of Chicago Press.

Zald, Mayer and John D. McCarthy
   1979   *The Dynamics of Social Movements: Resource Mobilization, Social Control, and Tactics*, Cambridge, Mass.: Winthrop.

Zald, Mayer N. and Roberta Ash
   1966   "Social Movement Organizations: Growth, Decay, and Change," *Social Forces*, 44 (March):327-341.

SUBJECT INDEX

Abundant Life Fellowship, 186
Administrative Officer (see Director)
Administrative Succession, 7
 defined, 9
 described, 72-74, 187
 finding summarized, 157-162
 hypothesized impact on institutionalization, 18, 27
 impact of economic resources on, 106-107
 impact of leadership on, 100, 103
 impact on LUM's institutionalization, 105-106
Adult Basic Education, 66, 74, 101, 114, *125-126*, 149
Adventure Club, 66, 81, 101, 104-105, 114, 121, *124-125*, 141, 149, 178
Alcoa, 173
Advocates, 67, 71, 84, 85, 95, 101, 107, 113-114, *117-118*, 119-121, *127*, 141-142, 144-145, 148-149, 152-153, 168, 177-178, 189
American Indian Movement, 87
Anderson, City of, 46
"Appeal for Theological Affirmation," 89
Appendix A, 69, 174, 181-182
Appendix B, 86, 140, 169, 173, 185-191
At-Large Members (see Leadership; Membership)

Benton County, 51
Bethany Presbyterian Church, 37, 53, 63, 69, 172
Bible (see Ideological Justification)
Big Brothers-Big Sisters, 50
Black Power Movement (see Social Conditions)
Blacks (see Board of Directors', Integrated Hands, Membership, Place Factors)
Blessed Sacrament Church, 63
Board of Directors (see Bureaucratization, Distribution of Authority, Leadership, Membership)
Board of Health
 Indiana, 177
 Tippecanoe County, 118
Book of Common Prayer, Episcopal, 88
Brethren, Church of, 53, 55, 63, 124
Bureaucratization, 6
 defined, 9
 described, 68-71, 187
 finding summarized, 157-162
 impact of leadership on, 103
 impact of LUM's effectiveness, 148
 impact on LUM's institutionalization, 109
Busing, 88

Call to Action, 90
Calvary Baptist Church, 186
Campaign for Human Development (see Community Infant Care Center, Ideological Justification, Personnel, Resources in Support Groups, Spanish-Speaking Persons Task Force)
Carroll County, 51
Cass County, 51
Case Study Method, 29-32, 164-165
Caterpillar Tractor Company, 97
Catholic Charities, 24
Catholic Congregations (see Cooperation, Resources in Support Groups, Support Groups)
Census Data, 32
Center for Christian Growth, 176

"Central Peace" Function (see Community Size)
Central Presbyterian Church, 38-39, 53, 63, 73-74, 122-123, 172, 190
Centralized Emergency Fund, 66, 82, 84, 114, 120, *126-127*, 137, 142-145, 148, 152, 178, 190
Champaign-Urbana, City of, 51
Charisma, 171
Charismatic Movement, 88
Chicago, City of, 66, 176
Christ United Methodist Church, 63, 119, 152-153
Christian Campus House, 186
Christmas Project, 66, 113-114, *120, 134*, 135, 152-153, 169-170, 178, 187-189
Church Membership (see Economic Resources, Resources in Support Groups)
Church Women United, 96, 178
City Council, Lafayette (see Political Climate, Revenue Sharing Task Force)
City Council, West Lafayette (see Political Climate)
Civil Rights Movement (see Social Conditions)
Clergy (see Personnel, Professional Staff Support within Support Groups, Support Groups)
Clinton County, 51
Clothing Give-a-Way, 187-188
Columbian Park, 124
Columbus, IN, City of, 187
Commission on Aging, Indiana State, 123
Committees (see Leadership)
Committee Chairs (see Distribution of Authority, Leadership)
Community Infant Care Center, 67, 74, 87, 105-106, 114, *126*, 149
Community Service Administration, 117
Community Size
 defined, 23
 findings summarized, 157-162
 hypothesis, 18, 23
 impact on LUM's effectiveness, 145
 impact on LUM's formation, 51
 impact on LUM's institutionalization, 97
Competition
 defined, 22-23
 findings summarized, 157-162
 hypothesis, 18, 22-23
 impact on LUM's effectiveness, 145
 impact on LUM's formation, 50-51
 impact on LUM's institutionalization, 96-97
Complexity, 6
 defined, 8-9
 described, 66-67, 187
 findings summarized, 157-162
 hypothesized impact on effectiveness, 28
 impact of administrative succession on, 105
 impact of economic resources on, 106
 impact of leadership on, 100
 impact of purpose on, 104
 impact on LUM's institutionalization, 107
Conflict, Liberal-Conservative (see Cooperation, Religious Policies and Practices)
Congregation of Reconciliation, 22
Congregations, Local
 Affluence (see Resources in Support Groups)
 Catholic (see Cooperation, Existence of the Problem, Membership, Resources in Support

Groups, Support Groups)
financial support of LUM (see Economic Resources from Support Groups, Stability)
Jewish, 102
liberal and conservative, 97-98
as member churches, 60-63, 82-83
Protestant (see Cooperation, Existence of the Problem, Membership, Resources in Support Groups, Support Groups)
religious beliefs, 94-95
social attitudes, 94
social concerns priorities, 4, 92-94
social concerns programs, 92-93
support of Tippecanoe County Federation of Churches (see Cooperation)
supporting LUM's formation, 52-55
survey of, 31
Congress Street United Methodist Church, 186
Conservatism
political (see Political Climate)
religious (see Cooperation, Religious Policies and Practices)
Constitution/Bylaws (see Formalization)
Construction, New Church (see Economic Resources in Religious Sphere)
Consultation on Church Union (see Cooperation)
Contributions, Per Capita (see Economic Resources in Religious Sphere)
Cooperation (Ecumenism)
defined, 19, 22
findings summarized, 157-162
hypothesis, 18-19, 22
impact on LUM's effectiveness, 142-143
impact on LUM's formation, 42-43, 50
impact on LUM's institutionalization, 89, 96
Council on Aging, 67, 114, 116, *122-123*
Counter Culture Movement (see Social Conditions)
County City Data Book, 92
Covenant Presbyterian Church, 37, 52-53, 106, 108
Criminal Justice (see Social Conditions)
Cross-Lines Cooperative Council, 135

Data Collection Procedures (see Congregations, Local; Evaluation; Literature and Research, Other; Newspaper, Local; Participant-Observation; Records and Documents; Tippecanoe County Federation of Churches)
summarized, 30, 171-172
Dayton, IN, City of, 100
Dayton, OH, City of, 22
Dayton United Methodist Church, 63, 119, 153
Dedication/Commitment (see Leadership)
Democrats (see Political Climate)
Denominational Agencies (see Economic Resources from Support Groups, Inter-Organizational Relations)
Detroit, City of, 90
Differentiation (see Complexity)
horizontal, 8, 66-67, 187
vertical, 8, 66, 187
Diocese of Indianapolis, Episcopal, 83-84
Direction/Competence (see Leadership)
Director (Administrative Officer, Pastor-Director, Urban Minister)
job description, 68-70, 182
Distribution of Authority, 6
defined, 9
described, 71-72, 187
findings summarized, 157-162
impact of complexity on, 107
impact on LUM's institutionalization, 109
impact of leadership on, 103
Dolphin, Rev. Judson
becomes director of LUM, 72-76
leadership, 74-75, 99-102, 148, 187
Dow Jones Industrial Average (see Economic Conditions)
Downtown Neighborhood Council, 36, 52

East Harlem Protestant Parish, 135
Economic Conditions
defined, 19
findings summarized, 157-162
hypothesis, 18-20
impact on LUM's effectiveness, 142
impact on LUM's formation, 43
impact on LUM's institutionalization, 89-90
Economic Resources in Religious Sphere, 6
defined, 8, 20
findings summarized, 157-162
hypothesis, 18, 20
impact on LUM's effectiveness, 142-143
impact on LUM's formation, 43, 172
impact on LUM's institutionalization, 90
Economic Resources from Support Groups
defined, 26
described, 38, 63-65, 186-187
findings summarized, 157-162
hypothesis, 18, 26-28
impact of effectiveness on, 110
impact of leadership on, 100
impact of purpose on, 104
impact of size on, 108-109
impact of stability on, 108
impact on LUM's effectiveness, 147-148
impact on LUM's formation, 56
impact on LUM's institutionalization, 106-107
Ecumenical Urban Ministries
goals, 3
problem of effectiveness, 12-13
problem of formation, 3-6
problem of institutionalization, 6-12
Ecumenism (see Cooperation)
Education (see Existence of the Problem, Support within Support Groups)
Effectiveness
addressing poverty on behalf of churches, 115-127
changing priorities, attitudes, beliefs, 135-140, 190-191
changing social policies, 116-118, 189
cultivating relations with and among the poor, 118-121, 189-190
defined, 12-13
findings summarized, 157-162
hypothesized impact on institutionalization, 18, 27-28
increasing resources among the poor, 121-126, 190
impact of different dimensions in total effectiveness, 28
impact on LUM's institutionalization, 109-111
Measurement of, 114-115
over the years, 139-140

policy implications, 168-170
problem of, 12-13, 155
promoting programs within churches, 133-135
providing emergency relief, 126-127, 190
relationships between goals, 150-153
summarized, 140, 189-191
summary of factors affecting, 153-154
within local churches, 127-140, 190-191
Effects on Individuals, LUM's, 128-130
Electronic Church, 89
Elly, Rev. Ronald
as seminarian, 36
becomes director of LUM, 38
convenor of Human Development Coalition, 116-117
describes clergy who supported LUM's formation, 55-56
interest in pastoral counseling, 72
interviewed for job as director of LUM, 38
job description as Urban Minister, 68
leadership, 52, 74-75, 99-102, 148
pastor at Hope Chapel, 36-38, 172
resigns from Hope Chapel, 38
resigns from LUM, 72-76, 91, 105-106, 108, 147, 174
Elston Presbyterian Church, 63, 172
Encyclopedia Americana, 87-89
Energy Fast Day, 187-188
Episcopal Church (see St. John's Episcopal Church; United Episcopal Charities)
Equal Rights Amendment, 87
Equality (see Ideological Justification)
Evaluation
of LUM, 29-33, 100, 102, 105, 171-172
of Tippecanoe County Federation of Churches, 30, 32
Evansville, IN, City of, 187
Executive Committee, 30, 66, 71, 73, 78, 107, 117, 174, 187
Existence of the Problem
defined, 21-22, 171
findings summarized, 157-162
hypothesis, 18, 21-22
impact on LUM's effectiveness, 144
impact on LUM's formation, 46-50
impact on LUM's institutionalization, 92-95, 174-175
summarized, 95
Expenses (see Economic Resources from Support Groups)
Expo '72, 88

Fairfield Township Trustee (see Township Trustee)
Faith Presbyterian Church, 37, 53, 63, 172
Family Service Agency, 72, 116, 123
Farm Labor Organizing Committee, 135
Federated Church, 63, 83
Federation of Churches (see Tippecanoe County Federation of Churches)
Finance and Funding Committee, 66, 71, 74, 78, 105-106
First Baptist Church, 63, 136
First Christian Church, 53, 63, 119, 135, 137, 152-153
First United Methodist Church, 63
Flexibility, 7
defined, 11

described, 79, 187-188
findings summarized, 157-162
impact of administrative succession on, 105-106
impact of purpose on, 104-105
impact on LUM's effectiveness, 148-149
impact on LUM's institutionalization, 109
Food Buying Club, 67, 84, 114, *120-121*, 142, 144, 147, 149-150, 152, 187, 189
Food Pantry, 96, 176
Formalization, 6
defined, 8
described, 66, 187
findings summarized, 157-162
impact of leadership on, 103
impact on LUM's institutionalization, 109
Formation
defined, 156
LUM's Analyzed, 41-57
LUM's described, 35-39
policy implications, 165-167
problem of, 3-6, 155
summary of factors affecting LUM's, 57
Free Speech Movement, 41
Friends, Society of (see Lafayette Friends)
Fuel Crisis Task Force, 67, 113, *118*

Gary, City of, 51
General Education Diploma, 126
Goals (see Purpose)
Good Friends Visitation, 66, 81, 87, 105, 114, *120*, 149, 169, 178
Good Shepherd, Church of, 53, 63
Goshen, IN, City of, 187
Grace United Methodist Church, 63
Greater Lafayette Community Centers/GLCC (see Lincoln Community Center, Southside Community Center)
Gross National Product (see Economic Conditions)
Grow-a-Row, 67, 71, 83-84, 100, 104, 113-114, *124*, 133-134, 136, 142, 144, 147-149, 152-153, 178, 190

Habitat for Humanity, 188
Hartford Seminary, 89
Hispanic American Day, 119
Holy Trinity Lutheran Church, 108
Hope Chapel, 35-39, 50, 52-54, 101, 121, 172
Host-Hostess Program, 187-188, 190
Human Development Coalition, 67, 113, *116-117*, 149
Human Relations Council, 50
Human Service Agencies (see Inter-Organizational Relations, Membership, Purpose)
Hunger Hike, 38, 55
Hypotheses
summarized, 18, 28

Ideological Justification
defined, 20
findings summarized, 157-162
hypothesis, 18, 20
impact on LUM's effectiveness, 143
impact on LUM's formation, 43-44
impact on LUM's institutionalization, 90-91
Immanuel United Church of Christ, 63, 108, 119, 152-153, 186

Implications
  for religious leaders, 162-170
  for theory and research, 162-165
Income (see Economic Resources from Support Groups, Place Factors)
Indiana Council of Churches, 85, 172
Indiana Counseling and Pastoral Care Center, 72-73
Indiana-Kentucky Conference of the United Church of Christ, 63-64, 84, 102, 108, 186, 188
Indiana, State of (see Political Climate)
Indiana Task Force on Poor Relief, 118, 186-189
Indianapolis, City of, 51, 72, 187
Indianapolis Star, 32
Indices
  exposure to LUM, 127, 178
  horizontal belief, 127, 178
  importance of social concerns, 127, 178
  individualistic explanation of poverty, 127, 178
  LUM's effects on individuals, 127, 178
  personal involvement in LUM, 127, 178
  response to community problems, 127, 178
  structural explanation of poverty, 127, 178
  vertical belief, 127, 178
Institutionalization
  defined, 6
  impact on LUM's effectiveness, 146-150
  key dimensions affecting total institutionalization, 98-99
  LUM's described, 59-86, 186-189
  LUM's analyzed, 87-112
  LUM's summarized, 59, 86
  model, summarized, 7, 12, 156
  policy implications, 167-168
  problem of, 12, 155
  process components (see Administrative Succession, Flexibility, Inter-Organizational Relations, Intra-Organizational Relations, Leadership, Productivity, Stability)
  process components
    defined, 6, 9
  process components
    described, 72-85
  structural components (see Bureaucratization, Complexity, Distribution of Authority, Economic Resources, Formalization, Membership, Size)
  summary of factors affecting, 111-112
Integrated Hands, 66, 113-114, *121, 135,* 149, 169, 170
Inter-Organizational Relations, 7
  defined, 11-12
  described, 82-85, 174, 188-189
  findings summarized, 157-162
  hypothesized impact on institutionalization, 18, 27
  impact of administrative succession on, 106
  impact of complexity on, 107-108
  impact of effectiveness on, 110-111
  impact of leadership on, 101-103
  impact of membership on, 109
  impact of productivity on, 108
  impact of purpose on, 105
  impact on LUM's effectiveness, 149-150
  impact on LUM's institutionalization, 109
  with denominational agencies, 83-84
Internal Revenue Service, 103
Interviews, 30-32
Intra-Organizational Relations, 7
  defined, 11

described, 79-82, 188
impact of distribution of authority on, 109
findings summarized, 157-162
hypothesized impact on institutionalization, 18, 27
impact of administrative succession on, 106
impact of bureaucratization on, 109
impact of economic resources on, 107
impact of effectiveness on, 110
impact of leadership on, 101, 103
impact of purpose on, 105
impact of stability on, 108
impact on LUM's effectiveness, 149
impact on LUM's institutionalization, 109

Jesus Movement, 88
Journal-Courier, 30, 32, 45, 91, 116, 119, 122, 124, 150, 172
Jubilee Christmas, 67, 82-83, 101, 104, 106, 113-114, *118-119, 133-134,* 136, 143-145, 147, 149, 152-153, 169-170, 187, 189-190
Judicatories (see Economic Resources from Support Groups, Membership)
Justice (see Ideological Justification)

Key '73, 88
Kokomo, City of, 46

Lafayette, City of (see Place Factors)
Lafayette Friends, 63
Lafayette Urban Ministry
  effectiveness, 113-154
  evaluation of, 29-33, 100, 102, 105, 171-172
  exposure to, 127-128
  formation, 35-57
  institutionalization, 59-112
  involvement in, 127-128
  proposed, 38
Leadership
  board, 9, 75-78, 102-104
Leadership, 7
  defined, 9-10, 24-25
  described, 74-78, 187
  findings summarized, 157-162
  hypotheses, 18, 24-25, 27, 28
  impact of administrative succession on, 105
  impact of effectiveness on, 110
  impact on LUM's effectiveness, 148
  impact on LUM's formation, 52-56
  impact on LUM's institutionalization, 99-104, 176-177
  staff, 9, 74-75, 99-102
Legal Aid, 116
Legal Services Program, 97
Liberalism
  political (see Political Climate)
Liberalism, Religious (see Cooperation, Religious Policies and Practices)
Lilly, Eli and Company, 173
Lilly Endowment, Inc., x, 65, 106, 147-148, 171-172
Lincoln Community Center, 121
Literature and Research, Other, 30, 32
Local Factors (see Place Factors)
Long Range Planning Committee (see Program and Planning Committee)
Louisville, Kentucky, City of, 36
Louisville Presbyterian Theological Seminary, 36
Low-Income Groups (see Existence of the Problem,

Inter-Organizational Relations, Membership, Purpose)
Maryville College, 36
Mascouten Family Institute and Mental Health Clinic, 123
Mayor, Lafayette (see Political Climate)
Mayor, West Lafayette (see Political Climate)
Medical Society, Tippecanoe County, 118
Membership, 6
  defined, 7
  described, 62-63, 173, 176, 186
  findings summarized, 157-162
  impact of leadership on, 102
  impact of purpose on, 104
  impact on LUM's institutionalization, 109
Membership Recruitment and Relations Committee, 66, 71, 78
Memorial Presbyterian Church of Dayton, 53, 63, 100, 119, 153, 172
Memphis, TN, City of, 22, 24, 41, 160-161, 171
Mennonite Fellowship, 63
Methods (see Case Study Method, Data Collection Procedures, Survey Method)
Metropolitan Inter-Faith Association (MIFA), 22
Minutes to Meetings (see Formalization, Records and Documents)
Money, 45
Montgomery County, 51
Moral Majority, 89
Mothers' Group, 67, 114, *121*, 149
Mt. Vernon, IN, City of, 187

National Association of Social-Workers Central Indiana Chapter, 117
National Council of Churches, 24, 44, 88-90, 142
National Homes Corporation, 173
National Organization of Women, 87
Neighborhood Development Project (NPP), 50, 55, 66, 79, 121, 124, 156, 161, 172-173
Neighborhood Development Project (NDP)
  becomes LUM, 38-39
  early supporters, 52-55
  history, 35-39
Networks, Social
  importance of, 25-26, 53
New Albany, City of, 36, 52
"New Breed" Clergy (see Religious Policies and Practices)
New Federalism, 88
Newsletter (see *Seed, The*)
Newspaper, Local (see *Journal-Courier*)
Newsweek, 32
New York Times, 32
North Central Labor Council, 186
Northern Conference of United Methodist Church, 52, 63, 83-84, 107, 174, 186, 188
Northside Area, 121, 135

Occupations (see Existence of the Problem, Support within Support Groups)
Office Manger (see Staff Positions)
Officers (see Distribution on Authority)
Older Citizens Visitation (see Good Friends Visitation)
One Great Hour of Sharing, 24
Open System Approach (also see Structural Conduciveness and Resource Mobilization)
  advantages of, 162-163
  defined, ix, 15
  summary of hypotheses, 18
  summary of findings, 156-162
Ordination
  of homosexuals, 89
  of women, 89
Organizational Environments (also see Open System Approach)
  effects of, 2
  texture of, 22, 171
Organizational Factors
  hypotheses summarized, 18
  hypothesized effects on LUM's effectiveness, 28 (also see Effectiveness, Institutionalization)
  hypothesized effects on LUM's formation, 24-26 (also see Economic Resources from Support Groups, Leadership, Support of Professional Staffs within Support Groups, Support within Support Groups)
  hypothesized effects on LUM's institutionalization, 26-28 (also see Effectiveness, Institutionalization)
  impact on LUM's effectiveness, 146-153
  impact on LUM's formation, 52-57
  impact on LUM's institutionalization, 98-112
Organizations, Complex
  as area of research, 32, 171
Other Side, The, 42
"Other" Sources of Funds (see Economic Resources from Support Groups, Inter-Organizational Relations)
Our Saviour Lutheran Church, 63
Overseer, The, 189

Parent Organizations (also see Ecumenical Organizations), 23
Participant Observation, 29-30
Pastor Director (see Director)
Pastoral Counseling Center, Lafayette, 67, 72-73, 100, 105-106, 114, *123-124*, 149, 174, 176
Patchwork Central, 187
Period Factors
  defined, 15-16
  hypotheses, 17-21
  hypotheses summarized, 18
  impact on LUM's effectiveness, 141-144
  impact on LUM's formation, 41-45, 57
  impact on LUM's institutionalization, 87-91
Personal Disposable Income (see Economic Conditions)
Personal Income (see Economic Conditions)
Personnel
  defined, 20
  findings summarized, 157-162
  hypothesis, 18, 20-21
  impact on LUM's effectiveness, 143-144
  impact on LUM's formation, 44-45
  impact on LUM's institutionalization, 91
Personnel Policies (see Bureaucratization)
Personnel Policies and Salary Review Committee, 30, 66, 70-74, 76, 103, 105, 174
Petition Drives, 187-188
Pine Creek United Methodist Camp, 121
Pittsburgh, City of, 100
Place Factors
  defined, 16
  hypotheses summarized, 18, 21-24

impact on LUM's effectiveness, 144-146
impact on LUM's formation, 45-52, 57
Plan of Analysis, ix, 32-33
Political Climate
  defined, 21
  findings summarized, 157-162
  hypothesis, 18, 21
  impact on LUM's effectiveness, 144
  impact on LUM's formation, 45
  impact on LUM's institutionalization, 91-92
Political Beliefs
  of clergy, 56
"Politics of Abundance" (see Economic Resources in Religious Sphere)
"Politics of Scarcity" (see Economic Resources in Religious Sphere)
Poor Relief (see Advocates, Indiana Task Force on Poor Relief, Inter-Organizational Relations)
Poverty (see Effectiveness, Existence of the Problem, Indices)
Presbytery of Crawfordsville
  National Missions Committee, 37-38, 52, 55
Presbytery of Wabash Valley, 30, 62-63, 72-74, 83-85, 107, 172, 174, 186, 188
Prince of Peace Lutheran Church, 186
Priorities, Community, 177
Productivity, 7
  defined, 11
  described, 79, 188
  findings summarized, 157-162
  hypothesized impact on effectiveness, 28
  impact of intra-organizational relations on, 109
  impact of leadership on, 101
  impact on LUM's institutionalization, 108
Professional Staff Support within Support Groups
  defined, 26
  findings summarized, 157-162
  hypothesis, 18, 26
  impact on LUM's formation, 55-56, 173
  profile, 55
Professional Workers (see Support within Support Groups)
Program Coordinator (see Staff Positions)
Program and Planning Committee, 29-30, 66, 71-73, 76, 82, 102, 103, 105, 117, 119, 138, 172
Programs (see Complexity; also Effectiveness and names of specific programs)
Project Commitment, 50, 121
Project Equality, 121
Project SAFE, 117, 152
Protestant Churches (see Cooperation, Resources in Support Groups, Support Groups)
Protestant-Catholic Relations (see Cooperation)
Public Policy, 66, 67, 71, 113, 117-118, 141, 144, 149, 169, 189
Pulpit Nominating Committee, 36
Purdue University, 5, 35, 53, 97, 118, 126, 135, 172-174
Purpose
  defined, 6-7
  described, 60-62, 113, 176, 186
  hypotheses, 18, 26-28
  findings summarized, 157-162
  impact on LUM's effectiveness, 147
  impact on LUM's institutionalization, 104-105
  impact of leadership on, 102
  relationship between goals, 28, 156

Purpose of Book, 2

Quest for Justice, 90
Questionnaire, 31, 172

Race (see Place Factors)
Reagonomics (see Social Conditions)
Records and Documents (also see Formalization), 30-31
Redeemer Lutheran Church, 53
Religion
  as area of reseach, 32
Religious Beliefs (also see Purpose, Religious Involvement)
  and social attitudes, 6
  Catholic, 5
  of clergy, 55
  of early LUM supporters, 53-54
  Protestant, 5
Religious Beliefs (also see Purposes; Religious Involvement; Congregations, Local)
  horizontal, 4-6, 94-95, 132-133
  vertical, 4-6, 94-95, 132-133
Religious Change (see Religious Policies and Practices)
Religious Involvement (also see Religious Beliefs)
  personal consequences
  prejudice, 5
  social attitudes, 5, 6
  social consequences, 5
Religious Policies and Practices
  defined, 17
  findings summarized, 157-162
  hypothesis, 17, 18
  impact on LUM's effectiveness, 141-142
  impact on LUM's formation, 41-42
  impact on LUM's institutionalization, 88-89
Repairs on Wheels, 67, 83-84, 100, 113-114, *124, 134-135*, 144, 147, 149, 152-153, 190
Reparations (see Religious Policies and Practices)
Republicans (see Political Climate)
Research Questions (see Ecumenical Urban Ministries, Effectiveness, Formation, Institutionalization)
Reserves (see Economic Resources from Support Groups)
Resource Mobilization
  defined, ix, 16
  implications for theory and research, 163-164
  summary of findings, 160-162
  relation to structural conduciveness, 16, 163
Resources in Support Groups
  defined, 24
  findings summarized, 157-162
  hypothesis, 18, 24
  impact on LUM's effectiveness, 145-146
  impact on LUM's formation, 51-52
  impact on LUM's institutionalization, 98
Resources: Religious Sphere (see Economic Resources, Ideological Justification, Period Factors, Place Factors, Resources in Support Groups, Support Groups)
Resources: Secular Realm (see Community Size, Economic Conditions, Period Factors, Place Factors)
Revenue Sharing Task Force, 67, 74, 87, 106, 113, *116*, 150-169
Revised Ol-er Americans Act, 123

205

Roles, Ministerial, 55-56
Roman Catholic Church (see Cooperation, Support Groups)

St. Andrew United Methodist Church, 63, 75, 83
St. Boniface Church, 63
St. John's Episcopal Church, 63, 102, 108, 138
St. Thomas Aquinas Center, 63, 83, 190
School Corporation, Tippecanoe County, 118, 126
Secretary (see Staff Positions)
Seed, The, 31, 67, 83, 104, 114, *137-138*, 143, 147, 149, 152, 178
Seeds of Vision, 67, 71, 83, 95, 104, 106, 114, 118, *135-137*, 138, 143-145, 147, 149, 152-153, 170, 178, 190-191
Self-Interest (see Professional Staff Support within Support Groups)
Seminary Consortium on Urban Pastoral Education (SCUPE), 66
Seminaries (see Personnel)
Senior Center, 122-123
Senior Citizens Visitation, 38
Service Cite Committee, 72, 73
Shamrock Park, 67, 114, *124*, 149, 178
Size, 6
  defined, 7-8
  described, 63, 186
  findings summarized, 157-162
  impact of effectiveness on, 110
  impact of inter-organizational relations on, 109
  impact of leadership on, 102
  impact on LUM's institutionalization, 108
  membership, 8, 63
  staff, 8, 63
Social Attitudes (see Congregations, Local; Existence of the Problem)
Social Change (see Social Conditions)
Social Concerns Priorities (see Congregations, Local; Effectiveness; Existence of the Problem)
Social Concerns Programs (see Congregations, Local; Existence of the Problem)
Social Conditions
  defined, 17
  findings summarized, 157-162
  hypothesis, 17, 18
  impact on LUM's effectiveness, 141
  impact on LUM's formation, 41
  impact on LUM's institutionalization, 87-88
Social Movement Organizations (see Ecumenical Urban Ministries)
  defined, 1, 171
  parent organizations, 1, 2
  problem of effectiveness, 2
  problem of formation, 1-2
  problem of institutionalization, 2
  proliferation in 1970s, ix
  radical, 1
  reform, 1
Social Stratification
  as area of research, 32, 171
Societal Factors (see Period Factors)
Sojourners, 42
Sorrento Seminar, x
South Bend, IN, City of, 187
Southside Area, 35, 38, 124, 172
Southside Community Center, 30-31, 37, 101, 105, 121, 125, 135, 174-175

Spanish-Speaking People (see Board of Directors, Membership, Place Factors, Spanish-Speaking Persons Task Force)
Spanish-Speaking Persons Task Force, 67, 74, 106, 114, *119-120*, 149-150, 169, 177-178
Special Transportation Committee, 122
Spouses of Professional Workers (see Support within Support Groups)
Stability, 7
  defined, 9-10
  described, 78-79, 188
  findings summarized, 157-162
  impact of leadership on, 100
  impact on LUM's institutionalization, 108
Staff Meetings (see Intra-Organizational Relations), 30
Staff Positions (see Bureaucratization, Distribution of Authority)
Statistical Abstracts, 98
Stidham United Methodist Church, 63, 100
Stockwell United Methodist Church, 63
Structural Conditions: Religious Sphere (see Competition, Cooperation, Existence of the Problem, Period Factors, Place Factors, Religious Policies and Practices)
Structural Conditions: Secular Realm (see Period Factors, Place Factors, Political Climate, Social Conditions)
Structural Conduciveness
  defined, ix, 15-16
  effects of, 16
  findings summarized, 157-162
  implications for theory and research, 163
  relation to resource mobilization, 16, 163
Summer Camp, 66, 104, 114, 118, *121-122*, 125, 137, 145, 148, 174-175, 177-178, 190
Support Groups
  defined, 23-24
  findings summarized, 157-162
  hypothesis, 18, 23-24
  impact on LUM's effectiveness, 145
  impact on LUM's formation, 51, 173
  impact on LUM's institutionalization, 97-98
Support within Support Groups
  defined, 25
  findings summarized, 157-162
  hypothesis, 18, 25-26
  impact on LUM's formation, 52-56
Supreme Court, 172
Survey Method, 29, 164-165
Survey/Consultation with Local Congregations, 30-31, 67, 83, 106, 114, 127, *138-139*, 143, 147, 149, 152, 170

Tax Revolt, 88
Teen Leadership Development, 66, 105, 114, *125*, 149
Theory (see Open system approach)
Time, 32
Tippecanoe County (see Community Size, Existence of the Problem, Support Groups)
Tippecanoe County Council on Aging (see County Council on Aging, Social Conditions)
Tippecanoe County Federation of Churches (see Evaluation, Inter-Organizational Relations) x, 30-31, 50-51, 85, 96, 173, 176, 178
Title III Funds, 65

Title XX Funds, 65
Township Trustees (see Advocates, Indiana Task Force on Poor Relief, Inter-Organizational Relations)
Transportation Coordinator (see Staff Positions)
Trinity United Methodist Church, 53, 63, 100

"Underground Church" (see Religious Policies and Practices)
Unemployment (see Economic Conditions, Place Factors)
Union Theological Seminary, 45, 190
Unitarian Fellowship, 63, 66, 100, 103, 108
United Church of Christ (see Indiana-Kentucky Conference, Immanuel United Church of Christ)
United Episcopal Charities, 63, 102, 108, 138, 186, 188
United Methodist Church (see Congregations, Local; Northern Conference of United Methodist Church)
United Nations, 172
United Presbyterian Church USA (see Presbytery of Crawfordsville; Presbytery of Wabash Valley; and names of specific congregations)
United Stand for Children and Youth, 117
United States Catholic Conference, 90, 142
United Way, 55, 92, 117, 174, 177, 187
University Church, 53, 63, 75
University Lutheran Church, 63

Urban Area (see Community Size)
Urban Mass Transportation (UMPTA), 122
Urban Minister (see Director)

Vatican II (see Cooperation)
Visiting Nurse Service, 118
Volunteer Transportation Service (VTS), 66, 81, 87, 114, *122*, 145, 169, 178, 187, 190
Volunteers (also see Support within Support Groups), 36
Voter Registration, 187-189

Wabash Center, 116
Wabash Township Trustee (see Township Trustees)
War on Poverty (see Social Conditions)
Warren County, 51
Washington Post, 32
West Lafayette, City of (see Place Factors)
White County, 51
White House Conference on Aging, 87
Women, Infants, and Children (WIC), 118, 144, 177
World Council of Churches, 89, 90
Wounded Knee, 88

Yale Divinity School, 45
Youth Coordinator (see Staff Positions)
YWCA, 136

NAME INDEX

Ade, Carla, x
Aldrich, Howard E., 6-8, 15, 22, 193
Aleshire, Daniel, 5, 195
Altizer, Thomas, 42, 193
Amerson, Philip A., 24, 193
Amos, *5:21-24*, 4
Armstrong, Bishop James, 90
Ash, Roberta, 1, 25, 199
Aveni, Adrian F., 6, 8, 198
Axtell, Sue, 103

Bahr, Howard M., 5, 193
Bakely, Rev. Donald, 118, 135
Baldeoin, Burt R., 176, 198
Bartel, Louis Frantz, 193
Bendix, Reinhard, 20, 193
Benestad, J. Bryan, 90, 193
Berger, Peter L., 3, 42, 193
Beswick, Rev. William, 39
Biggar, Jeanne, 5, 197
Bissaillion, Francis, 42, 193
Blann, Veronica, 108, 147
Blizzard, Samuel W., 26, 193
Blume, Norman, 24, 193
Boncy, Virginia, 80, 108, 125, 147
Bornholdt, Laura, x
Bowen, Otis, 91
Boyd, Malcolm, 42, 193
Branigan, Roger, 45
Brewer, Earl D. C., 4, 193
Brown, Robert McAfee, 42, 193
Brown, William R., 11, 194
Buchanan, Rev. John, 96
Burkey, Rich and M., 52, 193
Butler, Francis J., 90, 193

Callahan, Rev. Roger, 82
Campbell, Thomas C., 4, 26, 193
Campolo, Anthony, 4, 193
Carmichael, Stokley, 41
Carpenter, Phil, 75
Carroll, Jackson W., 24, 44, 91, 193
Carter, President Jimmy, 88
Cavert, Samuel McCrea, 42, 193
Chadwick, Bruce A., 193
Champion, Dean J., 1, 6-9, 11, 15, 193
Chinn, Ron, 62
Clark, Henry, 44, 193
Clifton, Rev. Thomas, 136
Cloward, Richard A., 171, 197
Cornell, George W., 4, 195
Cox, Harvey G., 26, 42, 193

D'Antonio, William V., 5, 193
Darnell, Suzanne B., ix, 2-3, 13, 15, 22, 24, 29, 42, 160-161, 164-166, 171, 198
Davidson, Anna, x
Davidson, James D., 3, 5, 6, 11, 13, 50, 62, 74, 94, 96, 103, 138, 174, 193-195
Davidson, Jay, x
Davidson, Terry, x
Davis, Angela, 42
Davis, Dr. George, 123
Demerath III, N.J., 21, 43, 44, 194

Deuteronomy *24:17-22*, 4
Dixon, Robert, 4, 194
Dolphin, Mary Jane, 74
Dolphin, Rev. Judson, x, 30, 72-76, 78, 82, 83, 84, 99-102, 105, 117, 120, 137, 148, 174, 178, 187-188
Dykhuizen, Dan, 103

Earle, John R., 26, 194
Eddy, Richard, 176, 198
Edelman, Rev. Kenneth, 172
Edwards, Barb, 124
Egan, Rev. John J., 90, 194
Ekland-Olson, Sheldon, 25, 26, 164, 198
Elly, Rev. Ronald, x, 3, 13, 30, 31, 36-38, 52, 55-56, 68, 69-70, 72-76, 78, 79, 80, 91, 99-102, 105-109, 116-117, 122, 123, 147-148, 156, 171, 172-174, 176, 194
Emery, F. E., 22, 171, 194
Esman, Milton J., 24, 27, 194
Etzioni, Amitai, 9, 194
Evans, Bernard F., 24, 26, 44, 195

Falwell, Rev. Jerry, 89
Faue, Jeffrey, 4, 195
Feagin, Joe R., 5, 24, 195
Fichter, Joseph, 44, 195
Fischer, Claude S., 23, 195
Flacks, Richard, 25, 195
Forbes, Rev. James, 190
Ford, President Gerald R., 88, 91
Foreman, James, 42
Foster, Bruce D., 26, 198
Fuchs, Victor, 46, 195
Fukuyama, Yoshio, 4, 193

Gamson, William A., 1, 17, 195
Garrett, William R., 20, 89, 195
Gaustad, Edwin, 43, 195
Gaylor, Les, 38-39
Gibbs, David R., 5, 195
Glock, Charles Y., 3, 5, 44, 195, 198
Goldwater, Barry, 45
Gorsuch, Richard L., 5, 195
Graham, James, 3, 13, 195
Greeley, Andrew M., 52, 195
Greenwood, Elma L., 42, 51, 195

Hadden, Jeffrey K., 21, 24, 26, 42, 44, 195
Hall, Richard H., 1, 2, 6-11, 15, 19-22, 24, 27-28, 195
Hamilton, Richard F., 25, 195
Hamilton, William, 42, 193
Hammond, Phillip E., 21, 26, 44, 194-195
Hancock, Rev. David, 74, 100, 103, 106
Hanstra, Mrs. Peter, 35, 36, 121
Hanstra, Rev. Peter, 35
Harrison, Paul M., 21, 44, 195
Hawbaker, Joan, 117
Helmuth, Ned, 78, 103
Henriott, Gary, 82, 102-103, 186
Hessel, Dieter T., 24, 195
Hipshire, Mary Jo, 83
Hoffman, Gerbard, 11, 194

Hogan, Thaddeus, 89, 195
Hoge, Dean R., 4, 194-195
Hougham, Anne, 46, 195
Hull, Thomas, x, 13, 76, 78, 83, 100, 103, 194
Hunter, James Davison, 42, 195

Jackson, Maurice, 15-16, 199
Jacquet, Constant H., 43, 90, 195
Jamison, Michael, 171, 196
Jenkins, J. Craig, ix, 2, 15-16, 24, 26, 28, 44, 195
Jewell, Louise, 103
1 John 3:14-18, 4
Johnson, Arthur L., 5, 197
Johnson, Benton, 26, 195
Johnson, Douglas W., ix, 3-4, 20, 22, 27-29, 42, 44, 51, 89, 142, 195
Johnson, President Lyndon B., 41, 45
Johnstone, Ronald L., 43, 89, 195

Keedy, T. C., 5, 195
Kelly, James R., 89, 195
Kennedy, President John F., 41
Kennedy, Robert F., 41
Kitty, Rev. Paul, 123
Kim, Gertrud, 91, 195
King, Martin Luther, 22, 41
Kleva, Gerald A., 195
Knapp, Forrest L., 42, 195
Knoke, David, 16, 195
Knudsen, Dean D., 5, 174, 195
Kremlick, Rev. Kurt, 73, 100, 103

Lee, Robert, 42, 195
Lenski, Gerhard, 5, 195
Lerch, Stephen R., 194
Liechty, Rev. Ronald, 83
Litterer, Joseph A., 8, 195
Lofland, John, 171, 196
Longino, Jr., Charles F., 22, 26, 195
Luke 10:27, 4; *4:16-21*, 4
Lynn, Robert, x

Madron, Thomas, 197
Maniha, John, 2, 196
Marrett, Cora Bagley, 22, 196
Martin, William, 26, 197
Martinez, Rosetta, 62
Marty, Martin, 89, 197
Marx, Gary T., 5, 197
Matthew 25:31-45, 4
McCabe, Sharon Shrottenback, 108, 147
McCarthy, Eugene, 45
McCarthy, John D., ix, 15-16, 19, 24, 197, 199
McCullen, Rev. Kenneth, 73, 83
McGovern, George, 87
Mecklenberg, Mike, 103
Miller, William L., 6, 8, 198
Mitchell, Robert, 26, 44, 195
Miras, Ronald E., 42, 197
Montford, Tee, 103
Mueller, Samuel A., 195
Mulvey, Linda, 80
Murnion, Rev. Philip, 90, 194
Myers, Phyllis Goudy, 1, 94, 96, 197

Nead, Rev. Donald, x, 3, 13, 75, 83, 194
Nelsen, Hart M., 26, 197

Nichols, Sue, x
Nixon, President Richard, 45, 87, 91
Norman, Holly, x

Oberschall, Anthony, 164, 197
Olson, Dorothy, 103
Orr, Robert, 91

Parella, Jr., Fredrick J., 24, 197
Parvis, Byron, 50
Pettigrew, Thomas F., 26
Pennings, Johannes M., 22, 24, 197
Perrow, Charles, 2, 6, 165, 196-197
Perry, Everett, 195
Photiadis, John D., 5, 197
Picard, Paul W., 51, 195
Piven, Frances Fox, 171, 197
Pope, Liston, 26, 197
Potter, Harry R., 6, 8, 198
Potters, Bobby, 46, 197
Presti, Mike, 103
Proverbs 21:13, 4
Psalm 82:3-4, 4
Pugh, D. S., 8, 197

Quinley, Harold E., 21, 24, 26, 197
Quinn, Bernard, 51, 195
Quinn, Gary J., 5-6, 197

Reagan, President Ronald, 88-89, 91
Roach, Peggy, 90, 194
Roberts, Michael K., 94, 194
Roberts, Phil, 76, 103
Rokeach, Milton, 5, 197
Roof, W. Clark, 51, 197
Rosaria, Kathy, 186
Ross, G. Alexander, 1, 22, 197
Rothschild-Whitt, Joyce, 25, 171, 198
Rymph, Raymond C., 26, 44, 195

Sala, Rev. James, 35, 172
Salisbury, W. Seward, 5, 198
Santa Ana, Julio, de, 44, 198
Scherer, Ross P., 15, 198
Schlangen, Joseph A., 5, 193
Schurr, Richard, 38
Semmes, Clarence, 178
Shriver, Jr., Donald W., 194
Sider, Ronald J., 44, 198
Siffin, William J., 2, 198
Smelser, Neil J., 15, 198
Smith, David Horton, 176, 198
Snow, David A., 25-26, 164, 198
Sorge, Dennis, x, 82, 102-103, 138
Stark, Rodney, 3, 5, 26, 44, 195, 198
Starr, Paul, 171, 198
Stinchcombe, Arthur L., 2, 17, 20, 24, 198
Stuhr, Walter, 24, 198
Swanson, Guy B., 43, 198

Takayama, K. Peter, ix, 2-3, 13, 15, 17, 19-20, 22, 24, 29, 32, 42, 160-161, 164-166, 169-171, 198
Thomas, Woods, 6, 8, 198
Tilly, Charles, 16, 198
Trist, E. L., 22, 171, 194
Tritschler, Dee, 38, 100, 103

209

Ullman, Edward, 23, 198

Vamos, Rev. William, 176
Vander Werf, Nathan H., ix, 89, 142, 199
Vanfossen, Beth E., 25, 199
Velasquez, Baldermar, 135-136

Warren, Chief Justice Earl, 172
Warren, Roland L., 19, 199
Webber, George M., 135
Weber, Max, 171, 199
Whitcomb, Edgar, 45, 91
White, Joyce, 83, 103
Wilcox, Maria Broughton, x
Wilkerson, Bonnie, x
Wilson, John, 17, 24, 26, 43-44, 199
Wilson, Robert, 44, 91, 193
Winter, J. Alan, 20-21, 26, 42, 199
Wood, James L., 15-16, 199
Wood, James R., x, 2, 16, 20-21, 27-28, 44, 195, 199
Wortham, Marty, x
Wuthnow, Robert, 5, 43, 199

Yokley, Raytha, 197

Zald, Mayer N., ix, 1, 15-17, 19-20, 24-25, 197, 199
Zurcher, Louis A., 25-26, 164, 198